AF605856

Beyond Biology

Selected Titles from the Moral Traditions Series
David Cloutier, Darlene Weaver, and Andrea Vicini, SJ, editors

The Vice of Luxury: Economic Excess in a Consumer Age
David Cloutier

Diverse Voices in Modern US Moral Theology
Charles E. Curran

Consumer Ethics in a Global Economy: How Buying Here Causes Injustice There
Daniel K. Finn

Kinship Across Borders: A Christian Ethic of Immigration
Kristin E. Heyer

Keeping Faith with Human Rights
Linda Hogan

Humanity in Crisis: Ethical and Religious Response to Refugees
David Hollenbach, SJ

The Fullness of Free Time: A Theological Account of Leisure and Recreation in the Moral Life
Conor M. Kelly

Reimagining Human Rights: Religion and the Common Good
William R. O'Neill, SJ

Hope for Common Ground: Mediating the Personal and the Political in a Divided Church
Julie Hanlon Rubio

Love and Christian Ethics: Tradition, Theory, and Society
Frederick V. Simmons, editor

All God's Animals: A Catholic Theological Framework for Animal Ethics
Christopher Steck, SJ

Beyond Biology

RETHINKING PARENTHOOD IN THE CATHOLIC TRADITION

Jacob M. Kohlhaas

GEORGETOWN UNIVERSITY PRESS / WASHINGTON, DC

Library of Congress Cataloging-in-Publication Data

Names: Kohlhaas, Jacob M., author.
Title: Beyond biology : rethinking parenthood in the Catholic tradition / Jacob M. Kohlhaas.
Description: Washington, DC : Georgetown University Press, 2020. | Series: Moral traditions series | Includes bibliographical references and index.
Identifiers: LCCN 2020051103 | ISBN 9781647121129 (hardcover) | ISBN 9781647121136 (paperback) | ISBN 9781647121143 (ebook)
Subjects: LCSH: Parenting—Religious aspects—Catholic Church. | Families—Religious aspects—Catholic Church. | Sexual ethics. | Christian ethics.
Classification: LCC BX2352 .K64 2020 | DDC 248.8/45—dc23
LC record available at https://lccn.loc.gov/2020051103

22 21 9 8 7 6 5 4 3 2 First printing

Printed in the United States of America

To my colleagues at Loras College,
with deep admiration and appreciation

CONTENTS

PREFACE

The origins of this book project lie in a debate that took place in a graduate seminar. Several years ago my classmates and I were heatedly discussing the significance of gender complementarity between parents as a precondition for a "real" family. The concern revolved around the claim that a complementary relationship between a woman and a man, as mother and father, is an indispensable foundation for authentic family life. At some point in our discussion, I interjected that if parental complementarity were truly essential for child well-being, then the Catholic Church would be required to disavow its long tradition of providing care for the orphaned through religious orders because single-sex monasteries could hardly be considered fitting environments for children under such parameters. Not surprisingly, this assertion received strong pushback. These reactions grew more visceral as I followed up by questioning whether the only significant difference between Catholicism's apparent approval of single-sex institutional childcare and categorical disapproval of parenthood by same-sex couples concerned the sexual activities of caregivers. Could it be that the presumption of a sexual relationship was itself the decisive factor in determining whether a single-sex commitment to caregiving is a praiseworthy act of Christian charity or an unconditionally condemnable act of harm?

As I have studied such issues in more depth, hopefully I have learned to ask more precise and careful questions. Nonetheless, I remain convinced that this initial discussion revealed problematic disjunctions in contemporary Catholic thought. Most notable is the disproportionate influence of concerns about gender roles and sexual ethical norms in present Catholic discourse around parenthood. As a consequence of these issues, which have often played center stage in the culture wars of the twentieth century and into the present, our ability as Catholics to think theologically about the nature of Christian parenthood has been affected. Too often, culturally reactionary posturing around sex and gender has led Catholics to neglect attending to the riches and complexities of our own tradition. Such preoccupations lure Catholics into believing that theological consideration of parenthood is possible without considering the actual caregiving capabilities of adults beyond gender, marital status, and presumed sexual activity. This book seeks to address this restrictive way of thinking by articulating its restraints and sketching a broader anthropology of parenthood.

Theological anthropology and moral theology, the investigations of who we are and what we ought to do, respectively, are intimately connected within the Catholic theological tradition.[1] The turn toward personalist moral methodology confirmed at the Second Vatican Council centers moral reflection on the "human person integrally and adequately considered" and posits human flourishing as its end.[2] Theological anthropology is foundational for moral theology, given that without an adequate conception of the human person, ethical norms fail to meaningfully contact the realities of human lives and are thereby hampered in pointing to a life of happiness. As Christina Traina has observed, many limitations in past and present Catholic moral teaching have to do with the limitations and biases of the anthropological vision employed, not the reliance of moral theology on anthropology itself. She writes: "The key is to walk the line between tentativeness and absolutism: to develop descriptions credible and detailed enough to yield morally normative, prophetic claims yet flexible enough to accommodate a degree of cultural pluralism and historical change; and to do so inductively, developing and refining descriptions."[3] Due to the close relationship of anthropology and moral theology, this book's search for a more adequate theological anthropology of parenthood wades into contested moral waters as it explores how contemporary Catholic teaching and scholarship have engaged, and neglected to engage, with parenthood as a theological subject in its own right.

Because I have two children of my own and have spent several years in youth ministry and higher education, this book undoubtedly has been influenced by my own experiences and the ways in which my theological education has and has not addressed my own experiences. Over the past fourteen years, my wife and I have exchanged periods of being primary caregiver, primary income earner, and both working full time. As a married, White, Catholic, Midwestern, heterosexual man with a stable family and a middle-class income, I recognize that my family checks most of the "good Christian family" boxes within the American Christian imagination. As such, even as I argue for a more expansive understanding of how Christians ought to think about parenthood, I recognize that my own experience is both limited and limiting. I do not intend to speak for others but to raise critical questions about how dominant modes of discourse have framed Catholic conceptions of parenthood. I fully acknowledge that my limited insight, resources, and abilities merely scratch the surface of this task. Nonetheless, I hope to offer the foundations for a revised framework that might expand the concerns of scholars and students of theology to facilitate more robust and inclusive conversations.[4] I further hope that this project will help those who are excluded by, or uneasy within, now-dominant Catholic presentations of parenthood to find resources for claiming the integrity and validity of their experiences as Christian parents and families.

This book is the continuation of research that began several years ago with a lively theological debate. Since then, it has yielded many opportunities for theological engagement as it has matured into its present form. I wish to thank all those interlocutors who have read or listened to aspects of this research and have offered their insights in response. These include especially my colleagues at Loras College, fellow participants in the Dubuque area theological writing group, and peers within the College Theology Society.

NOTES

1. See Traina, *Feminist Ethics*.
2. This phrase derives from the official commentary that accompanied the conciliar constitution, *Gaudium et spes*. See Janssens, "Particular Goods," 55–59. Christina Traina also warns that human flourishing is not a neutral concept, as it relies on the views of those who articulate it. Traina writes that "standard, 'neutral' accounts of flourishing may not account for women's needs and experiences; that women (and all others) are and should be responsible moral agents-in-community; that their concrete material, political, and spiritual fulfillment is a criterion of moral judgement; and that they are to have a hand in defining what constitutes this fulfillment." Traina, *Feminist Ethics*, 302.
3. Traina, *Feminist Ethics*, 43.
4. Sandra Sullivan Dunbar offers a distinct but related argument to the one made here. Aside from differing sources and methodology, her concerns are less specified at the anthropological level (as the present argument concerns parenthood particularly) and concentrated at the moral level regarding how inattention to the moral reality of care practices have worked to ignore caregiving as a moral concern and therefore disregarded those who provide care. See Sullivan-Dunbar, *Human Dependency*.

Introduction

In 2011, the Illinois Religious Freedom Protection and Civil Unions Act prohibited all adoption providers from prioritizing married couples over same-sex partners in civil unions.[1] Catholic social service agencies, which had played a significant role in adoption services throughout the state for decades, believed the new law required them to equate marriage with same-sex unions. Even though many agencies were reliant on public contracts to fund large portions of their budgets, they nonetheless announced their intentions not to comply, and each was subsequently notified that its state contracts would not be renewed.[2] In the ensuing lawsuit, lawyers for the Catholic agencies framed the issue as a matter of religious freedom. In contrast, the court ultimately viewed it as a matter of obligations between contracting parties.[3] Because no private entity can assert a right to a government contract without a legally binding reason, the Catholic agencies were found to lack grounds for claiming unfair treatment.[4] In the years since this decision, several religious organizations in Illinois have worked toward independent funding and now practice even more restrictive adoption standards than they had before the 2011 law.[5]

For the purposes of this book, this case and its consequences are less important than the arguments used to defend the Catholic agencies' position that their faith absolutely prohibited placing children with same-sex couples. This argument was made despite the fact that some Catholic agencies in the United States had permitted adoption placements with same-sex couples in recent memory.[6] The newfound absolutism being upheld in Illinois was based on a 2003 document and a 2006 clarification from the Congregation for the Doctrine of the Faith that placed an unqualified prohibition on the assertion that allowing children to be raised by same-sex couples constitutes an act of violence toward children.[7] Following this teaching, Catholic agencies could no longer take account of the actual conditions of children or their potential same-sex adopters. In line with such reasoning, the court arguments expended little effort on delineating the actual parental capacities, relevant to the day-to-day tasks of caregiving, that same-sex couples unconditionally lack. The specific deficiencies that were acknowledged tended to revolve around gender and sexual behavior, centering on the claim that a lack of sexual complementarity between same-sex caregivers prevents healthy child development.[8]

The case in Illinois is just one of many controversies that have surrounded Catholic institutions' varied attempts to uphold official Catholic moral teachings, often against growing oppositional public sentiment.[9] Catholic moral teaching dictates a host of specific sexual norms, including absolute prohibitions of all nonmarital sex, same-sex intercourse, masturbation, contraception, sterilization, abortion, pornography, and artificial reproductive technologies.[10] Yet nothing in Catholic teaching appears to prohibit intimate friendships, sharing a common life, or even some level of romantic affection between same-sex partners. Nonetheless, same-sex partners are regarded as violating Catholic norms via a presumption of sexual activity. Heterosexual Catholic couples are rarely similarly scrutinized on the presumption of sexual practice, despite abundant evidence detailing the infrequency with which they fully abide by Catholic sexual norms. The positive justification guiding these differentiated practices is generally articulated as an aim to protect the family based in heterosexual marriage. In this view, the sexual activity between same-sex partners matters less than their public participation in a relationship that blurs the unique boundary between marriage and other human relationships. Such contentions rest on a particular conception of the family that is itself worth critical examination. As recent history amply demonstrates—within the realms of sexuality, relationships, marriage, and family life—reactionary responses often have a way of presenting rigid ideals that mask the deeper diversities of the Catholic theological tradition.

THE ARGUMENT IN BRIEF

This book critiques the present state of Catholic moral thinking on parenthood and argues for more robust theological anthropological foundations. It contends that the prevailing framework for parenthood is significantly influenced by the reactionary posturing of the institutional Catholic Church in response to the rapid social developments of the twentieth and twenty-first centuries. This posturing includes trenchant assertions of traditional sexual ethical norms that have absorbed a great deal of energy to maintain while the social landscape has continued to shift. Importantly, the concerted efforts focused on these reassertions has been so weighty as to distort the related considerations of the family itself. Moreover, in response to disruptions in Western gender norms, the institutional Catholic Church has similarly recommitted itself to an essentialist theory of gender that conceives of maleness and femaleness as discrete and complementary categories. This, too, has led to intense intellectual sparring and has exerted a powerful influence over Catholic conceptions of the family.

Today, Catholic teaching tends to favor the differentiated gender roles of the father as the primary financial provider and the mother as the primary caregiver within autonomous biological-nuclear families. Though such thinking is often justified as natural or traditional, in fact it relies substantially upon the particularities of the industrialized West.[11] Many Catholic scholars have reacted critically to these developments in Catholic thought, but the implications of these preoccupations for Catholic reflection on parenthood have been limited. This has created a significant lacuna in the present Catholic theological imagination, whereby sex and gender constitute the primary foundations for conceptualizing parenthood while overshadowing questions about caregiving practices, capabilities necessary for parenting, and the complex nature of kinship itself.

This constricted theology of parenthood governs thought on childrearing without meaningfully engaging the Catholic Church's long and diverse history of negotiating kinship while tolerating various arrangements for the purposes of raising children.[12] Moreover, its culturally reactionary origins limit the ability to integrate contemporary social scientific studies of children's well-being into Catholic understandings of parenthood. This limitation only further restricts Catholicism's ability to respond thoughtfully to social developments with due concern for the demonstrated needs of children. In response, this book engages various sources of knowledge in order to reframe Catholic theological reflection on parenthood.[13] Although same-sex adoptive parenthood receives attention throughout, this is largely due to the clarity of questions its public rejection by Catholic leaders has raised more than any specific advocacy on the author's part. Beyond this issue, the book considers broader diversities in parenthood, including adoption and nonbiological parenthood, fathers as primary caregivers and nurturers, caregiving by nonparental kin such a siblings and grandparents, and functional conceptions of parenthood that recognize multiple participants in parenting such as communal parenting and co-parenting beyond the spousal pair.

This articulation of a broader Catholic conception of parenthood is guided by a commitment to personalist moral methodology that observes both the common embodied realities of human experience and the value of subjective experiences.[14] Moreover, it aims to assure the good of persons by considering both the needs and well-being of children as well as the potentials and capabilities of adult caregivers. These concerns are supplemented with a historically conscious methodology that attends to variation and development in theological perspectives while attempting to balance respect for the convictions of the Catholic Magisterium with critical examination and an intention to articulate resources for a more expansive and nuanced theology of parenthood.[15] Proceeding from the conviction that God proscribes only what is not truly good for persons, this book intends to establish a mutually critical dialogue between theological and nontheological sources in order to clarify and assess the claims of each as contributions to a broader theological vision of parenthood.[16]

CHAPTER SUMMARIES

Although each chapter of this book addresses a different topic, all intend to build upon one cohesive argument. Each chapter begins with a brief introduction acknowledging its place within the argument and, therefore, should be accessible on its own terms. Part I (chapters 1–3) provides a critical review of the present Catholic framework for conceptualizing parenthood and points both to its recent historical origins and theological limitations. Part II (chapters 4–7) initiates a reframing of parenthood by appropriating insights from a variety of sources in order to establish foundations for a more robust theological vision.

Chapter 1 argues that from the publication of the first modern encyclical on marriage, *Arcanum divinae sapientiae* of 1880, through Paul VI's publication of *Humanae vitae* in 1968, trends in official Catholic teaching led to limitations of the framework for parenthood in Catholic thought. These trends include a culturally reactionary aspect that sought to clarify and define the family and gender norms against changing social patterns. Ironically, these assertions were both fueled by anti-Modernist sentiments and linked Catholic thought on the family and parenthood to structures and conditions that were themselves largely indebted to conditions of the industrialized modern era. In the 1960s, as overt anti-Modernism waned and Catholicism came to embrace expanded social opportunities for women, rapidly changing social norms for sexuality and gender again provoked reactionary responses. The publication of *Humanae vitae* served as a linchpin in the shifting anxieties of the time, as concerns began to center on sexual ethical norms and the ecclesial authority that clarified these. Consequently, the late twentieth century saw the completion of an underlying framework for parenthood centered largely on issues of sexual ethics and gender norms.

Chapter 2 explores the mixed legacy of John Paul II's post–Vatican II synthesis, which crystallized a number of key positions of the Catholic hierarchy in response to the social trends of the contemporary West. John Paul II fortified a turn toward personalist moral methodology and elevated engagement with scripture in magisterial moral teaching. At the same time, his thought solidified thoroughly Modernist assumptions about the family and gender roles while centering concern about parenthood on sexual and reproductive ethics. This approach found favor in certain quarters but was rebutted by numerous academic theologians.

Chapter 3 explores the recent work of academic theologians and demonstrates the extent to which the prevailing framework for parenthood broadly shapes Catholic thought, even in the midst of contested theological differences. Despite rejecting the gender essentialism found in magisterial teaching and contesting many sexual norms, revisionist theologians often neglect parenthood as a theological issue in its own right. Instead, concern for parenthood tends to arise as a by-product of discussions on sexual ethics or is justified primarily on the grounds of sociological data, with thin theological support. This chapter also considers the present papacy of Pope Francis and his influence in shifting the terms of these debates, but it argues that the framework forged throughout the late twentieth century remains dominant.

Chapter 4, which begins part II of the book, addresses resetting the boundaries of Catholic thinking on parenthood and the family to create space for an anthropology of parenthood that is not buried beneath a labyrinth of anxieties about gender essentialism, sexual ethics, and the doctrine of marriage. The chapter recognizes the family as both a society in itself and a foundation for larger societies; but in taking this view seriously, it rejects the tendency of magisterial thought to apply the doctrine of marriage directly to considerations of the family. The chapter then challenges the tendency to associate irregular family forms more strongly with personal moral failings than with social and economic forces.

Chapter 5 further questions the idealization of a specific family structure and parental functions driven by historically situated ideals, including gendered and sexual norms. By drawing upon interdisciplinary research, it contends that how families function as social systems of stability, intimacy, and support is a more significant consideration than the structure of any given family. The chapter challenges the centrality of biological kinship and parental gender complementarity in Catholic thought, and it asserts commitment and stability as being more significant factors for promoting familial flourishing.

Chapter 6 demonstrates that diverse perspectives on kinship, children and childhood, and the nature of Christian caregiving have existed throughout the tradition. It argues that kinship is primarily a set of obligations constructed from various foundations, including, but not limited to, biological relationship. Christians across history have been willing to negotiate kinship beyond biological relatedness through commitment to the common bond of baptism and recognition of a common human identity as children of God. Thus, an anthropological account of parenthood must be rooted in both the natural human capacity to nurture and provide care for others as well as the Christian tradition of extending kin obligations to those in need.

Chapter 7 argues that Catholic Social Teaching provides important resources for reconsiderations of parenthood as a form of relational labor. Attention is directed to the anthropological vision of labor offered by John Paul II's 1981 encyclical *Laborem exercens,* as well as the relational anthropology of Pope Francis's 2015 encyclical *Laudato si'*. These documents help sketch a theological vision of parenthood vis-à-vis the goods of both caregivers and children with respect to the fuller realization of personhood.

The conclusion of this book returns to some of the questions raised in this introduction to reconsider such issues in light of the vision of parenthood that has been developed. It then points to trajectories for scholarly inquiry that could continue to expand and refine a broader contemporary Catholic conception of parenthood.

NOTES

1. "Illinois Religious Freedom Protection and Civil Unions Act." The Defense of Marriage Act was in effect at this time so that Illinois could legally recognize same-sex civil unions with many parallel implications to legal marriage at the state level, but the federal government restricted benefits and reserved the words "marriage" and "spouse" for marriages between one man and one woman.
2. McEwen, "FY12 Foster Care." Catholic leaders were assured prior to passage that the relationship between the state and religious agencies would not be altered. Nonetheless, soon after its passing, the attorney general of Illinois clarified that the state's interpretation of the new law required all adoption agencies to comply with its standard, regardless of religious affiliation.
3. Medlin, "Illinois Bishops."
4. Although this was clearly not the informal understanding, because no formal agreement bound the state to future contracts, the relationship was legally year-to-year. To allow an informal understanding as grounds for obligating future contracts would have set a potentially dangerous precedent for the state. Schmidt, "Summary."
5. In 2012, the fate of Catholic adoption services in Illinois became an important reference point for the US Conference of Catholic Bishops as a nationwide debate about

religious freedom arose in response to the contraceptive coverage requirement for most religiously affiliated employers under the Patient Protection and Affordable Care Act of 2010. Documents from the US Conference of Catholic Bishops suggest that the discontinuation of adoption services was the direct result of laws that forcefully intruded upon the conscience-bound beliefs of religious organizations. See US Conference of Catholic Bishops, Ad Hoc Committee for Religious Liberty, "Our First, Most Cherished Liberty"; and US Conference of Catholic Bishops, "Discrimination."

6. Before 2006, common practice included ranking applicants based on factors including marital status. While single and same-sex candidates were generally ranked beneath married applicants, they were not eliminated from consideration by all Catholic agencies. Catholic Charities of Boston placed thirteen children in the care of same-sex couples over a twenty-year period while Catholic Charities of San Francisco placed five children with same-sex couples between 2000 and 2006. William Cardinal Levada, former archbishop of San Francisco, explained these decisions as exceptional circumstances in which prudential considerations of the children's needs warranted the placement. See Buchanan, "Catholic Charity"; Filteau, "Catholic Charities."
7. Congregation for the Doctrine of the Faith, "Considerations," sec. 7.3. William Cardinal Levada both oversaw the Archdiocese of San Francisco while adoptions to same-sex couples were permitted and, after his promotion to prefect of the Congregation for the Doctrine of the Faith, authorized the 2006 letter to the archdiocese of San Francisco that clarified the absolute prohibition of this practice. "Catholic Charities in San Francisco"; Schmalz, "SF Catholic Charities."
8. Congregation for the Doctrine of the Faith, "Considerations," sec. 7.3.
9. Recent news reports include Silverman and Hassan, "Teacher Fired"; Associated Press, "Priest"; Coran, "Teacher."
10. Reimer-Barry, "How to Be Fired."
11. For a detailed study of changes in Western conceptions of marriage throughout the modern era, see Coontz, *Marriage.*
12. For a review of some of this historical diversity, see Cahill, *Family.*
13. This project centers on theological consideration of the nature of parenthood itself as it relates to parental function and children's needs. For this reason, it cannot address a number of questions related to means of reproduction and family formation that are nonetheless important, including but not limited to the used of assisted reproductive technologies, surrogacy, and international adoption.
14. See Traina, *Feminist Ethics.*
15. See Cahill, *Sex.*
16. This is expressed by Thomas Aquinas in the phrase "we do not wrong God unless we wrong our own good." Aquinas, *Summa contra Gentiles,* 3, 122.

PART I

The Catholic Framework for Parenthood

This project begins with a review of the historical roots of the prevailing Catholic framework for parenthood, by which I mean the pattern of conceptualizing parenthood that is guided by dominant patterns of thought that both reveal and conceal aspects of reality. Abstracting the concept of parenthood from its basis in experience, in order to conceptualize and understand it reflectively, necessitates guidance by inherited thought paradigms—that is, frames. These frames help us understand the reality we seek to intellectually interrogate, yet also do so according to their own particular concerns and constraints. As history moves onward, aspects of reality that were firmly centered within a conceptual frame can become displaced while aspects that were shielded from view may begin to come into focus. The Catholic philosopher Charles Taylor, for example, has explored such frames in his study of the "conditions of belief" that make atheism possible in the contemporary world, when it would have been taken as a sign of insanity in previous ages.[1] What shifted was not so much the definition of nonbelief but its position within the commonly accepted frame for understanding reality, as Christendom gave way to the rise of secularity.

This book engages in a related project by questioning how one particular form of the family (autonomous, biological, and nuclear, with associated male and female gender roles) came to define authentic family in Catholic thinking, despite much greater historical diversity and this model's historically contingent reliance on an industrialized, wage-based social context. On one hand, this movement toward idealizing a particular form of the family is due to the reactionary posturing that characterized many Catholic responses to the disruptions of modernity. On the other hand, it admits to common cause with the concerns of Modernism in a desire for intellectual clarity and discrete categories of classification.

Shifts in the imaginative framework for parenthood not only make the prevailing Catholic conception of the family possible but seemingly incontestable as well. Taylor writes, "all beliefs are held within a framework of the taken-for-granted."[2] Such frameworks map the terrain in which the human imagination engages the world while also constraining perspectives so as to make this engagement possible and plausible. Transcendent certainty in our present particular and historically bound idealizations of the family exists because this pervasive framework guides conceptualizations of the family along these lines while shielding both itself and alternative possibilities from view. Although frames operate invisibly, they can be exposed and critiqued through critical attention to how we think and why we think in such ways. Again following Taylor, taking a historical step back to before a particular framework emerged as dominant provides a compelling methodological lens for observing its rise and the transformation of thought it entailed. In so doing, greater imaginative possibilities are opened from which the theological recovery of a more expansive framework might be articulated. The next three chapters argue that the contemporary Catholic approach to parenthood is unmistakably shaped by historical realities that gave rise to a particular framework for parenthood that has both spurred new understandings and constrained imagination.

Expanding theological possibilities through a recovery of history implies a need for care in one's historical method because the process of constructing a historical narrative necessarily implies engaging in some level of rhetorical discourse. Among the most common rhetorical tools utilized by social and religious leaders' historical retellings is the declension narrative. Such stories portray a pattern of growth and decline in order to substantiate a present call for revival.[3] Declension narratives have been used with particular efficacy on matters concerning the family, by contrasting a preset crisis of values with an idyllic past.[4] Institutions have in fact risen and fallen throughout the course of history (e.g., the Roman Empire and the manufacturing economy), but critical historical engagement limits its scope of concern, avoids simplistic causal reasoning, and recognizes the complex and nonlinear developments of most movements throughout history. Conversely, rhetorically motivated declension narratives tend to be grand and simplistic while intending to convince their audiences of a certain way of understanding the past so as to encourage action in the present.

The return envisioned by such narratives is never actually possible. At best, calls for revival offer a recapitulation of certain aspects of the past. Although many historical practices and values may seem worth recovering, these existed within social contexts that both provided the conditions for their existence and supplied their meaning. Recapitulations of such realities in the present may function quite differently. Moreover, these realities are commonly linked to historical realities that are not worth retrieving. Concerning the family, any honest review of the past cannot help uncovering overt patriarchal patterns that restricted the freedoms and malformed the lives of countless women. Particularly within the US context, the historical functions of race and racist policies have likewise unavoidably restricted freedoms and malformed families and individuals. In a broader view, the realities of colonialization and its Eurocentric concerns decisively shaped the modern sociopolitical world as well as the demography of global Christianity.

Although the family seems uniquely prone to idealized historical memory, families have continuously adapted and changed in myriad complex and intertwined ways throughout history. Accordingly, the next three chapters review the modern development of thought on family and parenthood within the Catholic tradition so as to expose and clarify the origins of the contemporary Catholic conceptual framework. Some of the views expressed are deeply rooted within the tradition, while others have shallow roots stemming largely from reactions to changing modern social realities. This review begins with the origins of modern Catholic Social Teaching and modern Catholic teaching on the family at the close of the nineteenth century. Throughout, the chapters attempt to avoid the methodological pitfalls mentioned above while pointing to elements of the tradition that may be helpful for rethinking a contemporary Catholic theological anthropology of parenthood.

NOTES

1. Taylor, *Secular Age*, 3.
2. Taylor, 13.
3. The enduring efficacy of declension narratives may rest in cognitive biases that allow listeners to be continually captivated, no matter how often the same narrative arch is repeated, as well as the human mind's preference for positive memories and tendency to lend even difficult memories more positive valences over time.
4. For an excellent study on how the imagined past continues to shape present conceptions of family life, see Coontz, *Way We Never Were.*

CHAPTER 1

Origins in Modern Catholic Teaching

This chapter surveys the teachings of the Roman Catholic Magisterium on subjects pertaining to family and parenthood, beginning with the first modern encyclical on marriage, Leo XIII's *Arcanum divinae sapientiae* of 1880, through the papacy of Pope Paul VI in the mid–twentieth century. Although generations of scholars have already amply engaged with these resources, this review offers only limited engagement with the existing secondary literature, instead favoring a close reading methodology.[1] Through a close reading approach, the chapter calls attention to the decisions of the authors regarding their construction of these documents. This approach allows the chapter to shed light on the historical pathways that have led to the currently dominant Catholic framework for parenthood. With this reality in mind, the chapter highlights both consistent themes within this corpus and developments over time. In particular, it identifies two major patterns of restriction in the recent history of magisterial texts, both related to an underlying concern for protecting norms of gender and human sexuality.

The first restriction arises most prominently within the documents of the late nineteenth and early twentieth centuries and is characterized by an anti-Modernist tendency to reject social developments perceived to stem from the misguided claims of the Enlightenment's atheistic, rationalistic, materialistic, and reductionist ideals. Ironically, in its opposition to Modernism, the Catholic hierarchy concretized a particular view of the family that owes much to the ideals of that particular historical moment. This vision of the family is autonomous and nuclear, and comes with associated parental gender roles for motherhood and fatherhood that are cleanly divided by their participation in the private and public spheres. In addition, each gender is characterized by inherent virtues to support these roles—the nurturing, domestic, deferential female; and the protecting, providing male head-of-household.

The second constriction arises most profoundly in the wake of Vatican II, with Paul VI's publication of *Humanae vitae*. This document intended to provide a robust theological vision of marital love and human sexuality, yet its decision on the moral norms surrounding the regulation of conception tightly focused these considerations into a biologically reproductive frame. This exacerbated a tendency to reduce parenthood to procreation and to constrict moral considerations of parenthood to sexual ethical norms.

The modern framework that emerged is characterized by a conception of the family as private, biological, and nuclear. Within this model, an essentialist theory of gender limits consideration of diverse parental roles, while a continual concern to defend sexual ethical norms focuses attention on procreation. Although these trends do not entirely obfuscate earlier views, both work to marginalize broader historical conceptions of parenthood that have long characterized the Catholic theological tradition.

THE MODERN MAGISTERIUM, 1880–1958

Europe's social, political, and religious transition into the modern world did not come easily for the Catholic Church. Although the Industrial Revolution reshaped European economies, political and social changes reshaped the continent from the late eighteenth century through the late nineteenth century. As the institutional Catholic Church lost social capital and suffered repeated humiliations, the Roman Magisterium became increasingly defensive, authoritarian, and centralized.[2] The revolutions of the mid–nineteenth century, in particular, struck close to home, as Pius IX was forced to flee the city of Rome. After his return, he worked to counter the liberalism that accompanied the changes taking place in Europe. He wrote the 1864 encyclical *Quanta cura* and its attached syllabus, which condemned the errors of Modernism, including the infamous condemnation of the opinion that "the Roman Pontiff can and should reconcile himself to and agree with progress, liberalism, and modern civilization."[3] In July 1870, he successfully directed deliberations of the First Vatican Council toward a narrow dogmatic affirmation of the doctrine of papal infallibility. Even this proclamation did not stand in the way of forces reshaping Europe, and the council was soon disrupted by the invasion of Piedmontese Italian forces, who captured and annexed Rome into the Kingdom of Italy in autumn of the same year. Although earlier papacies had tended to be conservative and at times reactionary, Pius IX's condemnations of the ideas and ideals of modernity, coupled with his own gains through the declaration of papal infallibility in *Pastor aeternus*, reshaped the modern papacy. As his successors assumed the anti-Modernist mantle, papal engagement in moral teaching also increased in scope, frequency, and detail.[4]

Following the lead of his predecessor, Pope Leo XIII lived as a self-imposed prisoner of the Vatican throughout the entirety of his papacy. But unlike Pius IX, Leo sought to challenge modernity by mounting a Catholic intellectual renewal that could examine, clarify, and defend Catholic positions against modernist errors. During his twenty-five-year papacy, the remarkably prolific pope wrote ninety encyclicals on a wide array of topics. His 1880 encyclical *Arcanum divinae sapientiae* was the first encyclical devoted entirely to the subject of marriage and family.[5] This letter initiated a way of recounting the story of Christian marriage in the form of a declension narrative that would be retold continuously in successive teaching. Namely, the original form of marriage was good in accordance with the divine plan but, through human sin, suffered corruption; yet marriage was restored by Christ, who raised the institution to a sacrament.[6] *Arcanum*'s major themes include the divinely established hierarchical structure of the family, the Church's role as proclaimer and protector of divine truths, the benefits of love for marriage and spouses, the proper roles of church and state in regulating marriage, the contemporary corruption of morals, and the spread of divorce.[7]

Leo XIII was succeeded by another vigorous anti-Modernist, Pius X, who initiated the task of codifying canon law in 1904 (a project that would not be completed and promulgated until three years after his death, by Benedict XV). Pius X appointed Pietro Cardinal Gasparri to lead the arduous task of collecting and sorting through obsolete and contradictory canons from various sources while consulting with the world's bishops. The 1917 code was intended to collect and clarify the existing ordinances of the Church, but, as Todd Salzman and Michael Lawler document, the section on marriage introduced an innovative new perspective that reflected Cardinal Gasparri's own theological perspective on marriage developed twenty-five years earlier in his book *Tractatus canonicus de matrimonio*. Gasparri advanced three significant arguments in this book: "Marriage is a contract; the formal object of the contract is the permanent and exclusive right of the spouses to each other's bodies for sexual intercourse that leads to procreation; and the primacy of procreation over every other end of marriage."[8] Salzman and Lawler observe that "these three notions were not traditional in magisterial teaching but were all novel opinions in Gasparri's work, and therefore, in the code that his work dominated."[9] Gasparri himself admitted the novelty of considering marriage as a contract, and subsequent scholarship revealed that no prior magisterial document substantiates the right to a body as the "juridical essence of marriage" or as the "object of consent." Likewise, the treatment of the ends of marriage as a hierarchy of goals, as codified in canon law, held little basis in prior teaching.[10]

Benedict XV's successor, Pope Pius XI, wrote two significant encyclicals related to family and parenthood: the 1929 encyclical on education, *Divini illius magistri*; and the 1930 encyclical, *Casti connubii.*[11] The latter built upon *Arcanum* and established Catholic teaching on marriage and family in a way that, with few exceptions, was not substantially altered until the Second Vatican Council.[12] In addition to *Casti connubii's* reliance on *Divini illius magistri*, both of Pius XI's encyclicals relied heavily upon scripture, Saint Augustine,[13] the 1917 *Code of Canon Law*, and the encyclicals of Pope Leo XIII.[14] Among these, the *Code of Canon Law* supplies a juridical understanding of marriage and the obligations of parenthood, clarifies the rights and duties of the Church, and supports existing ecclesial practices.[15] Leo XIII's *Rerum novarum* provides support for asserting limits to the power of the state and helps define state obligations.[16] Like *Arcanum*, *Casti connubii* conceives of the family as a unit of society whose duties are fundamental as they are established by God's will.[17] As such, the goods of marriage and family life are prior and external to particular marriages and understood through the organic connections of society. *Casti connubii* itself introduced the mutual love of spouses as not only a good of marriage but an end of sexual intercourse as well. This being the first instance of such a claim, it constitutes an expansion by Pius XI of the framework for understanding marriage and "the marital act" by extending consideration to the interpersonal relationship of spouses.[18] David Matzo McCarthy has traced how this view subsequently evolved as the conceptual foundation of the family, shifting from the social context to the couple themselves.[19]

Pius XI's earlier encyclical, *Divini illius magistri*, devotes much consideration to the proper relations of the family, the Church, and civil society—the three "societies" with interests in children's education.[20] The encyclical also responds to a number of contemporary issues, including the dangers of sex education in schools, Catholic children in non-Catholic schools, and the coeducation of boys and girls.[21] Here Pius XI argues that "there is not in nature itself, . . . in temperament, in abilities, anything to suggest that there can be or ought to be promiscuity, and much less equality, in the training of the two sexes." Boys and girls are destined for dichotomous vocations, which makes coeducation not only senseless but also potentially harmful. Rather, the "perfect union of the sexes" rightly occurs only in matrimony. Failure to properly separate the sexes in the educational process is especially problematic because it threatens female modesty.[22]

The first part of the companion encyclical, *Casti connubii*, is structured according to Augustine's goods of marriage: procreation, fidelity, and sacrament.[23] Pius XI identifies procreation as the chief end of sexual intercourse but surmises that, while the procreation and the education of children remain the primary ends of marriage, the mutual aid of spouses may be considered the "chief reason and purpose of matrimony."[24] The second part of the encyclical identifies and responds to challenges facing marriage, including the mass media's spread of moral distortions and the growing belief that marriage is not a divinely established institution but a human construct with mutable forms and purposes.[25] The encyclical condemns contraception, abortion, and state or personal intervention in the body's procreative capabilities along with ideologies favoring women's emancipation from the domestic sphere and equal social rights with men.[26] *Casti connubii* concludes by advocating for a return to the divine intention for marriage as articulated in Catholic teaching. Like Leo XIII in *Arcanum*, Pius XI presumes that the propositions of the Magisterium are absolute, authentic interpretations of God's will for humanity that are not subject to the possibility of reform or alteration.[27] Likewise, these teachings are assumed to be nearly universally applicable.[28]

Both Leo XIII and Pius XI were critical of the growing women's movements in the West. Between *Arcanum* and *Casti connubii*, the goals of the European and American movements had shifted more firmly toward suffrage as women had gained the right to vote throughout Northern and Northeastern Europe, Canada, Australia, and the United States.[29] Spain and Portugal followed the year after *Casti connubii*, while Italy, France, and most of Southeastern Europe held out until the close of World War II. For his part, Pius XI describes the movements toward women's participation in public life as "unnatural" and in support of a "false liberty" that fails to recognize the natural distinctions of the sexes. Pius XI claimed that these movements would lead to women's own harm, ultimately making them slaves and mere instruments of men.

In contrast, the pope presents the domestic sphere as a women's proper place, where she has been raised by the Gospel to a "truly regal throne." Recalling Saint Paul and Saint Augustine, Pius XI confirms the subjugation of wives to their husbands and presents this as a manifestation of, not in contradiction to, women's dignity.[30] Their noble status notwithstanding, wives owe their husbands "honorable and trusting obedience."[31] Throughout the era, a hierarchal complementarity is repeatedly asserted, whereby the fundamental equality and social inequality of men and women are simultaneously upheld as unchangeable, natural, and inherent to the Christian tradition. Male primacy in the home is supported with reference to the bond between Christ and the Church by directly associating husbands with Christ and wives with the Church.[32] However, *Casti connubii* also limits male authority by clarifying that no wife is compelled to comply with demands from her husband that are not in accord with reason or her own dignity. Further, Pius XI offers complementary primacies: "For if the man is the head, the woman is the heart, and as he occupies the chief place in ruling, so she may and ought to claim for herself the chief place in love."[33]

Hierarchal complementarity, upheld earlier by Leo XIII and reiterated with some modifications by Pius XI, remained the prevailing conception of spousal and family order for another three decades, until Vatican II introduced a more egalitarian vision of marriage. Within this ordered home, parenthood is at least partially an act of caretaking, supervision, and educating, though the details of these functions are generally undeveloped.[34] *Divini illius magistri* upholds Aquinas's view that a father's rights over his children, including the duty to educate, are natural extensions of biological paternity.[35] *Casti connubii* clarifies that God "would have failed to make sufficient provision for children that had been born; . . . if He had not given to those to whom He had entrusted the power and right to beget them, the power also and the right to educate them."[36] Thus, by God's providence, the biological procreative capacity is trusted to assure *both the right and capacity* of parents to educate their children. This appeal to God's providence certainly overrode much observational evidence to the contrary. Nonetheless, as marriage was set within clearly ordered social relationships, actual responsibilities for educating did not depend entirely on individual parental capacities. After Vatican II's shift to a more personalist understanding of marriage, the conceptual autonomy of the family likewise increased, such that the parental pair became more central as attention to the socially embedded nature of families decreased.[37]

Beyond the changing social landscape, *Casti connubii*'s concerns were also driven by developments in married sexual norms. Among affluent Catholics, family sizes had begun to shrink, suggesting private use of contraceptives even amid public opposition.[38] Simultaneously, scientific advances made mapping fertility possible, and Protestant denominations began rethinking their longstanding opposition to contraception. Knowledge of fertile and infertile periods during the menstrual cycle had been available for some time, but in the early 1920s the Japanese gynecologist Kyusaku Ogino tracked the ovulation cycle precisely enough to reliably estimate these periods. His work, along with that of the Austrian obstetrician-gynecologist Hermann Knaus, was quickly employed to develop calendar-based methods for regulating conception. In the spring of 1930, a Catholic physician in the Netherlands produced the first ovulation calendar for the purpose of assisting married couples to avoid pregnancy. Only a few months later, in July 1930, the Anglican Communion's Lambeth Conference ratified a resolution approving the use of contraception within marriage. This constituted the first major denomination to break with the long-standing Christian moral condemnation of contraception, a position the same conference had reaffirmed at its previous meeting a decade earlier.

Casti connubii was promulgated on December 31, 1930; the close of the year in which both these developments had taken place. In response to the Anglican development, the encyclical appeals to the "uninterrupted Christian tradition" and declares contraceptive acts as offenses against both divine and natural law. It condemns all deliberate frustration of "the marital act" as a "sin against nature" and "a deed which is shameful and intrinsically vicious."[39] Moreover, it recalls God's judgment of this "horrible crime," who at times has "punished it with death."[40] Pius XI did not express the same stern judgment regarding periodic abstinence. His adherence to Augustine would have certainly raised suspicion of deliberate use of infertile periods to prevent conception, but his introduction of love as something more than a secondary end of the sexual act provided a legitimating rationale for knowingly infertile intercourse.[41] Although avoiding pregnancy certainly raised moral suspicion, the prevailing moral methodology of the time focused on the physicality of the act so as to make intention relatively inconsequential for moral judgment.[42] Clear magisterial guidance on this latter question would not be forthcoming for another two decades through the intervention of Pius XI's successor, Pius XII, who assumed the papacy in 1939.

Despite never writing an encyclical on family and parenthood, Pius XII's many public speeches demonstrate great concern for the subject. Like his predecessors, he affirmed the family as the basis for society, with primary rights that oblige social respect and protection.[43] Likewise, he disdained social acceptance of divorce and criticized the negative moral influence of mass media.[44] Along with the nascent social encyclical tradition, then including only *Rerum novarum* and *Quadregesimo anno*, Pius XII urged familial stability through secure housing, just wages, and rights to private property.[45] He also showed a unique concern for instructing fathers. He asserted that the entire health and well-being of the family—not only physically but also intellectually and spiritually—rested upon the virtue and hard work of the father.[46] He likened fatherhood to God's original act of creation and surmised that fatherhood communicates "the superior life of intelligence and love."[47] And, appealing once again to the hierarchal complementarity of the day, he asserted that fathers not only fulfill the "priestly" role of parenting but by their position of authority also hold an "episcopal" role within the home.[48]

Like his predecessor, Pius XII engaged with those contemporary issues that continued to reshape familial and parental norms. Informed by the new field of genetics, he deemed avoiding pregnancy out of concern for hereditary disease potentially licit, but he reminded doctors not to infringe upon the spousal right of procreation.[49] He also clarified the moral status of tracking fertility to prevent conception through a historic statement to midwives in 1951, in which he approved what came to be known as the "rhythm method" under certain limited conditions.[50] This judgment reified his introduction of love as a secondary end of sexual intercourse and further cast Catholic conceptions of marriage into an interpersonal frame. However, suspicion of immoral motivations still prevailed, such that permission and guidance by a priest was mandated for couples seeking recourse to this method.

In addition to this significant judgment, Pius XII also relativized the importance of biological kinship that had been central to his predecessors' vision of the family based on marriage and procreation. For him, the primary bond between children and parents was the passing on of faith, which "is a thousand times more precious" than biological parenthood.[51] He urged infertile couples, or those fearful of transmitting hereditary disease, to consider adoption, and he described adoption as "usually crowned with happy results" and "free of moral objections."[52] Yet his views on adoption are neither comprehensive nor entirely optimistic and, adding further ambiguity, he taught that "sterility is very often the punishment for the sinner."[53]

From Leo XIII through Pius XII, magisterial teaching demonstrates significant continuity along clear lines of development. For example, each pontiff presumes an essentialist understanding of gender, whereby male and female are stable and distinct categories, and legitimates differentiated consideration on the basis of gender. This includes gendered roles within the household and society, separate educational opportunities corresponding to these social roles, and a hierarchal differentiation of male over female within marriage. However, Pius XII's acceptance of birth regulation through periodic abstinence and his willingness to diverge from the biological, nuclear model of the family in a way that emphasizes spiritual kinship does not fit seamlessly with the earlier documents. Likewise, the documents demonstrate some tensions in their conception of parenthood within the family. This is caused by an apparent desire to prioritize both marital love and procreation, driven by the differences in Augustine's "goods" and Aquinas's "ends" of marriage, as well as the desire for the legalistic clarity that characterized the theology of this period. Leo XIII and Pius XI emphasized the spousal bond but avoided a hierarchy, whereas the 1917 *Code of Canon Law* presents the goods of marriage as a hierarchy. Likewise, the Holy Office in 1944 judged that all other ends of marriage are "essentially subordinate" to procreation and education—a judgment confirmed by Pius XII.[54] Consequently, the interpersonal relationship of parents as marriage partners is at times upheld, and even extended into sexual intercourse by Pius XI, but at other times is clearly subjugated to their responsibility to procreate.

There is also considerable irony in how the conception of the family promoted in these teachings is related to ideals and realities made possible by the Industrial Revolution, while the documents themselves purport to uphold tradition and frequently reject social advancements as evidence of moral and social decline. After the rise of the industrial economy had moved economic production out of homes and into industrial centers, the Catholic conception of the family could more easily distinguish between the public, economic lives of men and the private, domestic lives of women. Likewise, as wage labor in industry replaced more traditional forms of trade and craftsmanship, often passed down through families, the model of the nuclear family, headed by the male wage earner, became more plausible. This centered the conception of the family on the marital bond of the couple alone, rather than the joining of families. *Casti connubii* demonstrates acceptance of this shift in its emphasis on spousal love, while criticizing aspects of the modern age that had made this shift possible.

Catholic acknowledgment of marriage as a right of individuals stretches back well before the modern autonomous conception of the family to the begrudging medieval acknowledgment of the validity of clandestine weddings.[55] As marriage came to be officially recognized as a sacrament in the Late Middle Ages, ecclesial control became increasingly important. In the twelfth century, Pope Alexander III accepted a view of marriage based on consent and consummation, which notably disregarded parental consent and public celebration as essential for sacramental validity. Controversy about the centrality of the couple alone continued through the Council of Trent into the modern era. But this individualist commitment entered a new social reality as the Industrial Revolution further freed couples from traditional familial and social constraints through wage labor, allowing decisions to marry to be private to an extent rarely experienced before. Traditional familial authority and social controls weakened as individual freedom expanded alongside possibilities for self-sufficiency.[56] Yet within the documents considered above, recognition of and concern for this earlier social shift is remarkably muted. Instead, the private, nuclear model of the family has come to be accepted as normative, with relatively little awareness of social transformations that fueled its recent rise to ideological prominence.

This transition represents a significant disembedding of the concept of family from social life. Despite occurring within the historical context of Catholic anti-Modernism, the growing prominence of the autonomous nuclear family followed the broader modernist trend, identified by Charles Taylor, of framing values around the disembedded individual, or in this case the individual married couple.[57] Likewise, Sandra Sullivan-Dunbar has explored the rising prominence of individualistic conception of the person,[58] and the shifting view of dependency as innate and positive for persons and society to association with weakness and vulnerability throughout this period from the Enlightenment into modernity.[59] As Catholic Social Teaching developed in subsequent decades, it retained the idea of the family as a society and argued for the family's obligations to larger society, but these issues remained framed by the distinction of nuclear families as private cells within larger society that had became operative early in the modern period and came to dominate later thought.

Further, these changing emphases are influenced by elements of romantic thought. Romanticism was a multifaceted and broad social and intellectual movement. Like the Catholic hierarchy, Romanticism rejected many aspects of the emerging modern industrial world, while disagreeing significantly with the Church on the role and nature of religion. Each yearned for an idealized medieval past and was skeptical of the so-called advances of the modern world. Both also tended to recapitulate the "natural" family in ways that rejected what they viewed as modernism's excesses, while subtly assuming conditions for family life that modernity had made possible. The blindness to the upheaval of more diverse and communal family structures was supported by the rising Romantic movement's ability to tap into Western Christian ideals of gender and the family that gave the new conception of the family a convincing garb of traditionalism. To the private, nuclear conception of the family, Romanticism contributed visions of the innate virtues of each gender. This framework substantiated grounds for the conviction, shared by each of the pontiffs discussed above, that women and men operate in distinctive social spheres, despite the relatively recent origin of social patterns supporting these ideals. Moreover, appeals to innate differences in roles and virtues shaped the understanding of proper education based on gender, restrictions of women to their proper place within the home, and support for family wages for male heads of households. Interestingly, Romanticism's appreciation of the preciousness of childhood likewise supported a split-minded conception of children among Christians, in which children are envisioned both as gifts who bring joy and strengthen the bonds of marriage as well as rebellious adults-in-training, subject to "evil impulses," who stand in need of education and correction.[60]

Although all the popes of this period utilized the postindustrial separation of the male public sphere from the female domestic sphere, they were also aware of shifting gendered barriers, particularly about the role of women in public life.[61] Such changes were identified as unnatural errors of modernity opposed to women's essential character.[62] Holding on to one aspect of the preindustrial world, these teachings clearly articulate the family as a hierarchical society based in male authority. Observation of the social world of this time, the patriarchal patterns of the Christian tradition, and their understanding of divine law all supported these views.

THE ERA OF VATICAN II, 1958–78

John XXIII was elected to the papacy in the fall of 1958. Shortly thereafter, he shocked the world by announcing plans to convene a council. His predecessor, Pius XII, initiated rapprochement with the modern world by opening the use of the tools of modern biblical criticism to Catholic scholars and by initiating liturgical reforms. Within the realm of family and parenthood, he assessed advancing scientific knowledge and concluded that parental responsibility could include avoiding pregnancy in certain circumstances and that utilizing knowledge of natural processes to avoid pregnancy was morally permissible. In the late 1960s, Pius XII's observations would become central to Pope Paul VI's vision of responsible parenthood. However, before Vatican II, couples themselves were not considered competent to decide the moral justifications and means of avoiding pregnancy without the counsel of a priest. Moreover, many influential hierarchs and moralists rightly recognized the tension with long-standing tradition and therefore remained unconvinced of Pius XII's legitimation of separating sexual intercourse from a clear intention to procreate.

Vatican II's teaching on marriage and family is in many ways continuous with the content of earlier documents. Emphasis remains on the family as the foundation of society, the duties required of society by this fact, the primary rights of parents in their children's education, and the importance of familial stability.[63] Nonetheless, there is unavoidable discontinuity in the greater appreciation of gender equality ushered in by Vatican II. Although the conception of gender remains framed and conditioned by gender essentialism, the social equality of women is significantly broadened.

Six months to the day after the Second Vatican Council began its deliberations, John XXIII's encyclical *Pacem in terris* identified women's social progress as an outgrowth of women's own recognition of their natural dignity.[64] This remarkable statement sharply contrasts with earlier protectionist claims of prior popes, who clearly associated female dignity with modesty, submissiveness to male authority, and domestic life.[65] Before John XXIII, popes, interpreting the natural order and will of God, told women where and in what ways their dignity ought to be protected and promoted. This yielded deep suspicions of women's active involvement in the social spheres of paid labor and public leadership. Like his predecessors, John XXIII also appears quite unaware of the full historical scope of women's labor and tended to address middle- and upper-class individuals who were inclined toward greater alignment with the ideal of a private, nuclear family. Nonetheless, his divergence from earlier teaching initiated a more optimistic view of women's place in the workforce and influenced greater acceptance of coeducation.

As Vatican II progressed, the conception of the family likewise underwent transformation in response to this development. In conceptualizing the family, hierarchical language was replaced by ideals of spiritually enriching spousal partnerships. But as the social equality of women was more broadly affirmed, it was also conditioned by the continuing insistence on the primacy of women's domestic vocation. The term "legitimate progress" came to be employed as a way of asserting that the understanding of women's role in society was at once undergoing transformation and liberation from earlier restrictions, while at the same time upholding the ongoing validity of key values from within those structures.[66] The tensions inherent in holding these claims together would become more clearly evident decades later under John Paul II, whose support for women's rights to public participation is framed by his concern that women have come to neglect their obligations within the family.[67]

Other conceptual shifts in the documents of Vatican II are subtler but likewise mark important transitions that will come to fruition in postconciliar teaching. Among these is a shift from understanding divine law as dictating a particular hierarchical order of the family, in which essential gender roles are assumed, to articulating these essential gender roles themselves. Before the mid–twentieth century, the Catholic hierarchy explicitly promoted a hierarchical understanding of the family, centered on male headship and supported by female nurture. The relatively quick transition away from this overtly hierarchical model is remarkable given its defense as an unchangeable aspect of divine law only a few decades earlier. Since Vatican II, the Magisterium has, at times, suggested aspects of the earlier hierarchical ideal but has largely stood behind the turn, taken most explicitly in *Gaudium et spes*, toward a model of the family centered on spousal partnerships based in love.[68] David Matzko McCarthy argues that this shift forms the basis for John Paul II's further personalistic developments, in which the "interpersonal-organic communion" of the spouses comes to replace the earlier understanding of the "institutional-organic" social order as the foundation for family.[69] With this transition comes increased means of idealizing the private, nuclear family along with a diminishing appreciation for extended kin relations. Moreover, the shift creates the possibility for understanding families as individual cells that can critique and stand in opposition to the broader culture. This externalization and privatization of the family from the broader social context creates room for John Paul II's promotion of the social role of the family as ordered toward social transformation. Richard Gaillardetz has argued that this contrastive distinction of family from society may be strengthened by the reintroduction of the term "domestic church" in Vatican II's dogmatic constitution *Lumen gentium*.[70]

The concept of the family as "domestic church" was drawn from early Christianity and resonated with Eastern Orthodox usage.[71] Although much has been made about the significance of this term, its actual impact is difficult to assess. The introduction of this concept is commonly afforded greater significance than it actually warrants, especially in readings of Vatican II that posit relatively greater discontinuity with the prior tradition. The fact is, popes immediately before Vatican II conceived of the family, like the Church, as a society, and frequently spoke of parents as priests and even bishops of the home. What shifted was not the ecclesial imagery but the relative freedom that Vatican II permitted parents in making decisions about their familial and sexual practices without consulting a priest. Parents came to be seen as more responsible and autonomous, while husbands and wives were described in terms of equality rather than hierarchy. This shift, combined with the changing conception of the Church itself from a hierarchal "perfect society" to a community of the faithful as the "people of God," clearly relocated the way in which the smaller society of the family was conceptualized. The term "domestic church" serves as a convenient marker for this conceptual shift, but Vatican II certainly did not introduce it in and of itself. Moreover, the robust rethinking of the family in light of these transitions is manifest in numerous ways of conceptualizing the family that arise during and after Vatican II. The council describes the family as a "school of deeper humanity,"[72] "the primary mother and nurse of [cultural] education,"[73] "the first school of the social virtues that every society needs,"[74] the "foundation of all society,"[75] an "apprenticeship for the apostolate,"[76] the "domestic church,"[77] an "initial seminary,"[78] and a proclaimer of "both the present virtues of the Kingdom of God and the hope of a blessed life to come."[79] These varied statements emphasize the educational and evangelical dimensions of the family but also its institutional isolation. Although earlier hierarchal language on the definition of the family as an "imperfect society" was certainly limited, unlike the later terminology it naturally integrated the family within the larger social order.[80]

Even as Vatican II helped reimagine the social roles of women in contrast to earlier assertions of divine law, the shift toward greater familial and parental autonomy remained limited by concern for the objective moral order. At the close of the Second Vatican Council in 1965, the question of the legitimacy of oral contraceptives remained undecided. The race for an effective oral hormonal contraceptive had begun in the early 1950s. In 1960 "the pill" was approved for contraceptive use. In the United States, the pill was available only through prescription, and several states prohibited its sale. Within the Catholic context, these developments provoked two questions of intense interest. First, is the use of oral contraceptives technically contraception given that, like the rhythm method, they do not involve any direct interference with the physical sexual act? And second, and more ambitiously, given the sweeping reforms of Vatican II, might the hierarchy be willing to change the traditional stance against contraception? John XXIII chose to reserve such questions from the council's deliberations and created a secret commission to investigate the matter. After his death in 1963, Pope Paul VI came to oversee both the completion of the council itself and the work of this commission, which he made public and expanded.[81] After the close of the council, Paul VI invested heavily in implementing and guiding Vatican II's reforms but did not make a judgment on the matter of birth control until his encyclical *Humanae vitae* was issued a relatively long two and a half years later. Ultimately, he judged that oral contraceptives, unlike the rhythm method, fit within the Church's understanding of contraception, and he reaffirmed as exceptionless the traditional moral opposition to contraception.

Paul VI's actual decision on this matter is of somewhat less interest for this book than the impact of his reasoning on both the subsequent history of moral theology and the self-understanding of Catholics in relationship to the institutional Church.[82] *Humanae vitae* could not simply reject contraception on the basis of physical interference in the sexual act because Vatican II had already accepted the growing influence of "personalism" in moral methodology. Although obedience to the divine law remains essential, personalism does not allow explications of divine law to be both arbitrary in reference to the human good and binding on persons.[83] This contrasts with the earlier physicalist methodology that placed greater emphasis on divine law, known deductively as commands through analysis of the ends of particular acts.[84] Vatican II adopted the view that moral norms must be considered in light of God willing only what is good for persons and prohibiting only that which is not. Consequently, the fact of physical interference in the sexual act alone was no longer sufficient to explain the continued condemnation of contraception. In recognition of this, *Humanae vitae* explained its judgment within a personalistic framework that took account of the human goods of marriage and procreation and in so doing further centralized procreation and sexual ethics within Catholic conceptions of marriage, family, and parenthood.

Contraception was an issue of concern for a wide array of Catholics, such that *Humanae vitae* received immediate and widespread interest. This public attention and the unique posturing of the encyclical itself created conditions for a backlash that furthered divisions among Catholics. Although the document provides a personalist argument in support of its judgment, it first grounds the certainty of this judgment in the unquestionable authority of the Catholic hierarchy itself. In doing so, the encyclical undermines its own personalist positioning because the reasons delivered on this account are, in fact, divorced from the bindingness of its judgment.[85] Not only did Paul VI's judgment disappoint large numbers of Western Catholics who had hoped for, and even anticipated reform; it also couched its judgment in the unquestionable authority of the Magisterium, such that those who found the pope's argument wanting had no clear standing in rejecting its conclusions. Doing so placed one in immediate opposition to the moral authority of the Church itself.

Beyond *Humanae vitae,* the topics of marriage, family, and parenthood are not central to Paul VI's writings. His earlier social encyclical, *Populorum progressio,* is repeatedly silent on the role of the family where explicit references might be expected. Instead, its concern centers on the individual who is the "chief architect of his own success or failure" and who may be "helped, and sometimes hindered, by his teachers and those around him."[86] In fact, here Paul VI employs the terms "father," "mother," and "family" metaphorically (for God, Mary, and the Church or the human community) more often than literally. A single paragraph, titled "The Role of the Family," repeats many traditional issues but still objects to excessive familial influence over individuals.[87] In contrast, *Humanae vitae* contains a more sustained and positive reflection on the family. Most notably, it describes the family apostolate as allowing married couples to "become apostles to other married couples."[88] His later exhortation *Evangelii nuntiandi* of 1975 briefly touches on this theme to describe families as an evangelizing force and develops *Lumen gentium* by adding that aspects of the entire Church ought to be found in family life.[89] As such, Paul VI's general inattention to issues related to the family may have contributed to *Humanae vitae*'s impact as the only major document in which he gave sustained attention to the subject. How responses to this encyclical shaped Catholic self-understandings in relation to its judgment, other Catholics, and the Church at large is centrally important to understanding its historical impact. In concert with the embrace of personalism, which centralized the spousal pair in conceptions of the family, the encyclical and its reception further pushed Catholic conceptions of the family into a more tightly nuclear and biological frame.

The writings of John XXIII and Vatican II had sustained a traditional emphasis on the education of children as an essential component of "procreation," understood in its full moral context. In fact, from Pius XII onward, the ability to raise and educate children well began to be presented as a privileged good in considerations of birth regulation so as to displace the emphasis on procreation as a duty. In contrast, *Humanae vitae* only cautiously accepts the decision against conceiving a child, or more children, with repeated warnings about potential sinfulness. As such, *Humanae vitae* largely ended the trajectory toward an emphasis on education and complicated matters by inescapably tying its moral judgment to absolute magisterial authority. In its wake, the intimate links between sexual ethics and teaching on parenthood and the family produced a tendency to conceive of parenthood in a more restricted sense, centered on biological kinship. Although Paul VI's personalism closely associated the goods of procreation and education, he introduces the virtue of "responsible parenthood" within *Humanae vitae,* with its concern for sexual ethical norms and biological procreation. As the document became central to Catholic understanding, "procreation" likewise came to serve less as shorthand for "procreation and education" and instead was associated with biological reproduction alone, which the encyclical unambiguously framed as an exercise in the virtue of generosity.[90] Magisterial teaching into the present retains the conviction that spiritual education marks Christian parenthood at its fullest, yet this commitment is often overshadowed by a firm connection established between "responsible parenthood" and rejection of contraception.

The tradition's appeal to divine providence as assurance for parents' actual capabilities to educate children well further supported this reduced framework for parenthood even as the social contexts that had sustained this view were now thoroughly eroded.[91] In concert with the Church's own teachings, late modernity had created Western social contexts in which parental roles were matched to gender and supported by thick societal norms. The hierarchy was right to recognize the restrictiveness of this reality, particularly in relation to the freedom and dignity of women, but did not adequately consider how the loss of such structures would undermine supposedly natural parental capacities, which now rested more heavily in individual ability than social supports. Instead, the sufficiency of providence, often cast as the innate nurturing capacities of women and intellectual qualities of men, discouraged reflection on procreation as less than an unambiguous good. With respect to motherhood in particular, confronted with observable changes in women's roles, magisterial teaching shows a double-mindedness that attempts to both affirm women's freedom and dignity while articulating norms for behavior that demonstrate little evidence of significant historical or cross-cultural scrutiny. This allows a uniquely postindustrial feminine ideal to inform magisterial articulations of women's vocations while once socially supported capacities for childrearing are placed on individual parents alone, particularly through the supposedly innate parental aptitudes of women.[92]

CONCLUSION

Significant challenges in the relatively recent history of magisterial thought relate to how the goods of procreation and education are balanced, but the most significant points of concern in the shifting framework for parenthood are the effects of the Industrial Revolution and the changing status of women in Western society as well as the effect of *Humanae vitae* in bringing to the forefront contested sexual ethical norms and interpretations of magisterial authority. These trends have led to a framework for understanding parenthood that places considerable emphasis on gendered identity, particularly for mothers, while remaining relatively unaware of the recent historical roots of its own understanding of the "traditional family," which has increasingly been conceived as autonomous, biological, and nuclear. Chapter 2 considers the progression of magisterial teaching through the papacy of John Paul II. In this, certain established trajectories continue to develop, while John Paul II adds his own distinctive personalist moral methodology and introduces complementarity as an explanatory framework for differentiated yet egalitarian gender roles.

NOTES

1. Among the notable literature, see Von Hildebrand, *Encyclical*; Callahan, *Catholic Case*; Curran and McCormick, *Dialogue*; Smith, *Why* Humanae vitae *Was Right*; and May, Lawler, and Boyle, *Catholic Sexual Ethics*. More recent secondary sources within this ongoing discussion are presented in chapter 3.
2. Such disruptions include the confiscation of Church lands in the French Revolution, the coronation of Napoleon, the invasion and capture of Rome and the Papal States, and the growth of democratic governments separate from ecclesial authority.
3. Pius IX, *Quanta cura*, sec. 80. The Vatican's website posts only the Latin and Italian translations of this document. In Italian, it reads, "Il Romano Pontefice può e deve riconciliarsi e venire a composizione col progresso, col liberalismo e con la moderna civiltà."
4. Keenan, *History*, 30. See also Curran, *Development*, 176.

5. Pius XI, *Casti connubii*, sec. 4.
6. The first portion of this narrative parallels Jesus's words in Matt. 19 and Mark 10; however, the Gospels' perspectives are more moral than historical in nature. Consequently, they lead to an exhortation concerning the divine plan for marriage more than a reclaiming of a prior ideal. The inclusion of a sacramental understanding is the product of much later theological reflection. The corruption observed by the encyclical is most clearly manifest in polygamy and divorce. Leo XIII, *Arcanum*, secs. 5–8.
7. See Leo XIII, *Arcanum*, secs. 1–2, 11–15, 18–34. Two silences are notable. First, *Arcanum* does not view female subordination as a result of the fall; instead, it is part of the divine plan. Second, *Arcanum* is silent about love expressed through sexual intercourse. On the latter, see Obach, *Catholic Church*, 119.
8. Salzman and Lawler, *Sexual Person*, 37.
9. Salzman and Lawler, 37.
10. Salzman and Lawler.
11. Pius XI's first encyclical, *Ubi arcano* (1922), also lamented the harm that the social ills of World War I had done to Christian families. *Quadragesimo anno* (1931) and *Caritate Christi* (1932) consider the family in relation to social life. The constitution *Deus scientiarum Dominus* (1931) and the encyclical *Ad catholici sacerdotii* (1935) consider the priesthood in relation to the family. Finally, *Lux veritatis* (1931) considers the Holy Family as a model for Christian families, while the Apostolic Letter *Con singular complacencia* (1939) argues for the restoration of the family in light of Christ's headship and the model provided by the Holy Family.
12. The delay was not least due to World War I, reactions to which occupied much of Benedict XV's papacy (1914–22), as well as the relative newness of the subject for papal teaching.
13. Direct quotations of Augustine include *Casti connubii*, secs. 6, 17, 53, 101; and *Divini illius magistri*, secs. 10, 11, 17, 23, 26, 33, 36, 41, 55, 98. By comparison, Aquinas appears infrequently (*Casti connubii*, secs. 6, 70, 94; and *Divini illius magistri*, secs. 33, 31). The fifteenth centenary of Augustine's death between the publications of these encyclicals, in 1930, may have encouraged attention to his thought.
14. The encyclicals of Leo XIII referenced include *Arcanum divinae sapientiae* (1880), *Nobilissima gallorum gens* (1884), *Immortale dei* (1885), *Libertas* (1888), *Sapientiae christianae* (1890), *Rerum novarum* (1891), and *Militantis ecclesiae* (1897). *Casti connubii* also makes frequent reference to teachings of the Council of Trent. These function similarly to its use of the *Code of Canon Law*.
15. Pius XI, *Divini illius magistri*, secs. 6, 17, 39, 82, 89.
16. Pius XI, sec. 35; Pius XI, *Casti connubii*, secs. 8, 117, 118.
17. Pius XI, *Casti connubii*, sec. 105.
18. Selling, "Regulating Fertility," 1033.
19. McCarthy, *Sex*, 112.
20. Pius XI, *Divini illius magistri*, sec. 11.
21. Pius XI, secs. 65, 68, 79, respectively.
22. Pius XI, sec. 68.
23. Pius XI, *Casti connubii*, secs. 11–18, 19–30, 31–43, respectively.
24. Pius XI, sec. 24.
25. Pius XI, secs. 47, 49, respectively. Pius XI was cautious toward then-present developments in marriage and argued that marriage's form and purpose are fixed. Individual

choice is free to determine whether and whom a person will marry; but "the nature of matrimony is entirely independent of the free will of man, so that if one has once contracted matrimony, he is thereby subject to its divinely made laws and its essential properties." *Casti connubii*, sec. 6. In this light, and reiterating concerns of *Arcanum*, marriage's indissolubility is defended. *Casti connubii*, sec. 78–92.

26. Pius XI, *Casti connubii*, secs. 53–62, 63–67, 68–71, 74–77, respectively. Secs. 59–62 contain a defense of the Catholic Church's right and ability to define intrinsically evil acts.
27. Pius XI, sec. 1; Pius XI, *Divini illius magistri*, sec. 2. *Divini illius magistri* is more reserved as it seeks to establish the legitimate cooperation of Church, family, and society. In contrast, *Casti connubii* is not concerned with cooperation but with asserting the divine vision for marriage and family against erroneous opinions.
28. E.g., *Divini illius magistri* states that, although baptism provides the entry into the Church and salvation, children of non-Christians are not to be baptized, save for rare circumstances. Thus, despite baptism being a universal good, it is also occasionally withheld in light of the natural rights of parents. Pius XI, *Divini illius magistri*, sec. 39.
29. The initiation of these rights was not always uniform; for example, in Britain only women over the age of thirty were eligible to vote from 1918 until 1928, when the voting rights of men and women were ultimately equalized.
30. Pius XI, *Casti connubii*, sec. 27.
31. Pius XI, secs. 74, 75.
32. Pius XI, secs. 23, 26.
33. Pius XI, sec. 27.
34. Pius XI, sec. 15; Pius XI, *Divini illius magistri*, secs. 32, 34.
35. Pius XI, *Divini illius magistri*, sec. 33. The document quotes Aquinas and reads in part, "Now just as a carnal father partakes of the character of principle in a particular way, which character is found in God in a universal way, so too a person who, in some way, exercises providence in one respect, partakes of the character of father in a particular way, since a father is the principle of generation, of education, of learning and of whatever pertains to the perfection of human life: while a person who is in a position of dignity is as a principle of government with regard to certain things: for instance, the governor of a state in civil matters, the commander of an army in matters of warfare, a professor in matters of learning, and so forth." Aquinas, *Summa theologica*, IIa–IIae, q. 102, a. 1.
36. Pius XI, *Casti connubii*, sec. 16.
37. See McCarthy, *Sex*.
38. Digmann, *Sign*, 172, 179.
39. Pius XI, *Casti connubii*, sec. 54.
40. Pius XI, secs. 55–56. This is a reference to Onan. In subsequent decades, a consensus of biblical scholars came to regard Onan's crime as his disobedience of his father and failure to honor his brother through his obligation to produce children as heirs. "Onanism" is now generally understood as the means by which Onan made himself the object of harsh divine judgment, but not the full moral content of his sin; although in moral methodologies that closely link act and intention, Onan's contraceptive act remains sinful in itself, even as it carries further moral implications given his obligations. Historically, contraception was viewed as a crime against marriage, whereas abortion was considered a crime against created life and therefore God. This notwithstanding, here Pius XI asserts contraception as an abrogation of natural law.
41. Gallagher, "Magisterial Teaching," 75.

42. A 1933 commentary on *Casti connubii* illustratively wrestles with this still-uncertain question: "The marriage act between married people is in itself good. The frustration of conception by birth-prevention is in itself evil. Now, what is in itself good can be forbidden only when it is manifestly done for an evil purpose. Hence the difficulty of forbidding the marriage act at seasons when, according to vital statistics, conception is not likely. But as no good intention can make an evil act good, no good intention can allow the evil of birth-prevention." McNabb, *On Christian Marriage*, 1933. The tendency to admit no clear reason to restrict the practice while also being highly suspicious of its application is further demonstrated by Cardinal Hayes of New York, who in 1936 warned priests, "Instead of being freely taught and commended, it (rhythm) is rather to be tolerated as an extreme remedy or means of preventing sin." Tentier, *Catholics*, 117.
43. Pius XII, "Allocution to Parish Priests," 360; Pius XII, "Radio Message to the World," 353.
44. Pius XII, "Allocution to Newlyweds (1942)," 346ff.; Pius XII, "Radio Message to French Families," 363.
45. Pius XII, "Radio Message to the World," 330; "Letter *Testes obsequii*," 385.
46. Pius XII, "Allocution to Fathers of Families," 398.
47. Pius XII, "Allocution to Newlyweds (1941)," 325.
48. Pius XII, *Summi Pontificatus*, sec. 89.
49. Pius XII, "Allocution to the International Congress," 383. Pius XII also condemned artificial insemination regardless of the donor, but for varying reasons. See Pius XII, "Allocution to the Members of the II World Congress," 482; Pius XII, "Allocution to the Members of the Seventh Congress," 513.
50. Pius XII, "Allocution to the Midwives," 424; Pius XII, "Allocution to Associations," 440. The relation of this judgment to *Casti connubii* is not entirely settled. Many view *Casti connubii*'s moral acceptance of spouses who "use their right in the proper manner although on account of natural reasons either of time or of certain defects, new life cannot be brought forth" as the basis of Pius XII's development. Yet this passage is evidently directed at the elderly and infertile who are allowed to validly marry; a point of tradition defended by Augustine. Further Pius XI's tendency to justify sex through procreation and *Casti connubii*'s later assertion, within an extended consideration of moral marriage preparation, that knowledge of physiology ought not be used for "sinning in a subtle way" suggests that he may not have been inclined to agree with his successor. This statement could be an allusion to the rhythm method. It is consistent with Augustine's rejection of periodic abstinence in his opposition to the Manichees; although, until the twentieth century this was a theoretical debate only. See *Casti connubii*, secs. 59, 108; Obach, 149; Augustine "On the Morals"; and Hebblethwaite, *Paul VI*, 298.
51. "Above all, remember that when you call your children heirs of your blood, you must refer to something which is much greater than corporal generation only. You are, and your children ought to be, the source of a race of saints, . . . men sanctified and raised up to participate in the divine nature by means of supernatural grace. . . . As a consequence, in baptized people, when one speaks of transmitting inherited blood to descendants, . . . *there is no need to limit the sense of those words to a purely biological and material element,* but it may be extended to that which is, as it were, the nutriative liquid of the intellectual and spiritual life: the patrimony of faith, virtue, and honor transmitted by parents to their *posterity is a thousand times more precious than the blood*-be it ever so rich-infused into their veins" (emphasis added); Pius XII, "Allocution to Newlyweds," 312–13.
52. Pius XII, "Allocution to the Members of the Seventh Congress," 520.

53. Pius XII, "Allocution to Midwives," 408. This is likely an allusion to sexually transmitted disease.
54. The Rota asserted that marriage has both a primary and secondary end and this ordering is attested to by numerous popes, theologians, canonists, and moralists as well as recorded in Canon Law. The primary end of marriage is the procreation and education of children, the secondary is mutual aid and a remedy for concupiscence. The Rota contends that, because the rights of mutual aid and common living are "intrinsically dependent" on the right to "acts of generation," the ordering of the ends of marriage is certain in as much as the secondary is clearly dependent upon the primary. Holy Roman Rota, "Order," 553. "Now, the truth is that matrimony . . . has not as a primary and intimate end the personal perfection of the married couple but the procreation and upbringing of a new life. . . . This is true of every marriage, even if no offspring result." Pius XII, "Allocution to Midwives," 424.
55. See Christensen-Nuges, "Parental Authority," 51–72; Donahue, "Canon Law," 144–58; Finch, "Parental Authority," 189–204.
56. Brekus, "Children," 307.
57. Taylor, *Secular Age*, 147.
58. Hobbes proposed a thought experiment that considered persons "as if but now sprung out of the earth and suddenly (like mushrooms) come to full maturity without any kind of engagement to each other." Subsequent thinkers came to favor such an unattached individual as an anthropological given, despite the absurdity of such an assumption. Sullivan-Dunbar writes, "To seriously consider the realities of our beginnings harbored within the body of another, and of our deep connection and dependency on others early in life" causes such theories to collapse." Sullivan-Dunbar, *Human Dependency*, 36.
59. "In preindustrial English society, dependency was acknowledged as a universal condition; while women and children, for example, were certainly dependent on husbands and fathers, the husbands and fathers were also dependent on others in the economic and political ladder, and their interdependence with wives and children was also acknowledged. Dependency was the norm, and no cause for stigma; society was a complex system of dependencies. Furthermore, the word 'dependency' referred to a social relation rather than a state of an individual; the notion of psychological dependence did not exist. The word 'independence' was rarely used in preindustrial times, and when it first emerged, applied to groups (such as an independent church) rather than to individuals. When it did begin to be used more regularly, it often signaled a perceived social problem, such as a person who was too mobile, for example, free of the ordered local structures of social existence. In other words, 'independence,' not 'dependence,' was problematic prior to the rise of industrialization in England." Sullivan-Dunbar, *Human Dependency*, 53.
60. Pius XI, *Casti connubii*, sec. 15, 53; Pius XI, *Divini illius magistri*, secs. 8, 59, 68. *Divini illius magistri* recounts the proverb, "Folly is bound up in the heart of a child and the rod of correction shall drive it away."
61. See Reuther, *Christianity*, 10.
62. Pius XI, *Casti connubii*, sec. 75.
63. John XXIII, *Pacem in terris*, secs. 16, 17; John XXIII, *Mater et magistra*, sec. 195; Vatican II, *Gaudium et spes*, sec. 52.
64. John XXIII, *Pacem in terris*, sec. 41.
65. Pius XI, *Casti connubii*, secs. 74–75.

66. Vatican II, *Gaudium et spes*, sec. 52.
67. John Paul II, *Mulieris dignitatem*, sec. 10.
68. Vatican II, *Gaudium et spes*, sec. 48.
69. McCarthy, *Sex*, 118.
70. "To write of family as a domestic church, as Vatican II did, risks reducing the Christian household to a kind of spiritual refuge, and ecclesial 'oasis' from the hostile world." Gaillardetz, "School," 137.
71. Bishop Pietro Fiordelli was influential in the inclusion of this term within the document. He had been involved with the Christian Family Movement and knew of patristic sources that included references to "the Christian family as 'little church' or 'church of the home,' and to heads of households exercising an 'episcopal' role." The last of these was already in use by Pius XII. See Fahey, "Christian Family," 85–92.
72. Vatican II, *Gaudium et spes*, sec. 52.
73. Vatican II, sec. 62.
74. Vatican II, *Gravissimum educationis*, sec. 2.
75. Vatican II, *Gaudium et spes*, sec. 52.
76. Vatican II, *Apostolicam actuositatem*, sec. 30. Also see "training for the apostolate" and, in *Lumen gentium*, "school of the lay apostolate." Vatican II, *Lumen gentium*, sec. 35.
77. Vatican II, *Lumen gentium*, sec. 11.
78. Vatican II, *Optatem totius*, sec. 2.
79. Vatican II, *Lumen gentium*, sec. 35.
80. See Leo XIII, *Arcanum*, secs. 11–15; Pius XI, *Casti connubii*, sec. 12.
81. In his oversight of the council, Paul VI habitually intervened in support of the more conservative minority and provided their concerns with additional chances at incorporation into the documents. Yet he ultimately left the manner of incorporation open to the judgments of the drafting commissions. In the commissions, these suggestions were reinterpreted in light of the existing documents and substantially softened. Paul VI's interventions in the council are well documented, as is the circuitous path that Father Ermenegildo Lio's *De castitate* took from a rejected draft document, through its first return as papal *modi* in 1965 to finding its expression in *Humanae vitae*, a connection that Lio would celebrate in articles claiming he had written the "rough draft" of *Humanae vitae*. See Hebblethwaite, *Paul VI*, 298–300, 444, 470–71, 526.
82. Subsequent moral theology questioned assertions of absolute norms as framed by the Magisterium. Proportionalists and others differentiated the rightness or wrongness of an act from the moral goodness or badness of the actor, and therefore favored "virtually exceptionless" norms as more appropriate given the need to account for the particular situational conditions. Making the context and circumstances in which moral acts are performed integral to their moral assessment undercuts Paul VI's assertion that the act of contraception is, in itself, never morally permissible. Divisions within post–Vatican II Catholic personalism are profoundly influenced by this particular disagreement. See Traina, *Feminist Ethics*, 294; Fuchs, *Christian Ethics*, 44–45; and McCormick, "Ambiguity," 38.
83. As Traina explains, personalism essentially operates on this principle: "a legitimate norm advances the integral good of particular persons." Personalism grew from the melding of the natural law tradition with the Enlightenment concern for individual dignity and human rights. Traina, *Feminist Ethics*, 106.
84. The introduction of McNabb's commentary on *Casti connubii* is illustrative of the mentality of this early approach. He asserts, "Man's moral rule is a series of divine commands.

But commands are neither proved nor approved: they are obeyed." McNabb, *On Christian Marriage*, xiv.

85. According to Traina, because Vatican II emphasized both "the democratic implications of natural law epistemology and the collegial basis for a theology of hierarchal charismatic power. The result is an unresolved tension between the ultimately democratic implications of ethics' reliance on universal human reason and the hierarchal structure of the charismatic institution that purports to guard both dogmatic and moral truth." Traina, *Feminist Ethics*, 120.
86. Paul VI, *Populorum progressio*, sec. 15. This is especially striking because "formal education" is included.
87. Paul VI, *Populorum progressio*, sec. 36.
88. Paul VI, *Humanae vitae*, sec. 26. In the closing paragraph, Paul VI reminds that such moral teaching is ultimately directed at the attainment of happiness, for which a person "yearns with all the strength of his spirit, unless he keeps the laws which the Most High God has engraved in his very nature. These laws must be wisely and lovingly observed"; sec. 31.
89. Paul VI, *Evangelii nuntiandi*, sec. 71.
90. As Gallagher writes, canon 1113 of the 1917 *Code of Canon Law* makes clear that marriage is "an institution whose principal end is the total human good of the next generation." Gallagher, "Magisterial Teaching," 72.
91. Parents are clearly exhorted to educate their children in moral, practical, spiritual, and other matters. This question bears more on the extent to which these obligations ought to be a factor when considering avoiding conception.
92. Traina identifies Catholic magisterial teaching as playing into an essentialist feminist script in which "women have inborn capacities for tenderness and nurture that have been shut up in the home. If the doors of the household were thrown open, women's special influence would flow out into public life, transforming a world heretofore shaped only by men who, though not entirely depraved, tend to be rough and mean when beyond women's gentling reach. There are plenty of problems with this theory, not least among them the empirical fact that most women do not have the energy to be angelic in both household and public square." Traina, *Feminist Ethics*, 1–2.

CHAPTER 2

The Focus on Sex and Gender

This chapter continues the review of magisterial teaching through the writings of John Paul II and Benedict XVI. Like the first chapter, this chapter proceeds chronologically, with occasional assessments and explanations along the way. Ordering John Paul II's writings on issues relevant to our concerns is no small task, given their breadth and number. Distinct attention is given to his early papal and pre-papal writings to illuminate foundational elements of his perspective. During the 1960s, as he rose from auxiliary bishop to archbishop to cardinal, Karol Wojtyla wrote *Love and Responsibility* and *The Acting Person,* influenced Vatican II's *Dignitatis humanae* and *Gaudium et spes,* and corresponded with Paul VI as he prepared *Humanae vitae.* Early in his papacy, John Paul II began a series of addresses known as the "Theology of the Body"; called the 1980 Synod of Bishops on the theme of the family; and, in response to this synod, released both the apostolic exhortation *Familiaris consortio* and the "Charter on the Rights of the Family." Significant documents from the subsequent quarter century of his papacy include the encyclicals *Evangelium vitae, Centesimus annus, Sollicitudo rei socialis,* and *Laborem exercens*; the apostolic exhortation *Christifideles laici*; and his apostolic letters to women, children, and families. His legacy also includes numerous audiences, speeches, homilies, and books, in which he considered topics pertinent to this project.[1] Some of his predecessors were also quite prolific, yet no pope has shaped current Catholic discourse on parenthood and the family more than John Paul II.

In addition to works signed by John Paul II, significant documents were produced during his papacy by Vatican dicasteries, including the Congregation for the Doctrine of the Faith (CDF) and the Pontifical Council for the Family, as well as the United States Conference of Catholic Bishops (formerly the National Conference of Catholic Bishops and United States

Catholic Conference). For their part, the US bishops have issued a number of documents on marriage and family over the past forty years. Much of the content repeats or paraphrases teachings expounded by Rome, but these also contextualize the message for an American audience. The subsequent papacy of Benedict XVI pales in comparison with both the length and output of that of John Paul II. For the themes of this book, the impact of Pope Benedict XVI is relatively small, as he too generally extended the thought of his predecessor within these areas.

EARLY WRITINGS, 1960s TO MID-1980s

Bishop Karol Wojtyla's intellectual interest in the topics of love, marriage, and sexuality found expression in his 1960 book *Love and Responsibility*. Here he presents both marriage and family as founded in love. The former rightfully and naturally leads to the latter, but marriage precedes and is not absorbed by the formation of a family.[2] True conjugal love requires a conscious decision to "participate in the whole natural order of existence" through begetting children.[3] Wojtyla argues, "Sexual relations between a man and a woman in marriage have their full value as a union of persons only when they go with conscious acceptance of the possibility of parenthood."[4] If this possibility is rejected, especially by physical interference with the sexual act itself, the entire sexual act is reduced to mere pleasure seeking.[5] True conjugal love further entails preparedness to accept new human life and ensure a child's full physical and spiritual development.[6]

Wojtyla presents families as little societies and consequently surmises that parents and one or two children may not constitute a family in its fullest sense, because families arise "within the framework of a community of children, a collective of siblings."[7] In addition, Wojtyla discerns a basic asymmetry in male and female experiences of parenthood. He understands women to be powerfully and instinctually driven by desire for children, while men must cultivate paternal feelings.[8]

In what became a hallmark of his papal teaching, Wojtyla's views here combine repetitions of traditional positions (e.g., the distinction of marriage as sacrament from family as society, commitment to the value of large families, and presumed differences in gendered behavior) with his own, often innovative, argumentation.[9] This innovative perspective was driven in no small part by his commitment to personalism, based in the personalist norm: *respect persons as subjects in themselves and never use them as a means to an end.*[10] This universal ethical norm is based upon the uniqueness of human reason and the existence of a subjective "inner self."[11] Consequently, the task of ethics is to carefully differentiate acts of "loving kindness" from acts that intend to use persons as something less than respect for their full personhood permits.[12] In *Love and Responsibility*, this method finds unique application in sexual ethics, where lust provides a powerful motivation to violate the latter prohibition.[13]

Before his papacy, Cardinal Wojtyla participated in every session of the Second Vatican Council and contributed to drafting *Gaudium et spes*. As pontiff, John Paul II repeatedly returned to *Gaudium et spes* and its assertion, based on Luke 17, that "man . . . cannot fully find himself except through a sincere gift of himself."[14] This phrase became something of a mantra in his moral writings and corresponds to the personalist moral perspective he had been developing before his efforts at the council.

Wojtyla also served on the papal birth control commission, but, owing to his commitment to remain in solidarity with his fellow Polish bishops, whose movements were constrained by political authorities, he never attended a meeting and missed significant votes.[15] Despite this, speculation on his role in drafting *Humanae vitae* persisted throughout his own papacy. Recent reports based on Gilfredo Marengo's review of previously sealed documents suggest that Wojtya's influence was noteworthy but indirect. The future pope sent suggestions and "an extensive treatment of the theme" to Paul VI, but his words were not directly incorporated into the encyclical.[16] The drafting process itself apparently included considerable revisions to a draft document, while Paul VI personally labored to develop the encyclical's pastoral aspects. Marengo's research also uncovered a previously unknown request for reflections on the encyclical's theme made by Paul VI to the 197 prelates gathered for the 1967 Synod of Bishops. Twenty-five letters were ultimately received. Only seven, Cardinal Wojtyla's included, encouraged reaffirming existing teaching. Unlike those who felt that the reforms of Vatican II pointed toward lifting the ban on contraception, Wojtyla viewed both *Humanae vitae*'s conclusions and personalist methodology to be in clear continuity with the council's teachings.[17] As pope he repeatedly presented *Gaudium et spes* and *Humanae vitae* as harmonious documents.

John Paul II's personalist method recognized the potential for moral error in any means of regulating conception such that he remained suspicious of all methods of family planning; though this did not rise anywhere near the level of some bishops of the Vatican II era who believed that all licit sexual acts required a specific intention to procreate.[18] His concern led him to argue that married partners may commit adultery with one another and to remind spouses that fertility awareness methods may still be used immorally.[19] Skeptics noted that his personalism, with its fine-tuned analysis of the will's correspondence to physical acts, could also be viewed as a thinly veiled form of physicalism under a personalist guise. Such accusations fueled the larger rift growing among Catholic moral theologians that played a key role in centering Catholic concern for parenthood on reproductive issues. The next chapter pays more attention to the academic side of this intra-Catholic divide. For now, it is sufficient to acknowledge that some of the developments of John Paul II's moral reasoning provided grounds for significant intellectual opposition. Both the conditions of the times and the pope's own exercise of papal authority helped engender a situation where this opposition grew into a robust intra-Catholic divide that centered on the issue of contraception as the convergence point for many existing tensions. The claims and counterclaims leveled in this dispute exerted significant force in restricting the Catholic conception of parenthood by centering the understanding of parenthood on reproductive issues.

Less than a year after becoming pope, John Paul II began delivering catechetical instruction through a series of papal audiences, which would become known as the Theology of the Body.[20] The initial set of addresses, beginning in November 1979, built upon themes articulated in *Love and Responsibility* and laid the foundations for a personalist anthropology that supported the normative moral claims of *Humanae vitae.* This "Catechesis on the Book of Genesis" begins with Jesus's references to Genesis in his response to divorce in Matthew 19. From here, John Paul II applied his phenomenological insights to the imagery of prelapsarian humanity in order to ground his anthropological vision.[21] Although he begins by observing the bodily singularity of persons as fundamental, his anthropological account soon turns to the gendered manifestations of human embodiment. This moves through reflections on sexual differentiation toward a theological vision of the meaning and norms of sexuality.[22]

From 1980 to 1981, a second series of addresses provided a catechesis on the Sermon on the Mount. In these, lust acquires central importance in the account of the postlapsarian human, who has become "the man of lust."[23] John Paul II explains that a primary effect of the fall was that the differentiation between man and woman, particularly with reference to physicality, became a source of shame that persists through the human inability to realize authentic communion or to satisfy lust.[24] Thus, the heart "has become a battlefield between love and lust."[25] The human capacity to objectify and seek possession of other human beings is the great harm caused by this conflictive condition; a sinfulness that stands in direct contradiction to the personalist norm.[26]

The extent to which John Paul II understood these and subsequent catechetical cycles, which continued through 1984, as developing a fundamental anthropology in addition to a particular sexual anthropology is unclear, although he does indicate that the essential roots of Christian anthropology could be located in Genesis.[27] To some extent, more holistic accounts of his fundamental anthropology can be found in his earlier work *The Acting Person* and in the Christocentric anthropological vision developed in his first encyclical, *Redemptor hominis,* in 1979.[28] Particular anthropologies are presented in his reflections on the person as worker in the 1981 social encyclical, *Laborem exercens,* and his thoughts on womanhood in *Mulieris dignitatem.*[29] Accordingly, it is important to situate the sexual, intrapersonal, and nuptial dimensions of his anthropological thought, expressed in the catechetical addresses, within his broader reflections on the human person and condition—although the manner of relationship among these is not entirely self-evident.

The anthropological vision developed in the Theology of the Body bears strongly on the evolving Catholic framework for parenthood. In these addresses, the pope's views are mostly constrained to interpersonal realities of marriage and sexuality, such that little is said with respect to the nature and conditions of parents as caregivers. Although such an absence cannot be counted against a project that never sought to take up the topic as a matter of primary concern in the first place, the conditions of Catholicism at the time and the absence of this emphasis elsewhere helped center Catholic perspectives on parenthood more firmly on sexual and reproductive concerns.

The Theology of the Body received, and continues to receive, a differentiated reception within Catholicism. At the popular level, these reflections have been embraced by many Catholics, who often find in them both deep personal significance and a confirmation of their own religious commitments; but large swaths of the Catholic faithful also remain unaware or uninterested in their content. At the academic level, some have strongly embraced John Paul II's perspective; others have questioned how normative insights might be extracted through phenomenological readings of mythical characters.[30] Moreover, the project's end point in a defense of *Humanae vitae* suggests that it is driven by a clear doctrinal agenda despite presenting itself as an open reflection on biblical and experiential wisdom. At the doctrinal level, the speeches provide further intellectual bases for authoritative teachings, particularly those that pertain to gender and sexual ethics, within the framework of Vatican II. Despite not rising to a particularly high level of authority as addresses alone, several arguments found their way into more authoritative documents in subsequent decades.

Two key insights of the Theology of the Body quickly rose to prominence in the reasoning of magisterial documents. First is the norm specifying that morally praiseworthy sexual relations must be characterized by a mutual self-gift. Second is the assertion that men and women are created complementary in their persons—that is, as both distinct and equal. This complementarity has normative implications. Both these views could be found in the English edition of the *Catechism* published in 1994, and both hinge on John Paul II's development of the "nuptial meaning of the body" that is central to the anthropology constructed in the Theology of the Body.[31]

The idea of authentic love as self-gift and, consequently, of moral interpersonal actions as self-gift, arises from the union of John Paul II's personalist thought with the teaching of *Gaudium et spes*. Whereas Paul VI had taught that each and every specific sexual act must conform to the unitive and procreative purposes of the sexual act, considered in its objective meaning, John Paul II's concept of self-gift connected this mandate more clearly to the authenticity of human love. Within the unitive dimension, marriage safeguards the freedom and trust necessary for lovers to offer themselves interpersonally as self-gift. Within the procreative dimension, "openness to procreation" maintains the connection to physical self-gift as a lover is fully accepted, fertility and all. To intentionally render a sexual act infertile is to deny interpersonal fullness to both one's partner and one's self. This is because the human body has a "nuptial meaning" that finds its proper expression in marriage, where sexual intercourse may speak to the fullness of the human person as both subject and gift.

Likewise, the concept of "complementarity" explained both how gender shapes interpersonal relationships and the irreplaceable value of the partnership of woman and man in marriage. The concept behind the term "complementarity" had long functioned in papal writings but was historically bound within a hierarchal framework of male authority. With the more egalitarian model of marriage and social relations of Vatican II now holding sway, John Paul II revived the concept while attempting to strip it of an explicitly hierarchal import.[32] Masculinity and femininity are presented as "two ways of 'being a body'" that speak to and complete each other.[33] They are dual incarnations of humanity, both in the image of God, but also distinct.[34] And they are complementary because each, in a sense, "finds itself" in the other.[35] This recapitulated concept likewise proved useful for buttressing magisterial teachings on sexual ethics and provided a rationale for objectively linking all heterosexual marriages, through the bodies of the spouses themselves, to the good of procreation, even when factually childless or infertile.[36] This connection affirms the goodness of the marital relationship in distinction from its actual transformation into a family through reproduction while also drawing the conceptual origins of parenthood more tightly toward the physical, gendered bodies of the spouses.

At the same time as he was articulating his anthropological views through these addresses, John Paul II hosted the 1980 Synod of Bishops on the theme of the family, and he followed this with the apostolic exhortation *Familiaris consortio*. He described his exhortation as "a *summa* of the teaching of the Church on the life, the tasks, the responsibilities, and the mission of marriage and of the family in the world today."[37] The document begins by assessing the state of marriage and the family globally.[38] Despite occasional pessimism, John Paul II presents contemporary challenges as a mix of positive and negative developments that require careful discernment. Positive developments include greater appreciation for individual freedom, attentiveness to interpersonal relationships, support for women's dignity, and responsible procreation and education of children, as well as attention to "the development of interfamily relationships, for reciprocal spiritual and material assistance, the rediscovery of the ecclesial mission proper to the family and its responsibility for the building of a more just society."[39] Negative developments include erroneous conceptions of spousal independence, "the relationship of authority between parents and children," difficulty in transmitting values, divorce, abortion, sterilization, and the origin of a "truly contraceptive mentality."[40]

Reflecting the thought of his catechetical addresses, *Familiaris consortio* argues that conjugal love requires total self-giving, both spiritually and physically, as any reservation makes the physical self-giving a lie.[41] In wealthy countries especially, spouses seem deprived of "the generosity and courage needed for raising up new human life: thus life is often perceived not as a blessing, but as a danger from which to defend oneself."[42] In contrast to this challenge, John Paul II describes procreation as the "greatest possible gift" and laments that conception is often needlessly thwarted in the contemporary world.[43]

Familiaris consortio describes the fundamental task of marriage as communicating love, with four additional tasks flowing from this: to form a community of persons, serve life, build society, and share in the Church.[44] Citing *Humanae vitae*, *Familiaris consortio* recalls that marriage is directed to the total unity of heart and soul, demands fidelity and indissolubility, and is open to procreation. Correspondingly, the exhortation identifies selfishness as a primary cause of marital troubles.[45] It also contrasts support for life against contra-life mentalities that indicate God's absence and are driven by fear and selfishness. This culminates in a reaffirmation of opposition to contraception, sterilization, and abortion—especially when political power is involved.[46] To this end, *Familiaris consortio* provides an extensive review and defense of *Humanae vitae*. Here, John Paul II describes artificial contraception and natural methods of regulating conception that are supported by Catholic teaching as based on "two irreconcilable concepts of the human person and of human sexuality."[47] Respecting natural fertility encourages actions and dispositions compatible with an authentic vision of marriage. Therefore, "husbands and wives should first of all recognize clearly the teaching of *Humanae vitae* as indicating the norm for the exercise of their sexuality" and then seek the means to observe this norm.[48]

In contrast to the measured assessment that initiates the document, a more dualistic and authoritative perspective is displayed here. John Paul II describes the Magisterium as "the one authentic guide for the People of God," requests total adherence among theologians, and characterizes the world beyond Catholicism as "confused and contradictory."[49] This tension, between an openness to the changes of the contemporary world and a tendency to sharply contrast the errors of the world with the truth of the Church is, in fact, characteristic of John Paul II. In many respects, he was a moderate and synthetic thinker; but, particularly in matters of personal morality, oppositional dichotomies underlie his thought. These oppositions include the body and spirit, love and lust, reason and lust, and personhood and objectification. When this mode of thinking becomes prominent, he tends to reduce the complexity of human experience to stark contrasts between good and evil, truth and lies.[50] For example, if a sex act is not open to the possibility of conception, an act that can otherwise attest to the greatness of nuptial love becomes merely an act of lust.[51] Likewise, he tends to contrast the holiness of the private Christian family with the sinfulness of the world. As such, his own thoughts on the social obligations of the family are easily obscured by a private, protectionist reading that undermines essential Catholic commitments to solidarity.[52]

With respect to the tasks of parenthood, *Familiaris consortio* describes parents as "heralds of the Gospel" who fulfill their vocation toward children as both physical and spiritual progenitors.[53] Love conditions this obligation and perfects parents' "service to life."[54] Moreover, parental authority is described as both "unrenounceable" and a "true and proper 'ministry.'"[55] But the social mission of the family is deprioritized in *Familiaris consortio* as it treats the structural requirements of the family before considering essential functions. This pattern is quite typical of modern papal documents and tends to emphasize the sacramental reality of marriage over consideration of the family's social role.

Rather than baptism, John Paul II positioned sacramental marriage as the origin of the family as a domestic church.[56] This serves to prioritize the spousal relationship while distancing the family as a community of salvation from the sacrament that celebrates this salvation.[57] Moreover, the sacramental grace of marriage receives additional attention for enriching the parental vocation.[58] *Familiaris consortio* names the replication of God's fatherhood as a function of parenthood generally but also clearly distinguishes the parental roles of motherhood and fatherhood.[59] More common ground seems to exist between male and female experiences of parenthood in its evangelical dimension than in other tasks.[60] In the daily activities of parenthood, John Paul II assumes and supports gendered differentiations. For example, he argues for the importance of women's role in nurturing children and gives no indication that a father might also fulfill this task.[61] Considering the mutual task of education, he states that the love of parents is "the animating principle and therefore the norm inspiring and guiding all concrete educational activity, enriching it with the values of kindness, constancy, goodness, service, disinterestedness and self-sacrifice that are the most precious fruit of love."[62] Further, *Familiaris consortio* encourages parents to educate in ways that reduce materialism and emphasize the goodness of the human person.[63] The family itself is presented as a community of "life and love" such that, ultimately, "the essence and role of the family are in the final analysis specified by love."[64] Given the singular emphasis on the sacrament of marriage, it is unclear how nonmarried, single, foster, or stepparents relate to fully Christian parenthood, while John Paul II offers little to suggest that the domestic church can exist beyond the sacramentally married nuclear family with children.[65]

In these early writings, John Paul II developed and expressed many of the insights that would shape his legacy on parenthood and the family. They initiated a project of receiving Vatican II's commitment to personalist moral perspectives and a more positive relationship with the secular world. At the same time, like Paul VI, he sought to synthesize these reforms with established commitments to clear and absolute moral teachings while defending the ecclesial authority behind them. Many of the tensions inherent in this project crossed at the issue of contraception. As division and entrenchment over this issue grew, it became a nexus of Catholic identity that further shifted Catholic conceptual frameworks. In this context, thought on parenthood became increasingly bound up with sexual ethics and biological reproduction. Despite the complexity and nuances of his thought, John Paul II's own teaching did not stall this trend because he himself was firmly invested within the controversy.

LATER WRITINGS, LATE 1980s TO 2005

From the late 1980s through the mid-1990s, John Paul II continued to develop and affirm his teachings on family, sexuality, and reproductive ethics while responding to numerous social developments. Advances in technology and medicine raised increasingly complex moral questions in medical and reproductive ethics. Social awareness and an acceptance of homosexuality and same-sex relationships increased throughout Western nations and challenged traditional teaching. And women undertook a "quiet revolution" in the workforce, fueled by greater educational achievement, steady gains in highly skilled professions, and growing commitment to long-term careers.

Women occupy a unique place of concern throughout John Paul II's thought. Beyond being the first pope to address an apostolic letter directly to women, he repeatedly affirmed women's essential dignity and equality with men, rebuked the objectification of women, and was, to some extent, conversant with feminist scholarship. At the same time, he strongly supported distinctions in gendered vocations and, like his predecessors, contended that authentic respect for equality must acknowledge, not obscure, basic realities of gendered differences.[66] His apostolic letter on the dignity and vocation of women, *Mulieris dignitatem* of 1988, repeats many of the ideas developed in the Theology of the Body, frequently cites Vatican II documents, and devotes significant attention to anthropological reflection, in his distinctively personalist key. Once again, the differences between specifically gendered and more fundamental anthropological reflections are not entirely clear. For example, Mary's receptivity to accepting God's redemptive plan positions her as an exemplar for all humanity as a paradigm of self-gift.[67] But she is also presented as an exemplar of womanhood whose role in redemption, virginity, and motherhood recapitulate the biblical Eve as a new beginning for the "*dignity and vocation of women,* of each and every woman" (emphasis in the original).[68]

The letter also presents the divine life of God as another key to understanding the human condition as beings made in the image of their Creator. Here, John Paul II is careful to protect God's ultimate transcendence before appealing to divine generativity for anthropological insight. In doing so, he parallels the reality of human fulfillment in self-gift with the ultimate reality of the divine generativity that joins the Father to the Son.[69] Although the connection here clearly resonates with key themes in John Paul II's thought, *Mulieris digniatem* directs these observations exclusively toward biological procreation.[70] This movement is repeated later in an extended reflection on motherhood. One later chapter does consider spiritual motherhood, and links all female vocations to an innately motherly dimension of female personhood, but there is no specific mention of adoption or nonbiological means of family formation that could distinguish the reality of motherhood from an exclusive anchorage in biological reproduction.[71]

Throughout the letter, John Paul II labors to promote both the fundamental equality of men and women as persons as well as the distinctive features and irreplaceable value that masculinity and femininity add to the human experience. In this, his statements tend toward the conceptual, with relatively few practical norms. For example, women are cautioned not to allow social progress to "masculinize" and therefore damage the riches of their femininity, but the distinctive features of what constitutes "masculinity" go unarticulated.[72] Nor is femininity itself thickly articulated at a practical level. However, the operative conception is clearly defined by receptivity. This is exemplified by Mary's fiat that led her to "*the discovery of her own feminine humanity*" (emphasis in the original).[73] Additionally, the letter repeatedly connects femininity to the bodily realities of femaleness and motherhood and recalls Mary's primary embodiment of womanhood as "virgin-mother-spouse."[74] Although Mary is the paradigm for women, the divine oscillates between a grounding for general human anthropology and male anthropology more specifically. For example, Christ's love is specifically identified as the pattern of "all human love, men's love in particular."[75]

In 1989, exactly one year after *Mulieris dignitatem*, Pope John Paul II published the apostolic exhortation *Redemptoris custos.* This was further timed to coincide with the centenary of Leo XIII's encyclical on Saint Joseph, *Quamquam pluries.* Like this earlier encyclical, *Redemptoris custos* urges greater appreciation for the role of Joseph in the life of Jesus and underscores his significance as patron of the Church. The connections and contrasts to *Mulieris dignitatem* are particularly intriguing. The earlier letter undertook an anthropological exposition of womanhood founded in the figure of Mary, the virgin wife and mother, to demonstrate the inherent dignity of women and virtues of femininity. This complementary document does explore the person of Joseph, including his chastity and fatherhood, but does not articulate a parallel anthropology of masculinity. Instead, Joseph's virtues are construed as bases of broadly human attributes.[76] Joseph's roles as husband and father are characterized by his commitment, faith, protection, and guardianship, the same characteristics that ground his role as guardian of the Church.[77] The silence of Joseph in the Gospels is further taken as evidence of his strong and silent, contemplative, and faith-filled way of life. These are, of course, traditionally masculine attributes that the proceeding tradition and John Paul II himself ascribe in order to produce a compelling image of the saint whose actual life and personality remain opaque.

In *Redemptoris custos,* John Paul II is uniquely confronted with the unavoidable challenges that using the Holy Family as a model for marriages and families creates.[78] Mary and Joseph are traditionally presented as celibate spouses and parents to a child who is biologically only Mary's; clearly this is not the prevailing model of family, but nonetheless they are considered exemplars. John Paul II's vision of a complimentary relationship between virginity and married life sets both Mary and Joseph as foundations for either vocation as they each inhabit both spaces, but Joseph's nonbiological fatherhood presents a unique challenge. John Paul II asserts repeatedly that his is a true fatherhood, this is founded in both his marriage to Mary and his care for Jesus. Through his commitment and fidelity, Joseph the spouse and father gives himself as true self-gift to his wife and family.[79] Consequently, the exhortation relativizes the connection of self-gift to the sexual act as well as the roots of fatherhood in biological procreation, and in doing so suggests broader ways of conceiving of parenthood. Unfortunately, this mode of discourse, which opens broader possibilities for conceptualizing parenthood, is largely relegated to the unique challenges encountered within this particular document.

Like the challenges John Paul II faced in articulating a post–Vatican II moral approach that was both reformed and consonant with established teaching, he attempted to articulate how and why sexual differentiation still mattered in a world where the fluidity and cultural construction of gender roles were increasingly accepted. His response drew heavily upon the romantic ideals that had influenced his predecessors' essentialist understanding of gender.[80] These associated femininity with the qualities of receptivity, motherhood, purity, passivity, nurture, and the domestic sphere.[81] For John Paul II, the vocation of motherhood is every woman's "main" and "irreplaceable role" that corresponds to "the very essence of her womanhood."[82] The "fundamental contribution" of women to society is conditioned by the experience of motherhood in which women accept and love life for its own sake.[83] *Familiaris consortio* had asserted that women have a legitimate place in the labor force, but this must give due regard for women's roles as wives and mothers in order for social advancement to be "truly and fully human."[84] John Paul II repudiated social structures that compel married women to enter the workforce and viewed occupations that can be undertaken from the home as particularly appropriate for women's employment.[85] To this end, he urged deeper study of the relationship between work and family but directed this call primarily toward women.[86] Notably, he made no corresponding call to study men's participation in the workforce and home life.

Regarding women's role in the labor force, John Paul II taps into both real disparities in the way modern economic calculus has undermined and excluded the value of domestic caregiving and other forms on frequently unpaid interpersonal labor. At the same time, however, his unwavering commitment to defining persons by their gendered identities works to reaffirm the very assumptions that drove economic theory to exclude unpaid domestic work in the first place.[87] Like the late-nineteenth-century economists who shaped modern economic theories, John Paul II is prone to playing both sides with women's motivations. On one hand, he asserts a natural tendency in women to find fulfillment in the domestic sphere. On the other hand, he feels it necessary to push women toward this fulfillment, lest they assume roles beyond those suited to their gender. As Sandra Sullivan-Dunbar puts it in her review of economic theory, the tensions between the natural account of feminine desires and the gendered paradigm of women's workforce are a "curious flip-flop in attitude toward caring relationships" that is "symptomatic of an overly dichotomized account of motives."[88] John Paul II is more nuanced than the economists two generations his senior, but the same basic tension persists. The need to insist on particular gendered behaviors undermines the prior insistence that the dispositions behind these are in fact natural and flow from the identity of the persons themselves.

In John Paul II's thought, women are significantly defined by their parenthood and parental obligations in a manner and extent to which men are not. As with motherhood, John Paul II did not clearly articulate essential fatherly functions but nonetheless he associated these with economic contribution, love of wife and children, education, and involvement in the life of the family.[89] Thus, fathers are clearly more than income earners but occupy a secondary role in childrearing, while their parental obligations are routed through the motherhood of their spouse.[90] This position is exaggerated by the emphasis placed on reproduction, in which biological mothers have more direct physical experiences of parenthood through gestation, birth, and breastfeeding than do fathers. Although this difference in parental experience is a significant point of consideration, the limited effort to move past early childhood colors the entire construction of parental functions while emphasizing biological reproduction. The idea that this presentation of parenthood constitutes an egalitarian and complimentary vision of the genders and their relation strains the imagination, particularly as the old hierarchies of previous eras rest just below the surface. One significant consequence of failing to adequately attend to these assumptions about gender and parenthood is that the otherwise-ample possibilities for individual moral growth suggested by John Paul II's ethical perspective thin to a very limited vision of human adaptability in familial and social relations, particularly regarding women. To posit that a husband may find authentic fulfillment as his children's primary caregiver, or a wife do so as her family's primary economic earner, pushes human adaptability further from dichotomous gendered identities than John Paul II seems willing to allow.

At the national level, the US Catholic bishops likewise turned attention to women by initiating the pastoral letter "Partners in the Mystery of Redemption." This followed "The Challenge of Peace" in 1983 and "Economic Justice for All" in 1986. In each of these, the US bishops undertook drafting processes that were collegial among themselves, collaborative with theologians, and consultative with representatives of the lay faithful.[91] Although this approach complemented the communal ecclesiological vision of Vatican II as well as the personalist turn in moral theology, on the topic of women's role in the Church, the bishops discovered that their method was out of step from that preferred by Roman authorities, and they ultimately abandoned the project in 1994. This failure highlights how the era's desire to engage experiential knowledge was limited by an unwillingness to afford this knowledge's disconfirmative value in the face of authoritative, or simply sensitive, teachings. Holding such contradictory commitments in tension was no small challenge, and the US bishops learned that following the lead of John Paul II's own synthesis was the most pragmatic approach.[92]

This turn to the subject for verification only is fully displayed within the US bishops' 1988 publication *Faithful to Each Other Forever: A Catholic Handbook of Pastoral Help for Marriage Preparation*. The handbook's section on parenthood, itself published as a small volume in 1990, begins with a summary of marriage and then recounts the story of a young couple's first child.[93] This willingness to explore lived experience recalls the phenomenological concerns of John Paul II but also similarly employs this approach only to confirm existing teaching while avoiding more complicated experiential engagements. The booklet's subsequent reflection recounts greater awareness of both the challenges and joys of the gestational and caregiving processes of parenthood. Nonetheless, the one-sided method returns in the booklet's testimony by a husband and wife who have found personal and relational satisfaction in the use of Natural Family Planning.[94] The difficulties faced by some with regard to this teaching are acknowledged but ultimately given no bearing on the presumed correctness of the teaching itself. Rather, experiential knowledge that could be equally regarded as disconfirmation is treated as a difficulty in the faithful's reception of the teaching.

The bishops repeat John Paul II's assertion from *Familiaris consortio* that the Magisterium is the "one authentic guide for the people of God," but they also assert the importance of the conscience and repeat Vatican II's view that parental decisions rest ultimately with the consciences of couples.[95] To drive home this point, the bishops show how often the term "responsible" has been utilized in recent magisterial teaching about parenthood. These examples are doubly illustrative. First, they demonstrate a real commitment on behalf of the post–Vatican II Catholic hierarchy to secure decisions about the family within the consciences of the lay faithful. Second, they demonstrate the overwhelming association of "responsible parenthood" with narrowly reproductive choices. In the context of the original documents cited, every one of the five references to responsible parenthood refers explicitly to reproductive choices.[96] This remarkable reduction of parental responsibility to reproductive decisions might be taken as something of a touchstone for the completion of the shift in the framework for parenthood that had been developing for decades. By the early 1990s, it became possible for the US Catholic bishops to teach about parental responsibility without any reference to the actual practices of parenthood beyond reproductive decisions. This narrowing of Catholic discourse is further demonstrated by the format of the publication itself. The section heading "Responsible Conscience Decisions" is enough to notify any informed reader within post–*Humanae vitae* Catholicism that the section is about reproductive ethics.

The booklet itself devotes twenty-five of its forty-three total pages to this topic, while only a few scant sentences relate to the daily practices of childrearing. Practically speaking, the frame of Catholic parenthood had effectively been narrowed to matters of biological reproduction and did not need to explain how the daily tasks of caring for children could be virtually disregarded in a booklet titled "Parenthood."[97]

A few years later, however, the US Catholic bishops' 1994 pastoral "Follow the Way of Love" employed a more inclusive framing of the family centered on its social and evangelical mission as domestic church. It maintains common elements with John Paul II's framework and presents a theological foundation for family life before presenting the more typical starting point in marriage. "Like the whole Church, every Christian family rests on a firm foundation, namely, Christ's promise to be faithful to those he has chosen."[98] "Follow the Way" also addresses parenthood inclusively. After a note on the good of adoption, it states,

> Parenthood is indeed a Christian call and responsibility. It is the experience of acting as God's instruments in giving life to sons and daughters in various ways; but equally, it is an experience of being formed by God through your children.

> The life that you give as parents is not restricted just to your offspring. The children of other families need your guidance, as do other parents who can benefit from your hard-earned experience. Likewise, you cannot raise your own children alone. All families—even those with two parents—need a wider circle of aunts and uncles, grandparents, godparents, and other faith-filled families.[99]

Moreover, "Follow the Way" provides a more expansive vision of fatherhood and diversity in parental tasks:

> Flexible roles may appear difficult if your families of origin did not model them. Each family (couple) must decide what is best for them in a spirit of respect and mutuality. Especially when both spouses are employed, household duties need to be shared. . . .
>
> When children are born, both mother and father are important in nurturing and forming them. More and more, fathers have been discovering how their involvement in parenting enriches both their children and themselves. This is a hopeful development.
>
> We urge men to interpret their traditional role as "provider" for a family in more than an economic sense. Physical care of children, discipline, training in religious values and practices, helping with school work and other activities: all these and more can be provided by fathers as well as mothers.

These documents from the US bishops demonstrate both the trend toward more restrictive conceptions of the family centered on reproductive ethics as well as a recognition of greater complexities that include wider conceptions of the family beyond the nuclear family, family formation beyond biological reproduction, and an essentially social vocation of the family extending beyond private life. At the US level, the bishops in some ways challenged rigid parental gender roles, while in Rome romantic conceptions of gender largely carried the day. Both agreed on the unquestionable nature of *Humanae vitae*'s judgment and repeatedly returned considerations of parenthood to reproductive matters. Accordingly, despite significant countertrends, the operative concept of the family was drawn increasingly into a private, biological, and nuclear mold. Gender, sexuality, and marriage have a stepwise ordering in John Paul II's thought such that they neatly frame conceptions of the family and parenthood. This leaves the legitimacy of nonnuclear and nonbiological families in question as their reality and experiences are often ignored.

The emphasis on biological reproduction did encounter a clear challenge during this period as advances in medical technology led to increasing availability of reproductive assistance. Here the centrality of biological kinship in John Paul II's thought had to be balanced against firm magisterial opposition to artificial reproductive technologies (ARTs), expressed most notably in the CDF's 1987 instruction *Donum vitae,* and in John Paul II's 1995 encyclical *Evangelium vitae.*[100] On one hand, John Paul II's writings centered conceptions of parenthood on biological reproduction; on the other hand, these teachings prohibited couples from accessing certain assisted means of biological reproduction. In such a context, adoptive parenthood and other social commitments to children receive increased attention as possible alternatives to ARTs.[101] This strategy creates the impression that avoiding immoral acts is a greater issue driving this recognition of the value and legitimacy of nonbiological parenthood than goods intrinsic to adoption itself. Christina Traina has likewise found *Donum vitae*'s central emphases on marriage and biological reproduction troubling because the document misses relevant social ethical concerns, undermines the moral good of adoption, and advocates for the good of women only in view of their roles as wives and mothers rather than centering their inherent dignity.[102] As such, the document yet again repeats a tendency to centralize matters of sexual ethics and gender while surrounding and related moral concerns and theological convictions are obscured or bent toward these aims. John Paul II's thought on adoption is further circumscribed by his earlier assertion that parental rights are "unrenounceable," which seems to undercut the permissibility of placing a child for adoption.[103] His most developed authoritative reflection on adoption in *Evangelium vitae* promotes "adoption-at-a-distance," wherein the preservation of biological nuclear families is sustained through financial support.[104] Although this is certainly a laudable option, it does not capture all familial circumstances and again demonstrates the priority of biological relatedness in his thought.

John Paul II offered brief positive assessments of nonbiological family formation in both *Familiaris consortio* and *Evangelium vitae.* Because all people are children of God, he asserts, the bonds of the family rightfully extend to universal concern for children in need. Families may serve life by their willingness to "adopt and foster children who have lost their parents or have been abandoned by them." This benefits children, who rediscover the "warmth and affection of a family," as well as the family via its expansion.[105] Moreover, "true parental love is ready to go beyond the bounds of flesh and blood in order to accept children from other families, offering them whatever is necessary for their well-being and full development."[106] Stronger language on adoption comes from a short address that John Paul II delivered to adoptive families in 2000. Here, he speaks of adoption as a "great work of love" and a "true exchange of gifts."[107] He continues: "Adopting children, regarding and treating them as one's own children, means recognizing that the relationship between parents and children is not measured only by genetic standards. Procreative love is first and foremost *a gift of self.* There is a form of 'procreation' that occurs through acceptance, concern, and devotion. The resulting relationship is so intimate and enduring that it is in no way inferior to one based on a biological connection."[108]

Here, the explicit connection that John Paul II draws to procreation and self-gift is remarkable, yet this praise is prefaced with a lament over the use of assisted reproductive technologies and explicitly frames adoption as an alternative to such practices.[109] Thus, even as the family unit is centered in parental complementarity and biological procreation, the biological nuclear norm remains subject to exceptions in light of human need and the demands of the Gospel. Unfortunately, this recognition of the good of nonbiological parenthood is typically called forth only when the moral evils of ARTs or abortion constitute the driving moral concern.

John Paul II also indicated his desire that family life not be reduced to the nuclear family in calling for openness to grandparents and the extended family. Here, he favorably presents the extended family, especially as an aid to the nuclear family, but he also directs extended relations to respect the privacy of the nuclear family and its members.[110] In both considerations of nonbiological and extended family, the biological, nuclear model of the family stands in tension with broader theological conceptions of kinship and the social purposes of the family that the pope is also inclined to uphold. Although he willingly acknowledges the importance of these broader patterns of being family, his conceptual framework still leans heavily on the more restrictive model.

The conceptual model of the private, biological, nuclear family was also strengthened at this time through a moral reaction to the growing social acceptance of nonmarital cohabitation, civil unions, and same-sex partnerships. John Paul II assessed each of these in the late 1990s as "false alternatives" to the "irreplaceable value of the family based on marriage."[111] Such nonmarital sexual partnerships were considered harmful in themselves because they lack the full commitments of marriage while undermining the true meaning of marriage. Among nonmarital partnerships, same-sex relationships received particularly concerted attention.

Homosexuality had arisen as a focus of magisterial attention in the 1970s as the tradition's long-standing condemnation of same-sex sexual acts had come under scrutiny for its weaknesses in addressing both homosexuality as a sexual orientation and increasing public awareness of long-term, intimate same-sex relationships. Same-sex sexual acts could no longer be understood simply as deviant heterosexual behavior but instead seemed to emerge by natural or at least regular variations in human sexuality, which could lead to stable interpersonal commitments.[112] The initial Vatican response came in the CDF's 1975 letter *Persona humana,* which extends the method of *Humanae vitae* to a wider range of sexual ethical questions. The document condemns all sex acts outside marriage, all same-sex sex acts, and masturbation as failing to meet the procreative and unitive standard of moral human sexual expression. It also encourages growth in chastity and explains the great importance of magisterial teaching on these topics and the heavy moral weight of sexual matters.[113]

In 1986, the CDF's "Letter to the Bishops of the Catholic Church on the Pastoral Care of Homosexual Persons" refuted laxist pastoral interpretations of *Persona humana* and made the significant claim that, although the homosexual inclination itself is not a sin, "it is a more or less strong tendency ordered toward an intrinsic moral evil; and thus the inclination itself must be seen as an objective disorder."[114] Moving beyond the language of *Humanae vitae,* this document supports its argument by referencing John Paul II's thought in an appeal to the God-given complementarity of the sexes that sets the conditions for mutual self-gift.[115] Consequently, because same-sex sexual acts cannot be self-giving, all these acts manifest "a disordered sexual inclination which is essentially self-indulgent."[116]

In subsequent years, the magisterial response held firm while acceptance of homosexuality in Western societies expanded and concerns progressed from homosexuality to same-sex relationships to same-sex parenthood. The 1992 CDF document "Some Considerations Concerning the Response to Legislative Proposals on the Non-Discrimination of Homosexual Persons" asserts that sexual orientation cannot be considered a protected form of human diversity akin to race or gender. Instead, the document surmises, anyone who has made his or her homosexuality a matter of public knowledge thereby implies a willingness to engage in homogenital acts and consequently may rightly be subject to just discrimination in areas such as employment and housing.[117] In 1994, John Paul II himself described same-sex relationships as a "deplorable distortion of what should be a communion of love and life between a man and a woman in a reciprocal gift open to life."[118] In 2000, the Pontifical Council for the Family repeated John Paul II's claim and argued against same-sex partnerships being likened to marriage as they are not biologically procreative and cannot express the interpersonal complementarity of spouses.[119] And in the 2003 document "Considerations Regarding Proposals to Give Legal Recognitions to Unions between Homosexual Persons," the CDF argued that same-sex couples do not properly contribute to the survival of the human race because they cannot procreate biologically. Moreover, because they lack gender complementarity, neither can they be allowed to adopt children given that this absence would cause developmental problems for children.[120] As such, "not even in a remote analogous sense do homosexual unions fulfill the purpose for which marriage and family deserve specific categorical recognition."[121] Instead, legal recognition of same-sex unions is presented as an inherent threat to heterosexual marriage, children, and society.[122]

Throughout these arguments, aspects of John Paul II's own reflections on marriage and sexuality attain increasing significance. The importance of complementarity among parental partners and the significance of the biological capacity to procreate (at least in the physical form of sexual encounters, if not in actuality) become central planks in the argument. Thus, through arguments about what sexual relationships could not be, the Catholic conceptual framework for the family was driven toward greater emphasis on gender and sexual ethics, which once again reinforced a biological, nuclear norm. The latter CDF document in fact spells out the foundation of family in sexual ethics quite clearly as it declares, "There are absolutely no grounds for considering homosexual unions to be in any way similar or even remotely analogous to God's plan for marriage and family. Marriage is holy, while homosexual acts go against the natural moral law. Homosexual acts close the sexual act to the gift of life. They do not proceed from a genuine affective and sexual complementarity. Under no circumstances can they be approved."[123] This argument is not based primarily on persons or the quality of their relationships but instead on a moral judgment about gender and sexual acts that provides the response for everything else. Why sexual acts should be so definitive for the total relational quality of a partnership or the family is less clear, although it replicates a pattern that had become clearly established in magisterial documents.

The progression of magisterial teaching throughout John Paul II's papacy demonstrates the rise of his own perspective and terminology, driven largely by efforts to defend and explain reproductive ethics and gender norms as he both interpreted Vatican II and reacted against social developments. By the early 2000s, complementarity itself had become a key defense of the nuclear family in both Vatican and US documents. Similar to the influence *Humanae vitae* exerted in shifting conceptions of the family and parenthood toward reproductive ethics, John Paul II's papacy shifted concern from procreation to its own antecedent, sexual difference—giving theological weight to the concept of complementarity. As a consequence, the functional tasks of parenthood were displaced further from the prevailing Catholic framework as the private, biological, and nuclear family increasingly defined parenthood due to its foundation in gender complementarity and potential for licit sexual interactions. This trend advanced in part because engagement with the actual practices of parents themselves was given significantly less attention than the construction of theological arguments designed to oppose changing social realities that threatened established magisterial teachings. Vatican II's commitment to reading the signs of the times continued, but through selective experiential engagement designed to reinforce, but not challenge, existing teaching.

The trends were also driven by the heightened existential importance placed on reproductive ethics. In the hands of John Paul II, *Humanae vitae* came to epitomize a struggle over the value of the human person and the very meaning of human existence. This debate grew in complexity and importance as his central concern for truth, particularly "the truth about man," provided human sexual differentiation with metaphysical significance. Moreover, his belief in the clarity and precision with which absolute moral truths could be expressed through the teaching of the Magisterium removed ambiguity from the actions of those who used contraception, as their bodies enacted intentions known to be contradictory to moral truth.[124] For Paul VI, *Humanae vitae* spoke to Catholic spouses of a better way. For John Paul II, its moral judgment clearly differentiated truth tellers from liars.[125]

John Paul II encouraged some lines of argument that resist this prevailing trend, such as his support for including grandparents within the life of the family and his advocacy for the social mission of families. Nonetheless, his teachings tend firmly toward reinforcing the biological, nuclear model. Methodologically, this is reflected most clearly in his prioritization of structure before function. That is, an authentically loving marriage first requires the complementarity of male and female bodies, the sexual expression of authentic conjugal love first requires the uninterrupted hetero-genital sex act, the capacity for Christian parental education rests in the grace of a valid sacramental marriage, and the social mission of the family as an evangelizing community rests in the structural integrity of two married parents and their children. All these start with what is structurally prior in order to explain what is functionally latter. This pattern may be read within the Catholic tradition's understanding of grace as building upon nature. However, because the fundamental structural issues were at stake in broader social debates, such as reproductive ethics and same-sex relationships, the conversation became mired in gender and reproductive ethics, with decreased attention given to the latter functional issues. Exacerbating this, the pope's own propensity for dualistically pitting the authentic truth of magisterial teachings against the evils and confusions of the wider world, especially on these contested issues, further pulled attention away from his more optimistic assessments of culture and his understanding of the family's social obligations. Experiential evidence of families that are able to flourish despite structural differences from the nuclear model or parents who model Christian ideals of parenthood without gender complementarity or sacramental marriage could have been corrective, if the established methods had sought to incorporate experience as more than a confirmation of existing positions.

In a broader context, from the late nineteenth century through the mid–twentieth century, popes tended to employ private, nuclear conceptions of the family that were indebted to social realities made possible through industrialization. In 1968, Paul VI's encyclical *Humanae vitae* associated responsible parenthood with sexual decisions and further pushed Catholic attention toward narrow issues of biological procreation. After this, John Paul II's promotion of the encyclical's judgment and condemnations of certain social developments exacerbated this trend while highlighting gender difference as a key theological category. Other values and ways of conceptualizing the family persisted throughout. Pius XII emphasized the primary value of spiritual education, and John Paul II spoke of the social mission of the family. But these statements were overshadowed and increasingly marginalized as the prevailing framework moved Catholic understanding of the family toward a narrowing range of concerns.

BENEDICT XVI, 2005–13

Benedict XVI's unique contributions to the trends being traced are relatively limited. He was less innovative than John Paul II, and he articulated teachings with more classical theological language and greater concern for expressing the unity of Catholic teaching across time. For instance, the place of John Paul II's "sexual urge" is largely assumed by "eros" in Benedict XVI's writings, which added greater ambiguity to the role of desire in human sexuality.[126] Moreover, his encyclicals centered on theological virtues and drew attention to the fundamental realities of love and relationality. These could have provided unique starting points for a larger reflection on caregiving, but as Sullivan-Dunbar observes, such an opportunity was not explored.[127]

Like John Paul II, Benedict XVI saw artificial contraception as feeding numerous global social ills, and his 2009 encyclical *Caritas in veritate* specifically implicated artificial contraception within modern societies' destructive "anti-birth mentality."[128] In response to the problems of forced contraception, sterilization, and abortion in international aid, along with the spread of an "anti-birth" mentality, he wrote, "*Openness to life is at the centre of true development*" (emphasis in the original).[129] Elsewhere, Benedict XVI argued that an absolute witness against artificial birth control is "crucial for humanity's future."[130] Thus the emphasis placed on reproductive responsibility continued.

Benedict XVI's direct attention to women is likewise in line with, but nowhere near as developed as, John Paul II's. He upheld the importance of respect for human dignity and decried violence against women in situations where they are "still firmly subordinated to the arbitrary decisions of men, with grave consequences for their personal dignity and for the exercise of their fundamental freedoms."[131] Furthermore, he argued that women's employment should be freely chosen and effective in meeting the economic needs of families.[132]

Benedict XVI was pope at the time of the case study presented in the introduction to this book. The 2011 changes to the adoption law in Illinois witnessed evident frustration, ardent opposition, and concern that religious liberties were being violated, but they lacked clear articulations of the specific functional tasks that parenthood by same-sex couples necessarily fails to perform. Instead, justifications for the official Catholic position appealed to the necessity of parental gender complementarity with little interest in accumulating evidential supports, while the recent clarification by the CDF alone substantiated a faith-based claim. This fideistic reaction owed in no small part to the culture war mentality fostered under Benedict XVI and John Paul II. For example, John Paul II's teaching often pitted the light of the Gospel against the sinfulness of the world; he proposed Christian anthropology as fundamental for all social and economic organization, and he appealed to aspects of revealed knowledge, not common human reason, as essential for moral reasoning. Traina counts this as a giving up on traditional natural law commitments centered in universal human experience in favor of exclusive revelation.[133] This posturing limited the potential for open engagement with social developments and echoes the anti-Modernist sentiments of earlier papacies. With a wider appreciation of the historical and cultural context surrounding the legal case in Illinois, it is evident that the Catholic parties had been set up for failure in public debate by decades of increasingly narrowed conceptions of the family and parenthood driven by reactionary responses to both social developments and intra-Catholic conflict.

By the mid-1980s, both the Vatican and the American bishops had sufficiently narrowed concerns about parenthood such that reproductive ethics became not only an important moral dimension of parenthood but also its primary framing mechanism. In subsequent decades, the terminology of John Paul II became increasingly important within magisterial teaching, particularly in reaction to the rising social acceptance of same-sex relationships. By 2011, the American bishops were ideologically prepared to fight same-sex adoptive parenthood without any significant reference to the practical realities of parenting. As displayed in their 1988 booklet on parenthood, their operative frame had been largely reduced to sexual and reproductive ethics, and later developments had only further distanced the conceptual frame from the actual practices of parenthood. Appeals to gender complementarity largely carried the weight of the arguments, despite the concept itself and the practical differences it identified being only ambiguously articulated. The lived experiences of same-sex parental partners did not matter *because they could not matter* within the framework that became dominant by this time. Not only did this frame limit attention to parental practices after children are born; it was also coupled with a methodological opposition to engaging experiential knowledge that challenged existing teachings. Despite the social phenomenon of same-sex parenthood coming increasingly into public view throughout the preceding decades, the realities of these experiences were virtually ignored, then condemned in a blanket fashion. This was neither directly intentional nor entirely accidental; it was an eventuality that had been created by the narrowed Catholic framework for parenthood.

A NOTE ON THE SEXUAL ABUSE CRISIS

Rumors, allegations, and sporadic public reports of sexual abuse by Catholic clergy emerged with increasing intensity across the United States throughout the 1980s and 1990s. In 2002, the *Boston Globe*'s investigative reporting sparked widespread attention to sexual abuse by Catholic clerics and cover-ups spanning decades. The scandal gained national and then global attention as revelations in the United States unfolded alongside others in Ireland and Australia. The crisis expanded across the Western world for the following fifteen years with torturous regularity, until verified cases of abuse and cover-up spanned Europe, Australia, and the Americas. It is now known that national bishops' conferences and the Vatican had to some extent been aware of patterns of abuse by clergy since at least the 1980s, but the efforts undertaken to understand and redress the problem were limited and ineffective.[134]

As public scrutiny swelled after the 2002 reports, the US bishops commissioned the John Jay College of Criminal Justice in New York to conduct research into the crisis. The first report on the extent of abuse was issued in 2004, with a supplement released in 2006. A subsequent report of 2011 inquired into the roots of the abuse itself.[135] More recently, a 2018 Pennsylvania grand jury report exposed in even greater detail both the extent and gravity of the decades-long scandal in just that one state.[136] Several additional states have conducted, are conducting, or have announced plans to conduct investigations of their own. Across the Western world, national conferences of bishops and public authorities have likewise sought to understand the crisis.

Although the sexual abuse crisis is not directly related to the topic of our investigation, its occurrence during the time frame under review and its impact on the Catholic Church cannot simply be passed over. Moreover, the cover-up connected to the incidents of abuse shares a similarity with the methodological realities addressed above. Both demonstrate a willingness to protect the public reputation of the institutional Church while avoiding thoroughgoing engagement with contradictory evidence. A sufficient response to the abuse crisis required a firm commitment to engaging the problematic realities that would likely challenge Catholic self-understanding and certainly damage the Church's public standing. As with contraception and same-sex parenthood, this type of engagement was not something the hierarchy was well disposed to undertake. Unfortunately, the perception of a slow and halting response on the part of the Magisterium further damaged Catholicism's public standing. For years, the desire for a full and robust response went largely unanswered as allegations continued to grow. Many Catholics who resonated with certain aspects of John Paul II's thought were well prepared to frame events through the lens of a culture war, and they interpreted the crisis as a by-product of condemnable social realities, such as the lax reforms of Vatican II, the sexual revolution, and increasing public acceptance of homosexuality. For their part, reform-minded Catholics tended to link the crisis to any number of existing contentions with the Church's conservativism.

This book is not suited to adequately address the abuse crisis, except to acknowledge that the origins, institutional response, and reactions of the faithful followed patterns that had been cultivated within Catholicism throughout the preceding decades, some of which also influenced conceptions of parenthood. Notably, the crisis seems to have created a greater level of distrust in the institutional authority of the Magisterium while exacerbating rates of deconversion in the United States and elsewhere. These are challenges that the Catholic Church in America and beyond will need to deal with for the foreseeable future. Unfortunately, the dispositions and conceptual frameworks required to begin to respond adequately to this reality do not appear to correspond well to those that have been cultivated in recent history.

CONCLUSION

These last two chapters have traced historical developments in magisterial teaching on the family in order to show how the underlying theological conceptions of parenthood have developed over time. These developments were not accidental, but neither were they intentional products of reflection upon the tasks of parenting itself. Rather, consequential shifts in framing have tended to arise as reactions to social changes that impinged upon magisterial teachings related to gender, sexuality, and reproduction. From *Humanae vitae* onward, this has produced a growing tendency to center conceptions of parenthood on biological kinship. Magisterial teachings certainly retain the conviction that spiritual education marks Christian parenthood in its fullest, yet they also undermine this conviction through a narrow emphasis on gender, sex, and reproduction. The consequences of this emphasis have recently emerged in a general inability of the institutional Church to reflect clearly on the actual tasks, responsibilities, and functions of parenthood.

The next chapter reviews these concerns in light of the academic theological context and its tendencies to replicate the shortcomings of magisterial teachings, even when arguing from differing methodological standpoints and for differing conclusions. It also considers the present papacy of Francis and his influence in both reshaping and reaffirming these trends.

NOTES

1. Many of these are collected in the *Enchiridion on the Family: A Compendium of Church Teaching on the Family and Life Issues from Vatican II to the Present* by the Pontifical Council on the Family. An updated edition was released in 2011 but is not available in English.
2. "The family is an institution created by procreation within the framework of marriage." Wojtyla, *Love*, 242, 217.
3. Wojtyla, 53.
4. Wojtyla, 227.
5. Wojtyla, 235, 239.
6. "It is here that the full productive power of love between two persons, man and woman, is concentrated, in the work of rearing new persons." Wojtyla, 56.
7. Wojtyla, 242. This perspective is consistent throughout his thought because, like his predecessors, John Paul II maintained the conceptual connection between having children and the virtue of generosity and therefore praised large families.

8. Wojtyla, 259.
9. Authors writing favorably of John Paul II frequently explain his methodology as a creative traditionalism that employs theological and philosophical innovations at the service of clarifying traditional or objective truths; among others, see West, *Theology*, 33. Janet Smith offers a positive but more detailed explanation of how the newer commitments to personalism and phenomenology compliment more traditional concerns for natural law and Thomism. See Smith, "Natural Law."
10. Positively stated, the norm requires that all people be treated with love. Wojtyla, *Love*, 25, 41. In a later work, John Paul II gives a succinct account of his understanding of the fundamental nature of moral acts; see John Paul II, *Memory*, 34ff.
11. Wojtyla, *Love*, 22.
12. Wojtyla, 34. *Love and Responsibility* strongly critiques systems viewed as prone to this latter option such as Utilitarianism. Also included are "reductive" systems, including Freudian psychoanalytic theory, Manicheanism, and the views of numerous philosophers. John Paul II was consistently concerned with ideologies and movements that stem from reductive anthropologies, are destructive, or require violence for their propagation. This gives rise to a tendency to describe a range of disagreements with Catholic teaching as rooted in harmful ideologies; often with the implication that these are intentionally orchestrated. See John Paul II, *Memory*, 165–66.
13. The mention of "Onanism" is clear representation of physicalist thought as *Love and Responsibility* repeats the traditional identification of coitus interruptus with sin after the scholarly consensus had shifted to judging the act as merely the means by which Onan committed his real sin of disobedience, a perspective shared by scholars at the Papal Birth Control Commission.
14. Vatican II, *Gaudium et spes*, sec. 24.
15. As a member of the commission, Wojtyla did not attend any of the meetings that had persuaded like-minded members to change their views. Wojtyla did, however write a critical response to the commission's report. His book *Love and Responsibility* may also have been influential for Paul VI. See Hebblethwaite, *Paul VI*, 468ff, 597; and Smith, "Personalism," 229.
16. Wooden, "Birth." Marengo's book is available in Italian as *La Nascita di un'Enciclica: Humanae Vitae alla luce degli Archivi Vaticani.*
17. For Karol Wojtyla's argument for the anthropological harmony of *Gaudium et spes* and *Humanae vitae*, see Wojtyla, "Anthropological Vision," 731–50.
18. It is worth remembering that Pius XII had sanctioned the use of fertility awareness methods of family planning only nine years before the publication of *Love and Responsibility* and eleven years before Vatican II. Some council fathers still questioned the wisdom of this judgment and believed moral sexual acts required a specific intention to procreate. In contrast, Cardinal Wojtyla writes, "We cannot therefore demand of the spouses that they must positively desire to procreate on every occasion when they have intercourse. To say that intercourse is permissible and justified only on condition that the partners hope to have a child as a result of it would be an exaggeratedly strict ethical position." Wojtyla, *Love*, 233.
19. John Paul II, "Interpreting the Concept." Many of John Paul II's addresses to general audiences are only available in Italian, Spanish, or Portuguese on the Vatican website. For English translations of those in the Theology of the Body cycles, see John Paul II, *Man and Woman.*

20. These were mostly consecutive but special events and travel interrupted the series. The audiences are widely available in chronological order.
21. Matt. 19: 3–12; cf. Mark 10: 1–10. John Paul II, *Original Unity*, 15, 17, 28, 31ff.
22. John Paul II interprets the original human as nongendered before the creation of Eve. The original human, Adam, becomes male only in relation to the female, Eve. Adam is cast into a deep sleep before this differentiation, which, John Paul II claims, contains an element of "annihilation." Thus, despite the continuity between the original Adam and the male Adam, and the creation of Eve out of Adam, John Paul II emphasizes that this event suggests a recreation of humanity. The problem of the solitude of the original human is overcome by the creation of new humanity, now expressed in the duality of male and female. John Paul II, *Original Unity*, 64ff.
23. John Paul II, *Blessed Are the Pure*, 36.
24. John Paul II, 57, 63–65ff. John Paul II acknowledges that lust is associated primarily with men but asserts that its consequent shame is experienced deeply, though differently, by both genders. John Paul II, 69.
25. John Paul II, 75.
26. John Paul II, 79. "When we state that 'lust,' when compared with the original mutual attraction of masculinity and femininity represents a 'reduction,' we have in mind an intentional 'reduction,' almost a restriction of closing down of the horizon of mind and heart. In fact, it is one thing to be conscious that the value of sex is part of all the rich storehouse of values with which the female appears to the man; it is another to 'reduce' all the personal riches of femininity to that single value, that is, of sex, as a suitable object of the gratification of sexuality itself" (p. 126).
27. Secondary work on the Theology of the Body tends to present this project as fundamental anthropology. Certainly, the idea of self-gift is central to John Paul II's anthropology, but this only has overt sexual connotations in certain works, suggesting the Theology of the Body is a particular articulation of more fundamental anthropological commitments. The tension arises between John Paul II's broader anthropological reflections and commitments and the strong statements he made concerning the importance of sexuality. On the latter, see West, *Good News*, 17.
28. See Wojtyla, *Acting Person*; and John Paul II, *Redemptor hominis*.
29. See John Paul II, *Laborem exercens*; and John Paul II, *Mulieris dignitatem*. For further attention to female anthropology, see John Paul II, "Nuptial Meaning"; and John Paul II, "Mystery."
30. Hogan and LeVoir describe this as a unique methodological achievement in uniting the important yet dangerously subjective insights of phenomenology with the objective truths of moral teaching through the use Genesis, which communicates "objective truth which is at the same time central to human experience." Hogan and LeVoir, *Covenant*, 4.
31. *Catechism of the Catholic Church*, 2337, 2346, 2333.
32. John Paul II's critics have argued that his thought covertly continues female subordination. This criticism gains greater credibility by the fact that John Paul II did not always use complementarity as an egalitarian concept. He explicitly frames marriage and virginity as complementary while asserting virginity's preeminence. Curran, *Moral Theology*, 193.
33. John Paul II, *Original Unity*, 62.
34. John Paul II, 79, Cf. 23, 63ff. John Paul II also taught that together, man and woman are the image of God, an idea earlier expressed by Paul VI. Paul VI, "Pope Paul VI," 89.

35. John Paul II, *Original Unity*, 62ff. John Paul II emphasizes the theological significance of bodily existence which manifests itself as male or female. These reflections do not directly consider social gender roles; although a view of women's fundamental vocation to motherhood may be inferred. Throughout, John Paul II shows some hostility toward the sciences. His most explicit objection is to the reductionist anthropologies that over-reliance on these disciplines can produce. This is consistent with Paul VI's criticism of "scientism." Yet John Paul II also expresses hesitations with such things as evolutionary theory and suggests theology's superiority in potential conflicts.
36. Christine Gudorf observes that John Paul II avoided worn and unconvincing social stereotypes which led to reduced content in the categories themselves. Questioning why largely empty categories would be retained, she offers, "together with the principle that every sexual act must be open to procreation, it constitutes the moral bulwark against homosexuality." Gudorf, "New Moral Discourse," 54. Patricia Beattie Jung similarly concludes that magisterial accounts of complementarity are weak in light of present knowledge about sexual diversity. Jung, "God Sets the Lonely," 120–22.
37. Quoted by Garcia de Haro, *Marriage*, 333.
38. During the synod, some bishops complained of the First World priorities of the preparatory themes; see Reese, "Report."
39. John Paul II, *Familiaris consortio*, sec. 6.
40. John Paul II.
41. John Paul II, sec. 11. Before John Paul II's address, the idea that contraception is analogous to lying had emerged among defenders of *Humanae vitae.* Mary Rosera Joyce uses this argument in a book that was largely composed before the publication of *Humanae vitae*; see Joyce, *Meaning*, chap. 6.
42. John Paul II, *Familiaris consortio*, sec. 6.
43. John Paul II, sec. 14.
44. John Paul II, sec. 17.
45. John Paul II, sec. 9.
46. John Paul II, sec. 30.
47. John Paul II, sec. 32.
48. John Paul II, sec. 35.
49. John Paul II, sec. 31.
50. The tension between John Paul II's opposition to dualisms and the role of dualistic concepts in his thought persists throughout his writing. For example, in *Evangelium vitae* this tension is pronounced as the world struggles "between truth and error, between the culture of life and the culture of death." John Paul II, *Evangelium vitae*, sec. 21; See also Curran, *Moral Theology*, 25; and Curran, "*Evangelium vitae*," 123–25. Jennifer Bader sees a basic tension in his mature anthropology as well: "Wojtyla posits a distinctly hierarchical relationship between body and person. . . . John Paul II *identifies* the body with the person. Yet, at certain places in the papal writings, one still detects an echo of this previous way of thinking which seems to exist in tension with his new, more holistic view of the person"; Bader, "Engaging," 96.
51. Wojtyla, *Love*, 235, 239.
52. See Cloutier, "Wanting," 261.
53. John Paul II, *Familiaris consortio*, sec. 39.
54. John Paul II, sec. 36.
55. John Paul II, sec. 21.
56. John Paul II, sec. 49.

57. Bourg, *Where Two or Three Are Gathered*, 73.
58. John Paul II, *Familiaris consortio*, sec. 60.
59. John Paul II, sec. 41; see "Conclusions,'" 1220ff.
60. John Paul II, *Catechesis tradendae*, sec. 42; Wojtyla, *Love*, 260 ff.
61. John Paul II, *Familiaris consortio*, sec. 66.
62. John Paul II, sec. 36.
63. Sex education is described as the prerogative of parents who have the right to dictate how and when it is given. Such education should be done in light of the Church's teaching of sexual expression as a fully human act. John Paul II, *Familiaris consortio*, sec. 37. In 1995, The Pontifical Council for the Family released "The Truth and Meaning of Human Sexuality; Guidelines for Education within the Family," a document that offers guidelines for domestic sexual education.
64. John Paul II, *Familiaris consortio*, sec. 17.
65. Bourg, *Where Two or Three Are Gathered*, 76.
66. John Paul II, *Familiaris consortio*, secs. 22–25. This indicates that John Paul II distinguished motherhood and fatherhood as essentially different such that parenthood is more the overlap than the source of motherhood and fatherhood. Interestingly, John Paul II leaves room for cultures and customs to dictate how women's equality and participation in social life is expressed.
67. John Paul II, *Mulieris dignitatem*, sec. 4.
68. John Paul II, sec. 11.
69. John Paul II, sec. 8.
70. John Paul II, sec. 8.
71. Here again, there is no corresponding reflection on how the physical embodiment of men suits them for inherently fatherly tasks.
72. John Paul II, *Mulieris dignitatem*, sec. 10.
73. John Paul II, secs. 11, 30. The discussion of abortion makes a similar point: "Normally, a *woman's conscience does not let her forget* that she has taken the life of her own child, for she cannot destroy that readiness to accept life which marks her "ethos" from the "beginning" (sec. 14).
74. John Paul II, *Mulieris dignitatem*, sec. 22.
75. John Paul II, sec. 25.
76. John Paul II, sec. 24.
77. John Paul II, sec. 8.
78. For an alternative view that sees the use of the Holy Family in this document as entirely unproblematic while connecting the vision offered to the moral teachings of *Humanae vitae* in service to spousal spirituality, see Shivanandan, "Conjugal Spirituality," 485–506.
79. John Paul II, *Redemptoris custos*, sec. 7.
80. Although hierarchical language was largely avoided at Vatican II, John Paul II once again identifies men as "head" of the household in *Laborem exercens*. John Paul II, *Laborem exercens*, sec. 19. See also John Paul II, *Familiaris consortio*, sec. 25, where language of headship is avoided and equality is emphasized; and John Paul II, *Mulieris dignitatem*, sec. 10, where the dignity of women is contrasted to domination by husbands.
81. Earlier, he had suggested that gendered attributes extend into the sexual act where women, by "the very nature of the act" are the "comparatively passive partner, whose function is to accept and to experience; . . . it is enough for her to be passive and unresisting." Wojtyla, *Love*, 271.

82. John Paul II, "Woman," 854.
83. John Paul II, *Evangelium vitae*, sec. 99.
84. John Paul II, *Familiaris consortio*, sec. 21.
85. John Paul II, sec. 24. This is a revision to his earlier thought, in which the opportunity for employment outside the home itself was considered problematic; Wojtyla, *Love*, 238.
86. John Paul II, *Familiaris consortio*, sec. 24. This one-sided view was also expressed in the US bishops' concern that participation in the workforce could interfere with mothers' ability to provide full-time care for young children. US Conference of Catholic Bishops, "Putting Children and Families First," sec. VI.B.4.
87. Alfred Marshall's influential late-nineteenth-century textbook set the stage for contemporary exclusion of care work from the view of economic calculation. According to Sullivan-Dunbar, Marshall argued, for the sake of simplicity, to avoid including calculations of unpaid care work within calculations of social income. Nonetheless, paid work, such as that done by domestic servants, was to be included. Marshall himself recognized the contradiction but held the two should be accounted separately. His followers likewise excluded unpaid care work from economic calculations but did not further pursue the calculation of the value of such work independently. As such, work that was not actively commodified through a monetary exchange in practice came to be excluded from the purview of economic contribution. Sullivan-Dunbar, *Human Dependency*, 65.
88. Sullivan-Dunbar, *Human Dependency*, 66.
89. John Paul II, "Letter," sec. 16.
90. John Paul II, *Familiaris consortio*, sec. 25. The *Code of Canon Law* gives a broad articulation of the realms of education: "Parents have the most grave duty and the primary right to take care as best they can for the physical, social, cultural, moral and religious education of their offspring"; *Code of Canon Law*, 1136.
91. Hinze, *Practices*, 91.
92. At the 1980 Synod of Bishops, Archbishop Quinn of San Francisco learned this lesson after he called for greater dialogue between the Magisterium and theologians who opposed the judgment of *Humanae vitae*. Though his opinion was warmly received by some episcopal conferences that remained skeptical of the encyclical, he was attacked as a liberal in the Italian press and denounced by Cardinal Felici. Some believe his influence declined following the synod. See Reese, "Report," 199; and Reese, "Looking Back."
93. Bishops' Committee for Pastoral Research and Practices, *Parenthood*, 6.
94. Bishops' Committee for Pastoral Research and Practices, 23–28.
95. Bishops' Committee for Pastoral Research and Practices, 10.
96. Bishops' Committee for Pastoral Research and Practices, 11. Somewhat remarkably, a short subsequent mention of adolescent rebellion focuses exclusively on their lack of desire to have children in the future. Of all that might be said about parenting adolescents, their future reproductive choices do not seem to rise to such a singular level of concern.
97. Knowing what we now know about the cover-up of sexual abuse taking place among the US bishops at the time of this publication, *Parenthood*'s urging of those who intellectually disagree with the teaching of the Magisterium to courageously obey the teaching authority through faith, trust, and penance in spite of their own experience and perspectives is profoundly disturbing. Bishops' Committee for Pastoral Research and Practices, *Parenthood*, 30–31.
98. US Conference of Catholic Bishops, "Follow."

99. US Conference of Catholic Bishops.
100. ARTs are variously called "artificial" or "assisted" reproductive technologies, which are interpreted as either unjustifiable "artificial" interference with the natural order, as John Paul II would have it, or as "assistance" with natural processes, as some moralists have argued. See Congregation for the Doctrine of the Faith, *Donum vitae*, sec. II.
101. Congregation for the Doctrine of the Faith, *Donum vitae*, sec. 8. *Evangelium vitae* offers a parallel line of argument in presenting adoption as an alternative to abortion. John Paul II, *Evangelium vitae*, sec. 63.
102. Traina, *Feminist Ethics*, 324–26.
103. John Paul II, *Familiaris consortio*, sec. 25.
104. John Paul II, *Evangelium vitae*, sec. 93.
105. John Paul II, *Familiaris consortio*, sec. 41; see also John Paul II, *Evangelium vitae*, sec. 63.
106. John Paul II, *Evangelium vitae*, sec. 93. Families with economic advantages are encouraged to "adopt" whole families through economic support. This removes the separation from biological parents, which, John Paul II reminds us, is often caused by poverty and not parental desires.
107. John Paul II, "Address of the Holy Father John Paul II to the Meeting of the Adoptive Families," sec. 3.
108. John Paul II, sec. 4.
109. John Paul II, sec. 3.
110. John Paul II, *Familiaris consortio*, sec. 27; Pontifical Council for the Family, "Charter," sec. 6.C. The inclusion of grandparents is connected to John Paul II's effort to consider the needs of the elderly in relation to family life. This includes common living, or, when not possible, frequent visitation and contact. See John Paul II, "Rights," 927.
111. John Paul II, "Address of John Paul II to the Members of the Pontifical Council," sec. 2.
112. First published in 1976, this groundbreaking work of John J. McNeil was instrumental in laying out the limitations of existing Catholic sexual prohibitions regarding homosexuality and same-sex relationships. See McNeil, *Church*.
113. Congregation for the Doctrine of the Faith, *Persona humana*, sec. II.2.
114. Congregation for the Doctrine of the Faith, *Letter to the Bishops*, sec. 3.
115. Congregation for the Doctrine of the Faith, secs. 6, 7.
116. Congregation for the Doctrine of the Faith, sec. 7.
117. Congregation for the Doctrine of the Faith, "Some Considerations," sec. 14.
118. John Paul II, "Paternity of God," 868.
119. Pontifical Council for the Family, "Family," sec. 23.
120. Congregation for the Doctrine of the Faith, "Considerations," sec. 7.
121. Congregation for the Doctrine of the Faith, sec. 8.
122. The Pontifical Council for the Family had presented the same set of arguments against same-sex partnerships being likened to marriage. First, they are not procreative; second, they cannot express interpersonal complementarity; and third, they are "'a deplorable distortion of what should be a communion of love and life between a man and a woman in a reciprocal gift open to life.'" Pontifical Council for the Family, "Family," sec. 23.
123. Congregation for the Doctrine of the Faith, "Considerations," sec. 4.
124. John Paul II, *Veritatis splendor*, sec. 32.
125. See Pope John Paul II, "General Audience," January 12, 1983; and Pope John Paul II, "General Audience," August 27, 1980.
126. Benedict XVI, *Deus caritas est*, sec. 11.

127. Sullivan-Dunbar, *Human Dependency*, 203.
128. Benedict XVI, *Caritas in veritate*, sec. 2, 28.
129. Benedict XVI, secs. 28, 44.
130. Benedict XVI, "Human Person," sec. 1.
131. Benedict XVI, sec. 7.
132. Benedict XVI, *Caritas in veritate*, sec. 63.
133. Traina, *Feminist Ethics*, 125–26.
134. Keenan, *Child Sexual Abuse*, 23.
135. See John Jay College of Criminal Justice, *Nature*; John Jay College of Criminal Justice, *2006 Supplementary Report*; and John Jay College Research Team, *Causes*.
136. Office of the Attorney General, Commonwealth of Pennsylvania, "Report I of the 40th Statewide Investigative Grand Jury: Redacted."

CHAPTER 3

The Limits of Contemporary Discourse

Having traced developments in magisterial teaching behind the presently restricted framework for parenthood, this chapter begins with a short introduction to contemporary Catholic moral theology, and it then assesses the present theological context. In doing so, it considers the recent work of academic Catholic theologians and the documents of Pope Francis. The chapter identifies concerns that point toward more robust conceptions of parenthood while demonstrating the pervasive influence of a framework that focuses attention on gender and sexual ethics while displacing parenthood as a topic of serious theological consideration in its own right. This framework influences even those theologians who seek to expand the present tradition through criticisms of magisterial teaching. Such a commonality across differences suggests that inadvertent agreement on the means of conceptualizing parenthood has arisen within intra-Catholic disagreements over gender and sexuality. Pope Francis's vision of a more merciful and welcoming Church has shifted some of the terms of this conversation yet likewise remains substantively bound to aspects of the prevailing framework.

REVISIONIST THEOLOGY

Catholic academic theology has grown and diversified significantly throughout the past century through increased lay, female, and geographical representation as well as expanding fields of concern. At the same time, it has been marked by deep divisions, which were especially volatile in the first two decades of John Paul II's papacy.[1]

As Catholic moral perspectives overwhelmingly turned to personalist moral methodologies, academic moralists increasingly utilized historically conscious perspectives and engaged experience as a source of moral knowledge.[2] This move departed from earlier approaches that were based on natural law and were informed by a classicist worldview, where historical norms are taken as consistent and unchanging. Although personalism was broadly influential, the tensions between the new academic trajectory and older norms crystallized in differing reactions to Pope Paul VI's 1968 encyclical *Humanae vitae*. Despite the issue of contraception being a narrow focal point, behind this contention lay an array of simmering differences in the application of personalist moral methodology, the reception of Vatican II, the authority of the Magisterium, the continuing relevance and interpretation of natural law, and the Catholic Church's uneven responses to a changing world. These disagreements exposed deep divides, which were further aggravated by similar diversities in pastoral application.

Among scholars, these rifts grew and solidified into broadly defined "traditionalist" and "revisionist" camps, despite John Paul II's efforts to restrain dissent and clarify Catholic moral commitments.[3] The majority of academic moralists in the West leaned toward revisionism, while prominent traditionalists also stood close to magisterial conclusions despite occasionally employing novel arguments in their defense.[4] Germain Grisez is an exemplar of such a position. Although he generally upheld traditional Catholic moral teaching, particularly the prohibition of contraception, he pointed to flaws in the supporting magisterial argumentation and proposed his own moral methodology. In contrast, Josef Fuchs influenced revisionists by clarifying concern for the "preservation of a value" as of greater significance to the continuity of the tradition than a material "recurrence of a literal practical guideline."[5] Attempts to heal and overcome the ongoing division between traditionalists and revisionists continue today, even as moral theological perspectives continue to diversify.[6] Increasingly, a simple dichotomy has become ill fit for describing the actual diversities of the field, but this may be waning in significance, more on account of growing complexity rather than actual rapprochement.[7]

Such diversity should not hide the fact that Catholic moral theology remains substantially united by common commitments. In general, Catholic moralists work in dialogue with scripture and tradition and acknowledge the Magisterium as an authoritative guide tasked with interpreting these fundamental sources. Since Vatican II, Catholic moralists have broadly embraced personalism and the concomitant belief that morality ought to be based in the good of persons.[8] Moreover, commitments to moral realism and natural law remain pervasive. The first expresses confidence in objective bases for morality and the reality of sin, the second in the human intellect's ability to discern moral value through disciplined application. Differences in how these common commitments are interpreted largely fuel intramural disputes. Present disagreements are informed by the work of several mid-twentieth-century theologians (Louis Janssens, Joseph Fuchs, Bernard Häring, Bernard Lonergan, et al.) who advocated for reforms in moral theology, including greater attention to historical development and concern for the subject in understanding the Christian moral life. Subsequent work in Liberation Theology and Feminist Theology also broadly informs the field.[9]

Although revisionism is something of a catchall category for the generally progressive commitments informed by this history, its proponents are united by a few common concerns. First, revisionist theologians owe their moniker to their advocacy for revisions to specific sexual ethical norms, both before and in the wake of *Humanae vitae*. Revisionists are generally uninterested in moral laxism but tend to criticize the disproportionate emphasis and unique methods employed for considerations of sexual behavior within the Catholic moral tradition.[10] This perspective conflicts with the Magisterium's claims that existing sexual ethical norms are both unalterable and categorically grave moral matter due their intimate relation to theological anthropology and the divine law.[11] Consequently, revisionist proposals are also inextricably entangled with contested issues of ecclesial authority.

Second, revisionist theologians tend to be skeptical of assertions of the objectivity and clarity of the moral law that leave little or no conceptual distance between moral ideals and practical norms. John Paul II, for example, asserted that all morally permissible sexual expression requires a "total self-gift," which seems to place an exceptionally high bar on the quotidian sexual lives of even lovingly married couples.[12] Revisionists have identified this trend as betraying a misunderstanding of the actual complexities of sexual lives, and they claim that it substantiates a moral dualism in which anything short of the ideal is characterized as evil.[13] Darlene Fozard Weaver observes that though John Paul II overasserts the connection between particular acts and a person's orientation to the divine, revisionists tend to create an excessive distance between particular actions and intimacy with God.[14]

Third, revisionists tend to employ forms of personalism that differ substantially from those of the Magisterium.[15] Before the twentieth century, moralists generally employed a physicalist methodology that made moral determinations based on an act's conformity to a discerned natural moral end. This allowed categorical moral judgments based on the structure of the act itself. Physicalism's assumption that conformation to the natural order of things in itself assures moral practice displaced any immediate need to explain *why* certain acts are good or bad for persons. In contrast, personalism centered moral judgment precisely in the good of the human person. Nonetheless, the Magisterium has repeatedly taught that certain specific acts remain always and everywhere illicit because of the nature of their object. This object is determined apart from, or at least preceding, explicit attention to the context and subjective intentions of the acting person.[16] Both Paul VI and John Paul II utilized forms of personalism that allowed for such categorical judgments of selected physical acts, specifically those related to sex and procreation. Revisionists have argued that this approach actually undermines the basic commitments of personalism itself by prioritizing the interests of physicalist analysis.

Some have further charged the Magisterium with holding a "procreationist" bias that emphasizes biological reproduction as the ultimate end of the sexual act.[17] Christine Gudorf argues that this approach limits sexual ethical considerations by elevating coitus as the only "real" form of sexual expression while ignoring other pleasurable and emotionally gratifying interactions.[18] Relevant to present topics, such a procreationist bias draws concern for parenthood toward sexual ethics and away from the subsequent rearing of children.[19]

Fourth, revisionism presumes that moral perspectives have and will continue to adapt over time in response to changing contexts, changed understandings of human persons, and the workings of the Holy Spirit.[20] Revisionists have strongly criticized the "classicist" worldview, which presents the moral order as "static, necessary, fixed and universal."[21] They discern the influence of this worldview in magisterial presentations of particular moral judgments as definitive and immutable. In contrast, revisionists claim a historically conscious perspective that regards reality as "dynamic, evolving, changing, and particular."[22] This difference leads to divergent expectations of both the need for and possibility of change in authoritative moral teaching.[23]

As an implication of this historical consciousness, revisionists are also committed to using "experience" as a source for moral reflection.[24] Catholic theology holds *scripture* and its interpretation through the *tradition* as foundational, while *reason* is admitted as an essential tool for meaningfully interpreting these sources. Revisionists add *experience* as a source that connects morality to lived realities and provides grounds for dialogue.[25] In contrast, the Magisterium generally recognizes some informative and secondary role for experience but has criticized its prominence within revisionist methodology.[26] Christina Traina has argued that the method employed by some Vatican documents makes experiential knowledge irrelevant to the presumed validity the Magisterium's conclusions.[27] Revisionists have also criticized some magisterial interventions for posturing to protect magisterial authority rather than answering methodological concerns.[28] They further contend that magisterial hesitance to explicitly engage experience preserves the particular historical experiences that have shaped Catholic moral teaching (i.e., primarily that of elite Western European celibate men).

Fifth and finally, revisionists tend to approach gender in a markedly different manner from traditionalist and magisterial sources.[29] Recent magisterial documents often sanction differing masculine and feminine traits and an essentialist view of gender that asserts a clear connection between sexual phenotype and gender expression.[30] This understanding of gender is also commonly framed in moral terms, while gender essentialism is linked to safeguarding human dignity.[31] Gender, in turn, is associated with contrasting the supposedly complementary constellations of masculine and feminine characteristics.[32] In contrast, revisionist theologians accept greater influence of social construction in gender identities.[33] Some have questioned whether complementarity according to sex and gender is an irretrievably patriarchal concept,[34] or if, as an interhuman reality, it necessarily relates to gender at all.[35] Consequently, these perspectives disagree on the legitimacy and value of distinguishing "sex" (the biological fact of sexual differentiation) from "gender" (a collective interpretation of that fact). This distinction has gained wide acceptance in academic circles, although more recent theories of gender have made this construction appear overly simplistic. Meanwhile, the Magisterium continues to vociferously oppose this distinction.[36]

CONTEMPORARY SCHOLARSHIP

Academic Catholic moral theology encompasses a wide range of perspectives. Many scholars advocate for traditional moral norms, while others propose significant revisions to sexual ethics and the theology of marriage and family. A few have given explicit attention to parenthood, particularly about ethics, conceptions of kinship, and adoptive parenting.[37] Surveying several recent books on marriage and family scholarship reveals evidently disproportionate attention to sexual ethics and the sacramental theology of marriage.[38] Some argue that the predominance of the concern for sexual ethics is due to their inherent relation to a right understanding of human persons, such that the concentration of concern is realistic rather than imbalanced.[39] Yet the tradition's insistence on the family as the place of fundamental human formation and its historical balance of procreation and education makes this claim difficult to sustain in broader context. When authors do consider parenthood, the *spirituality of* parenthood is the preferred approach, while the term "fatherhood" does not even appear in all indexes. Excluding the few books focused explicitly on family life exacerbates this trend. As such, the products of academic theology appear open to the critiques already leveled at magisterial documents. Catholic moral theologians of the late twentieth and early twenty-first centuries appear well trained in articulating their methodological commitments and locating themselves within the field, yet they generally show less awareness of how these intramural distinctions have shaped the landscape itself.

Scholars working in the field of sexual ethics, where matters have been hotly contested, tend to replicate the pattern of moving from sexuality and gender to parenthood with limited reflection on either the practical realities of parenthood or parenthood itself as a subject of theological exploration. For example, Margaret Farley's *Just Love* engages both the framing and prominence of sexual ethics in Catholic moral theology but offers little reflection on parenthood, even when this would be relevant. Farley articulates grounds for supporting same-sex partnerships and argues that heterosexual and homosexual sexual relationships can be evaluated on similar standards.[40] She approves of same-sex parenthood yet stops short of supporting same-sex marriage, arguing that same-sex couples should be allowed to determine the suitable institutional form of their own relationships.[41] Although there are defensible motives for this reservation from the point of view of the adults concerned, it leaves same-sex parenthood resting in a conceptual gap. Farley does not thoroughly consider how the presence of children might have an impact on the evaluation of adult relationships. This is not to assert that same-sex couples with children must be married, but rather that negotiating stable relational contexts for parenthood is important to children's well-being and cannot be overlooked. However, the underdevelopment of theological discourse in this area exacerbates such oversights. Like the arguments of the Catholic adoption agencies presented in the introduction to this book, Farley allows her judgments in sexual ethics to carry over into parental fitness without meaningfully engaging considerations of children's needs and parental capabilities, despite her support of same-sex parenting.

Todd Salzman and Michael Lawler's *The Sexual Person* articulates a revisionist sexual anthropology to support a more robust and inclusive view of human sexuality. They criticize the idealization of sex in magisterial documents, particularly those of John Paul II, but similarly centralize sex in their conception of family and parenthood. Salzman and Lawler place good sex as foundational for family formation (by conception or adoption) and for sustaining healthy marriages, families, and children. Although sexual acts may play an important role in relational health and stability, this centralization replicates problematic Catholic moral preoccupations without being balanced by a clear theological vision of parenthood itself. The imbalance becomes evident by comparing their argument for the moral acceptance of homogenital sexual acts with their argument for same-sex parenthood. The former relies on a thorough rethinking of complementarity and the human person, and the latter is *exclusively* based on social scientific evidence.[42] Once again, parenthood is treated as an extension of sexual ethics, while experiential evidence bears the weight of its justification.[43]

Finally, William May's *Catholic Sexual Ethics* contrasts with the books above in its explicit defense of magisterial teaching.[44] May and his coauthors, Ronald Lawler and Joseph Boyle, declare that magisterial teachings must be regarded with complete docility as a matter of faith because the Magisterium "*always* teaches with the authority of Christ."[45] They further cite as "very weighty" the argument that sexual desires have been uniquely corrupted by original sin, which justifies the greater attention these matters receive.[46] The authors assert that the "procreative good is intrinsically and always good" and they clarify that any sexual act may be morally evaluated on the basis of openness to this good.[47] But despite these claims about the absolute goodness of precreation, the book is largely silent on the actual realities of parenthood. Moreover, it rejects same-sex parenthood on the basis of sexual ethical issues without meaningful reference to parental capabilities.

That May and his coauthors' book hews close to the magisterial perspective is not surprising. What is surprising, however, is that their perspective follows the patterns of other authors who strongly disagree with May and colleagues' methodological commitments and moral conclusions. Such arguments illustrate how easily Catholic ethicists allow sexual ethical concerns to function as justifications for parenthood.

Similar patterns also appear in the field of marriage and family, despite greater awareness of limitations in present ways of conceptualizing the family and parenthood. A number of significant questions related to marriage and sexual relationships have weighted the field in these directions, despite a few prominent books dealing with family life explicitly.[48] Unfortunately, theological engagement with the family has often been relegated to the periphery of intellectual moral theology. Writing on the family rarely receives the attention of more prominent moral issues, while the broader Catholic literature on the topic is largely populated by practical and spiritual writing aimed at popular audiences.[49]

A Catechism of Family Life, edited by Sarah Bartel and John Grabowski, provides an interesting case in point for demonstrating both the general biases of the field as well as the larger concerns it ought to encompass. The book is structured around 110 questions obtained from various sources, including students, family, friends, and adult learners. This results in a diverse and balanced collection of questions sorted into eight categories.[50] The editors respond to each with quotations from magisterial documents as well as occasional explanations and clarifications. As the questions progress to more concrete issues about childrearing, however, these responding texts become less direct, come from less authoritative sources, and are more frequently reused.[51] Remarkably, the book's index and recommendations for further reading reflect the concerns of the field more than the content of its own pages. Its recommendations for further reading do not even include the topics of parenting or the social role of the family, despite these being addressed in the text itself.[52] This disconnect between the book's body and its supporting material illustrates that, without the concerns of actual parents actively shaping the conversation, the structure of academic and magisterial discourse tends to revert to a narrower focus on sexual ethics and gender.

Additional recent works in marriage and family scholarship offer more concerted contributions to building a broader theological framework for parenthood. Many authors are contributing to calls for stronger engagement with the full set of moral concerns related to the family as well as authentic and concerted engagement with the realities of family life. Lisa Sowle Cahill, for example, disparages the "disproportionate energy" absorbed by sexual morality and claims that this imbalance distracts from the broader concerns of the family.[53] Florence McCaffrey Bourg laments how existing biases "stifle the imagination when it comes to theology of family as domestic church."[54] She argues this narrowness is supported by magisterial approaches that favor natural law, consistency, and deductive reason, which "amount to an assertion that, underlying everything unique in humans of various times and places, the most important human values are timeless."[55] Consequently, magisterial perspectives take on a strained relationship with the actual diversities and complexities of contemporary family life. Julie Hanlon Rubio similarly attends to the idealization of the family over actual engagement with lived experiences.[56] In an important recent work, Sandra Sullivan-Dunbar argues for the full moral value of the caregiving work that has been too easily and often overlooked.[57] Likewise, Christine Firer Hinze labels current economic systems as exploitative, inasmuch as unpaid care labor advantages some while often leaving care workers themselves economically vulnerable and socially marginalized.[58] Contemporary scholarship in the field of marriage and family is also advancing more robust views of kinship and social conceptions of the family. As such, the field is increasingly challenging the ideal of private, biological nuclear families that rose to prominence as Catholic discourse came to frame concerns related to the family, gender, and sexual ethics.

David Matzo McCarthy offers one of the more unique approaches to addressing the disproportionate role of sexual ethics in considerations of family life. He maintains that the turn to personalism encouraged a focus on intimate and idealized partnerships separate from the social conditions and practices that provide the actual context of human relationships.[59] This tendency seeks profound truth in isolated sexual acts apart from the surrounding context of marriage and home.[60] For McCarthy, this prioritization gets reality backwards; sex ought to serve the relational bonds that provide its context. He states, "The chief problem with the personalist account of sex is, not that it goes wrong, but that it says too much to be right. Every sexual act is defined as full and total, so that sex has no room to be ordinary. The act of sexual intercourse, in this theological framework, transcends its particular meaning in time, in order to reveal the complete contours of our two-in-one flesh humanity."[61] This "Earth-shattering" view of sex is incompatible with the realities of marriage and makes attentive consideration of marital realities meaningless because the sexual act says it all.[62]

Although McCarthy's characterization of personalism is at times slippery and tends to avoid implicating the Magisterium in theological currents that have clearly been driven by authoritative teaching, he uniquely grasps and explains how prevailing frameworks have influenced the contemporary theology of the family. In so doing, he identifies one reality of the prevailing conception of parenthood that is a real cause of concern: the presumption that moral sexual behavior is in and of itself sufficient to guarantee the moral value of the entire marital relationship, including parenthood. He memorably summarizes the problem latent in this approach: "Great lovers do not necessarily make for good housekeeping."[63] In addition to misplacing and exaggerating the role of sex in marital relationships, this elevation of sex as the pinnacle of marital love deviates from the tradition's regard for love of others, even to the point of self-sacrifice, as love's highest form.[64]

Several scholars have attempted to mitigate the preoccupation with sexual ethics by offering more expansive interpretations of the good of procreation so as to open sexual ethical discourse to a broader range of issues. In his book on adoptive parenting, Gilbert Meilaender, a Lutheran who is both influenced by and highly conversant with Catholic perspectives, points to John Paul II's introduction of a more expansive use of the term "procreation" in an address to adoptive families.[65] Meilaender is less comfortable than John Paul II here in distancing procreation, as a precise moral term, from biological reproduction, because such slippage could undermine the very arguments that keep Catholic sexual morality positioned against the use of contraceptives.[66] Scholars less concerned with this norm have gone further down the path suggested by John Paul II's brief comments to adoptive families. For example, Margaret Farley offers "fruitfulness" as a revised way of understanding the good of procreation that is inclusive of growth in loving relationships, care, and justice.[67] She recognizes that biological reproduction is not possible for all sexual relationships and argues that nonreproductive sex acts may still be fruitful in other ways.[68] Similarly, Richard Gaillardetz draws the concept of "generativity" from the Orthodox tradition in order to connect the good of procreation to the vocation of Christian discipleship, while disrupting its singular association with biological reproduction. According to Gaillardetz, the Orthodox tradition understands the love of the married couple as replicating the triune life of God, in which profoundly mutual and fecund love "overflows outward into the world." Christian couples should likewise aspire to see their love come to fruition beyond themselves in innumerable ways.[69] Finally, he argues that procreation is misconceived when it is tied to only specific sexual acts. Instead, the family's mission itself is procreative as it participates in both the creation and formation of persons. This procreative mission is greater than any single sexual act or any single couple can bear alone. Instead, the procreative mission of the family extents to the social relationships in which families are embedded, which give context and shape to the realization of this good.[70]

As with sexual ethics, several scholars have criticized the role gender plays in conceptions of the family. This is clearly manifest in reactions against idealizations of masculine and feminine traits and against insistence on gender complementarity as essential for ethical sex, the possibility of marriage, and the foundation of family life.[71] McCarthy criticizes John Paul II's pronouncements about gender for yielding impossible expectations of mutuality in marriage. He argues that no person can or should completely give all of one's self to another; nor can or should a person find total completion in a single relationship.[72] Human sociality is both deeper and more complex than a single romantic dyad can fulfill. For McCarthy, love is nurtured in marriage as well as friendships and social interactions. Ultimately, these diverse, complex, and interacting experiences of love point beyond human realities to love's source in God.[73] The tendency to idealize and emphasize the gendered sexual relationships of parental partners leads to the misconception that they are morally determinative of family life and parenthood.[74] McCarthy writes: "Masculinity and femininity make a difference to what men and women do, but it is not always clear what that difference might be. In other words, gender impinges on our identities and common endeavors, but being male or female is not equivalent to identity or function."[75] In the home, especially, personalities and preferences play an important role in determining individual functions. Idealizing marriage as a "self-contained whole" that hinges on a mutual complementarity of man and woman reduces the complexities of actual spousal roles through inattentiveness to individual human capacities and needs beyond preestablished gendered norms.[76]

Lisa Sowle Cahill sees "an irreducible ambivalence" in the papal assertion of both gender equality and gender essentialism.[77] Asserting her feminist concerns, she argues that such views can underwrite differentiated access to social benefits and preferential roles for men that are sustained "by ideology and by physical force, both direct and indirect."[78] She criticizes the impossible idealism of John Paul II's presentation of women in particular. Similarly, Julie Hanlon Rubio cares about the Magisterium's use of gender to present an idealized, fictional account of the Holy Family that makes it difficult for families and individuals in diverse situations to hear and respond to the Church's message.[79] Rubio strongly criticizes John Paul II's portrayal of the family, which "never steps out of the ideal realm to touch the reality of individual families."[80] Rather than reliance on such idealizations, she advocates for recognizing the limitations and challenges of real families without treating these as aberrations.[81]

Florence Caffrey Bourg is likewise concerned about the "pep talk" approach of papal writings that present all challenges as conquerable through exhortative language that tends to equate ideals with norms.[82] This portrays the reality of internal family conflict as essentially foreign to the family. Unrealistic ideals of family harmony become the starting point, and the world beyond this home is presented as the real threat to family tranquility.[83] Families do face many external challenges, yet internal harmony based in scripted gender identities is not the baseline of domestic life. Entertaining such notions limits meaningful engagement with reality while creating expectations of perfection that can make sharing actual familial worries and challenges unwelcome.[84]

Sacramentally, this same trend obscures the common Christian identity in baptism as a foundation for the domestic church, instead favoring the complementarity of man and woman in marriage.[85] Bourg suggests that the emphasis on marriage may result from a hesitance to receive Vatican II's ecclesiological vision against the backdrop of an older, stricter separation of lay from ordained that views marriage as primarily related to procreation and the education of children. Bourg entertains the possibility of considering both sacraments as foundational to the domestic church, and she notes the US bishops' view that marriage specifies and gives focus to the grace of baptism.[86] She is unwilling to accept a singular connection of the domestic church to sacramental marriage because this restricts the concept to nuclear families alone.[87]

Bourg's openness to more expansive conceptions of the domestic church beyond the nuclear family contrasts with juridical trends within Catholicism that favor structural definitions of the family while devaluing and excluding deviating family forms.[88] In so doing, the structural components of the family (i.e., a married mother and father and their children) are expected to carry the moral weight of the Christian understanding of family. Magisterial sources often exhort such families to a specifically Christian calling but rarely define their identities as families fundamentally in relation to this calling. Against this pattern, Cahill argues, the "Christian interpretation of family life must confront the possibility that traditional family structures should be replaced, not reinforced, in the domestic church."[89] In her view, an honest assessment of Christian ideals for the family challenges long-accepted cultural norms for family structure and function. Rediscovering the diversity of biblical and historical Christian views on kinship has played a significant part in this academic willingness to rethink familial bonds. Still, there is evident disagreement about how closely the Christian familial ideal ought to be bound to the "natural family," which is typically characterized as a married couple and their biological children.

On one hand, several authors have argued that the Christian call to discipleship relativizes biological kinship by calling Christians into the one family of Christ, united by a common identity as adopted children of God. Stephen Post argues that early Christianity prioritized love over biological kinship, as evidenced by a willingness to accept children beyond the obligations of biological kinship and to allow children to be raised by nonbiological kin when this suited children's best interest.[90] Rubio likewise claims that the New Testament's commitment to discipleship undermines absolute assertions of "natural" family patterns. She writes: "The kinship bond and all the ethical priority that comes with it are called into question, because the Jesus of the Gospels preaches that family, like money and power, can be dangerous to the person who wants to live a holy life."[91] This does not mean that the New Testament is antifamily, but she advises caution when seeking biblical support for family values. The New Testament stresses altruism beyond biological kin and commands love of the neighbor (who is further characterized as the foreigner or enemy). No priority seems to extend to biological kin because the moral emphasis is placed on concern for, and the making of, social kin.[92] This reality reorients parenthood within the Christian perspective. Rubio writes: "Christians love children not because children belong to them, but because children belong to God. Their commitment to their children is rooted primarily in love, not biology."[93]

On the other hand, assertions of moral obligations based in biological kinship and natural family patterns remain prominent. For example, Cahill roots family in biological kinship and presents nonbiological kinship as an analogous extension of these natural bonds. Her argument is grounded in a commitment to the natural abilities of persons and capacity for growth as well as a realistic recognition of the damage caused by sin. Grace exerts a transformative influence on families, even as this call to discipleship remains mired in the ambiguities of earthly existence.[94] As such, Cahill addresses the classic features of Christian anthropology (nature, sin, and grace) in the context of the family.[95] Her brief and realistic comments on adoption are evidence for her distinction between biological and nonbiological kinship.[96] She strips adoptive kinship of any romanticism, presenting adoption as a form of "crisis management."[97] Granting that adoption should not be considered an unambiguous good, her view notably lacks a felix culpa moment or strong vision of redemption.[98] Ultimately, she advances an "inclusive and supportive approach to family life, one that can hold up ideals such as male-female co-parenting and sexual fidelity without thereby berating and excluding single-parent families, divorced families, gay and lesbian families, blended families, or adoptive families."[99]

Gilbert Meilaender likewise connects kinship primarily to biological ties but makes room for adoptive parenthood by exploring how both blood and shared history constitute pathways to kinship.[100] He first contextualizes Christian kinship in relation to the ultimate and primary Christian identity as children of God: "Baptism is not primarily an event of importance for the biological family, even if relatives of the child are generally present. Rather, it signifies that at the deepest level the child's identity is marked by relation to God, who sets his hand upon us in baptism and calls us by name."[101] He orders kinship along the theological pattern of creation, reconciliation, and redemption. And he asserts that each of these dimensions helps us see biological kinship, adopted kinship, and our kinship in Christ in a larger and more balanced perspective.[102] Like Cahill, Meilaender recognizes that adoption is always tinged with loss, given that it implies a fracturing of biological ties. Choosing to place a child for adoption may be a supremely loving act of biological parenthood; nonetheless, it ruptures the future of that particular bond. Adoption is a good in itself and reflects an essential aspect of the story of faith, but it operates in reference to the natural ties of biological kinship, while the nuclear family grounded in the complementary spousal relationship provides the norm for the family.

In this way, Milaender argues that adoptive kinship is a real form of kinship that goes beyond fiction while also dismissing nonnuclear families as alternatives to the ideal. But his attempt to rethink adoption while maintaining a framework for parenthood based in gender and reproduction is tenuous.

For example, he argues against same-sex parenthood by considering how Catholic children of same-sex couples may find themselves divided between love for those who have raised them and love for God's plan for marriage. This thought experiment itself concedes that same-sex couples may be capable of raising thoughtful and faithful children who would be capable of entertaining such a dilemma, yet this implicit concession does not impact his conception of parenthood as rooted in gender and procreation.[103]

Moreover, Meilaender's view of adoptive parenthood attempts to map a voluntarist account of parenthood onto a largely causalist tradition without critically questioning the latter. Voluntarist approaches to parenthood root parental identity in the willing commitment to raise a child, whereas causalist approaches identify obligations as arising from acts associated with procreation. Meilaender simultaneously claims the former as an authentic foundation for parenthood while admitting that the latter is fundamental and, in a sense, primary. Thus, he strains to legitimate a chosen commitment as a foundation for parenthood while tying the moral possibility of such a commitment to family structures patterned on the biological, nuclear family. His effort is rightly concerned with the limited attention that adoption has received in recent theology, but it avoids exploring how the commitments of this discourse itself create an inhospitable context for thinking of adoption as a unique Christian good.[104]

In addition to expanding definitions of the family beyond biological and nuclear moorings, questions are also being raised about belief in the family as a private shelter from the world of social interaction. Contemporary magisterial teaching negotiates a challenging tension between its indebtedness to romantic influences that idealize private life in the home and its commitment to calling families to recognize their Christian vocation through social engagement as agents of change in the world. Cahill observes that the former trend risks idolatry and can support self-centeredness and greed.[105] She explains: "The primary values defining the Christian family are the same values that define the 'new family in Christ': other-concern and compassionate love that overlooks socially normative boundaries and is willing to sacrifice to meet the needs of others."[106] The family, as domestic church, participates in the full mission of the Church. For Cahill, this means protecting the eschatological edge of the Christian mission, even within familial life.[107]

McCarthy likewise criticizes the suburban ideal of self-sufficient, private families that is too easily accepted within Catholic thought. He believes the preservation of such an ideal is shaped and co-opted by capitalist economics, individualism, and the needs of the nation-state.[108] Families turned in on themselves can move freely to seek employment opportunities and become market-dependent consumer units disconnected from the informal networks of support and exchange that characterize healthy community life. Acquiescing to such ideals closes families to their essential social dimensions and insulates them from the grace of encounter that can come with response to the world's needs. When marriage is viewed as an interpersonal partnership of love that defines larger considerations of the family, it obscures the Christian ideal of "an open, socially reproductive household."[109] Open households draw upon the relational resources of kin, friends, and community for support, and in so doing create networks of exchange and dependence that cement social bonds.[110] McCarthy writes: "Love is ordered towards communion and mutuality and is therefore best served by open families in their necessary but incomplete expressions of love in a fragmented world."[111]

Open households recall more traditional family patterns tied to their surrounding community and reliant on high levels of shared support and resources. This contrasts markedly with the private familial ideal of self-sufficiency, centered squarely on the shoulders of two married parents. Magisterial documents provide wavering support in the direction of open households. Recent teaching makes room for a social and ecclesial mission of the family and advocates for the inclusion of family members beyond the nuclear household, particularly elderly grandparents.[112] Yet it also hesitates to extend the concept of parenthood beyond the spousal pair, which would be an implication of taking the social interconnectedness of open households seriously.

With similar reservations, Meilaender argues for permanency as an essential aspect of "parenthood," and in so doing he excludes practices like foster parenting from the term's authentic meaning.[113] This argument serves to protect sexual and gender norms that are most easily sustained under the framework of private, biological nuclear families. Yet engagement with parental experience self-evidently attests to the negotiated and divisible nature of parental roles. The historical rise of the nuclear family itself obscures the diverse history of parental responsibilities in which siblings, grandparents, aunts, uncles, and unrelated adults have often assumed partial or primary responsibility for parenting children. Such patterns remain evident today even in the West, despite ideals and practices that detract attention. For example, Catholic teaching firmly links parental responsibility to education but also supports schools and churches as a means of fulfilling this parental duty. Although teachers are not fully parents to their pupils, they undeniably participate in a responsibility of parenthood. The fact that certain individuals are primary parents of certain children does not exclude the participation of others in authentic acts of parenting in partial or impermanent ways. The mere fact that Catholicism can morally support parenthood in both single and two-parent families makes the divisible nature of parenthood obvious. Demeaning the contributions of caring adults as inauthentic to actual parenting serves idealization more than reality. This is particularly true of family experiences that have not been beneficiaries of the assets of socially privileged groups. Emphasis on the private nuclear family is emphasis on an upper-class ideal that many have not experienced. Among Latina/o families, for example, Victor Carmona has brought attention to how dysfunctional immigration systems often sever and undermine family unity,[114] while Nichole Flores has argued that extensive and extended family networks can serve as a model of solidarity.[115]

For Christians, open families are not just open to interdependence and communal ties for their own benefit. They are also called to this existence through a fundamental vocation to serve the common good and the evangelical mission of the Church. This dimension of family life consistently arises within Catholic teaching. Inspired by this tradition, Mary Roche Doyle suggests the family is "more of a verb than it is a noun." She explores the practical and particular ways in which Catholic Social Teaching calls actual families to participate in the world as well as the necessary conditions for enabling vibrant social vocations.[116] Echoing McCarthy's concern for the dominance of social forces in family ideals, Roche criticizes moral praise for families simply because they have access to the necessary supports for maintaining familial ideals when these are denied to others.[117]

In addition, Rubio's *Family Ethics* offers a sustained reflection on the interactions of both internally and externally oriented dimensions of family life and identifies the family as a point of convergence between private and social spheres.[118] Contrary to easy idealizations, Rubio highlights the tensions between family and discipleship in the New Testament. She writes: "Despite traditional theological claims to the contrary, family values are hardly prevalent in the New Testament. Jesus himself locates his vocation outside of his family. . . . Jesus poses troubling questions about the compatibility of discipleship with family duties."[119] Observing the prominence of discipleship in early Christianity, she argues that discipleship is not a natural outcome of family life but a hard-fought and often conflictive negotiation of values.[120] As such, Christian parents are called to a "dual vocation," directed both inwardly to the well-being of the family and outwardly to the betterment of society.[121] Rubio's moral concern for the privatization of families is well supported by Catholic Social Teaching, which counts families among the "intermediate associations" that can promote dramatic social change.[122] Despite general inattention to this reality, the family is in fact essential to magisterial teaching on social reform.[123] She writes: "The genius of Catholic teaching on the family is its refusal to limit families by telling them to simply focus on themselves. Christian families, from this perspective, are to grow in self-giving love within and outside the bonds of kinship."[124]

In all these ways, contemporary scholarship is questioning the private, biological nuclear family as an operative ideal in Catholic thought. Magisterial teaching has often been far too accepting of this ideal as a support for concerns related to sexual ethics and gender, but it nonetheless harbors a vision of the social mission of the family that challenges reliance on such ideals. The authors cited above demonstrate the limitations of each element of the private, biological nuclear norm and are each open to theological critique. Families may be formed in ways other than biological kinship, which may or may not represent a fundamental pattern for kin relations. Overemphasis on the legitimate privacy of families creates opportunity to neglect the more challenging aspects of Christian vocation. And family boundaries often and rightfully extend beyond two married parents and their children. In so doing, most authors entertain some notion of shifting from a singular emphasis on how families are structured to how families function. For example, Cahill argues that structural definitions of the family are less significant than assessments of family function in light of Christian commitments.[125] She writes: "If the socially radical meaning of Christianity is taken seriously, Christian families can become vehicles of social justice, even as they strengthen and build upon their bonds of kinship, affection, and faithfulness."[126] She finds a contemporary exemplar for this conviction in African American families, which, despite challenging circumstances, have often provided mutual support and maintained a marital and parental ideal while remaining broadly inclusive of diverse family structures.[127] Such an understanding of the family does not make all familial arrangements morally equivalent, but it shifts the lens of moral evaluation from the constituent parts of a family's structure to the family's functional ability to realize its Christian vocation. This shift opens Catholic thinking on the family to the possibility that many family structures may realize morally praiseworthy possibilities while growing in discipleship in socially significant ways.[128]

Nonetheless, only a handful of authors have critically engaged with the conceptual parameters of the family, let alone parenthood. Consequently, their advocacy for reinterpreting the tradition often lands within a larger framework that centers theological conceptions on the very preoccupations they hope to overcome. In addition, the absorption of interests of the wider field of moral theology in sex and gender tend to distract from and overshadow the significance of these contributions. Although the reception of revisionist issues has warmed in some ways during the papacy of Pope Francis, the larger Catholic theological context has remained remarkably persistent in its utilization of a framework for parenthood that is narrowly based on sexual ethics and gender norms.

FRANCIS

Pope Francis's first apostolic exhortation, *Evangelii gaudium*, set forth a vision of a joyful, invitational church that evangelizes by mercifully encountering the needs of the world.[129] This centering of the Church's mission on hospitable openness to the challenges of people's lives and other aspects of his papacy have led Francis to be widely regarded as a reforming pope. The trajectory of his papacy certainly deserves this recognition because he has continued to develop Catholic teaching while offering a renewed vision of the missional Church. Nonetheless, the differences between his teaching and that of his most influential recent predecessor, John Paul II, are frequently overstated, especially as related to teaching on the family. Like John Paul II, Francis has repeatedly reaffirmed his commitment to the teaching of *Humanae vitae*, and he frequently employs the concept of complementarity to describe the normative implications of gender difference. Again, following in the footsteps of John Paul II, Francis convoked the first synod of bishops of his pontificate on the theme of marriage and the family. Francis's approach to organization, oversight, and communication differed markedly from former synods; and his unique emphasis on mercy and pastoral care was influential throughout the process. Nonetheless, his subsequent apostolic exhortation, *Amoris laetitia*, stands in significant continuity with those of his predecessors. There are key developments taking place that call attention to the continuing development and possible expansion of conceptions of the family and parenthood. However, these are often muted by the document's recourse to the prevailing narrow framework. Francis's document reiterates earlier preoccupations, particularly with respect to sexual ethical norms, gender complementarity, and the basis of the Christian family in sacramental marriage. Yet the pope's own insistence on the missional dimensions of Christian life and the need for the Church to mercifully and meaningfully address the actual needs of families in the world today helps expose tensions latent in this pattern of routing concern for parenthood through sexual ethics and gender.

As the product of two unusually public synods, *Amoris laetitia*, Pope Francis's 2016 apostolic exhortation, evidences a desire to shift magisterial teaching on the family in a more pastoral direction.[130] In this, Francis himself appears content to lean into his conservative credentials on the topics of sexuality and gender while advocating for reform in pastoral care and missional outreach. However, *Amoris laetitia* is not a presentation of Francis's thought alone, given that its primary content emerged out of synod discussions that represented several competing views among the representative bishops. *Amoris laetitia* articulates a unified vision that encompasses the synod's agreement, but the path of its development also makes it particularly useful for understanding how the Catholic framework for the family and parenthood was being explored and questioned within the workings of the Magisterium itself.

Amoris laetitia's continuity with earlier teachings is evident in its tendency to accept the private, biological nuclear family as a natural foundation and ideal for family life, upon which the social mission of the family is added. The exhortation itself claims that there is "no stereo-type of the ideal family, but rather a challenging mosaic made up of many different realities, with all their joys, hopes and problems."[131] However, the statement seems directed at diversities aside from structure. Following John Paul II, *Amoris laetitia* exclusively centers Christian family life on sacramental marriage, even while clearly connecting marriage itself to baptism.[132]

Amoris laetitia states: "Only the exclusive and indissoluble union between a man and a woman has a plenary role to play in society as a stable commitment that bears fruit in new life."[133] Nonetheless, the document later characterizes family life based in sacramental marriage as the "fullest" realization of Christian families, while retaining openness to some structural differences. The interpretative key to discerning what amounts to an impartial realization of the Christian family versus a dangerous contradiction is not an assessment of the interpersonal relations, missional dimensions, or social commitments of any particular family. Rather, it is a structural assessment. Some *forms of union* "radically contradict" the ideal of family based in marriage, while others "realize it in at least a partial and analogous way."[134] Unions that are structurally nuclear but lack marriage require pastoral discernment to determine their relation to marriage. Considerations of same-sex couples do not appear in these references, but an earlier quotation from the Congregation for the Doctrine of the Faith clarifies that there are "absolutely no grounds for considering homosexual unions to be in any way similar or even remotely analogous to God's plan for marriage and family."[135] As such, same-sex relationships are categorically excluded, while heterosexual unions require discernment, which centers on their disposition toward sacramental marriage. In both cases, structural consideration of who composes a family are absolutely prior to considerations of family function.

During the 2014 synod's first week of discussions, the bishops considered making use of the inclusive framework employed by Vatican II in response to non-Catholic religions. In this view, the family based in sacramental marriage would remain central, while the relative goods of other family forms would be considered as standing in closer or more distant relations to this center.[136] As such, the Church could look for good in all family forms without excluding any as necessarily contradictory to the Church's vision of the family, while still upholding an ideal of the family based in sacramental marriage. This would have represented a significant departure from the categorical judgments of recent decades and was not ultimately employed by *Amoris laetitia.*

Despite ultimately framing concern for the family around a structural ideal, *Amoris laetitia* does not fully support a private, biological nuclear ideal. Its strongest resistance comes in its response to overly private conceptions of the family through insistence on the social mission of the family. Reminiscent of Farley's argument above, the document advocates for an expanded understanding of the "fruitfulness" of marriage and family that clearly extends to socially engaged action.[137] Recalling Rubio's work, *Amoris laetitia* encourages families to actively contribute to society by reaching out in solidarity to the needs of those around them, and it specifically calls upon married couples to recognize their social obligations.[138] The nuclear family is also presented as embedded within a larger family structure, with obligations to interact with and assist relatives. This link to the social obligations of the family as disruptive of overly private ideals goes so far as to include neighbors as a form of extended kin.[139] Nonetheless, this advocacy for socially oriented families with less rigid structural boundaries stands in tension with other aspects of an exhortation that opens with the imagery of a harmonious private home.[140]

Likewise, the exhortation remains protective of the biological norm by maintaining the separation of adoption from procreation. *Amoris laetitia* does go further than other recent authoritative documents in praising adoption as a good in its own right that is directed to the well-being of children. Moreover, it clearly recognizes adoption as a pathway to parenthood and includes foster care as a legitimate expression of parenthood. Both procreation and adoption are presented as manifestations of the fruitfulness of marital love, with adoption attesting to unique truths about parenthood.[141] Nonetheless, it replicates earlier documents by presenting the choice to adopt as a likely response to infertility.[142] As with Meilaender's argument above, this view of adoption attempts to assert the important truth that Christian parenthood is founded on freely chosen virtuous commitment to the good of a child while simultaneously restricting fully authentic Christian parenthood to households founded in sacramental marriage and guided by a norm of biological reproduction.

Francis's attempt to lean firmly into sacramental marriage as the foundation of Christian family life, and to protect the gender norms associated with this, exposes further tension with his concomitant desire to frame parenthood as a willful responsiveness to children's needs. Francis continues John Paul II's insistence on gender complementarity as a fundamental component of marriage and family life, but his concerns for familial diversity, pastoral care, and the social mission of the family prompt greater explanation as to why complementarity should remain so essential beyond mere assertion.[143] Ultimately, Francis's willingness to engage with the realities of family life counts as a significant weakness for his assertion of the necessity of gender complementarity. The exhortation insists on the importance of gender difference and its necessity for sacramental marriage, but it cannot sustain these commitments when issues shift from the idealized realm of sacramental theology to more practical considerations of family life.

Amoris laetitia insists on the importance of gender difference as essential mutuality in the marital relationship upon which the family is built. Moreover, it opposes theories of gender that distinguish biological sex from gender identity as harmful denials of anthropological realities that attempt to erase important differences.[144] Despite acknowledging some malleability in the categories of "masculine" and "feminine," and encouraging reciprocity in marriage, the document tends toward stereotype. For example, while both mothers and fathers are called upon to be involved in the life of the family, only women's role in motherhood is presented as essential to society.[145] As Hoon Choi has observed, the document makes very limited progress in acknowledging men's roles as caregivers.[146] Men are to love their wives and are encouraged to take on "some aspects" of childrearing if required for the good of the family.[147] Even as the document pushes toward greater parental mutuality and attempts to disrupt rigid gendered categories, it presents women as essential to parenthood, while men are to play a supporting role.

The document's fundamental struggle is with how to keep the functions traditionally ascribed to the family united to an essential structure in a world where structural alternatives are increasingly obvious. Like Vatican II, *Amoris laetitia* prioritizes the ultimate function of the family unit (i.e., socializing and evangelizing its members while serving and evangelizing society) while insisting that a particular family structure is essential for these tasks (i.e., a complementary union of married man and woman). For the popes of the early twentieth century, this link was hardly called into question. Their concern was with gendered responsibilities within the family, particularly women's place in the home, against the backdrop of changing social norms. By the end of the century, however, chosen diversities in family forms could hardly be ignored. For John Paul II, insistence on complementarity accomplished much of the work of holding the family structure and family function together. True marital love, expressed as mutual self-gift, was only possible, he insisted, through a married union of man and woman. The consequence, however, was the frequent accusation that his presentation of marriage and family drifted into ephemeral idealizations divorced from lived realities.[148] In contrast, Francis insists on engaging the lived realities and responding pastorally to present needs. This concern to engage with experience directs attention precisely to the point at which the tenuous insistence on an essential link between structure and function is weakest.

Amoris laetitia reveals this weakness in two ways. First, as a consequence of concern for pastoral care, *Amoris laetitia* is uniquely willing to admit exceptions and alternatives to the idealized family structure. Such a compromise with reality undermines the purported essentialness of marriage and gender complementarity. For example, if a spouse dies, it counsels single parents to find other supportive adults who can model mature masculinity or femininity for the children. In so doing, *Amoris laetitia* undermines its own argument for the absolute necessity of parental gender complementarity.[149] Circumstances alone are insufficient to justify why some families can seek balanced gender influences beyond the nuclear household and others categorically cannot. Consistency with this norm would advise remarriage as quickly as possible or would have to admit that parental gender complementarity is not an absolute requirement for families. Beyond this inconsistent pastoral exception, the Church's own concern for the social mission of the family further calls this unevenly applied norm of parental gender complementarity into question. At a fundamental level, families cannot simultaneously be regarded as open and engaged social units with respect to their social mission and self-sufficient wholes with respect to parental gender complementarity. Although the prevailing framework has worked to hide this tension, here the two streams of familial commitments have come to a head. Either social engagement matters or it does not; the pastoral exception for single parents indicates that the ideal of a privatized family is more negotiable than the families' innate social character. However, the barrier around the nuclear household has been fortified in recent decades to sustain the arguments against same-sex relationships and parenthood.

Second, *Amoris laetitia* itself is incapable of sustaining its descriptions of masculinity and femininity in light of its own engagement with familial realities.[150] Recent trends in magisterial teaching have increasingly upheld the centrality of parental gender complementarity. As Christina Traina points out, a 2019 document from the Congregation for Catholic Education goes so far as to believe that "our bodily sex is a product of our essential masculinity or femininity, not the other way around."[151] Nonetheless, this increasingly urgent magisterial concern seems to find little meaningful resonance in actual familial experiences. Tellingly, the closer *Amoris laetitia*'s concerns get to the lived needs and challenges of families, the less gender appears to matter in any significant way. In fact, the only time gender is meaningfully considered in *Amoris laetitia*'s entire chapter on the parental task of education, the primary responsibility of parenthood according to the modern magisterial tradition, is within an explanation of how gender roles are negotiable.[152]

As *Amoris laetitia* considers the actual functions of the Christian family, adaptable human capabilities take priority over gendered differences. Like John Paul II, Francis attempts to shore up this disparity through emphasis on the grace of sacramental marriage; but his argument struggles to convince, in large part because its flights to idealization are so obviously disconnected from its concerns to engage reality. The fundamental question is not if sacramental marriage contributes to parenthood and the development of Christian families, as it certainly does. Rather, the fundamental question is if this reality necessitates restricting the recognition of authentic Christian parenthood within this sacramental reality. Doing so appears to negate the priority of the fundamental Christian identity given in baptism, which *Amoris laetitia* itself recognizes as the foundation for the self-giving love required in matrimony.[153] Recognizing this tension in anything more than the brief exceptions typically directed at single and adoptive parents would encourage disconnecting capacities for Christian parenthood from sacramental marriage. The bishops briefly considered an inclusive framework for families at the 2014 synod that could account for such diversities; however, the approach was abandoned. Scaling back the absolute association between marriage and family would also weaken the bulwark of teaching on gender and sexuality that recent popes have worked diligently to construct and defend. Thus, despite minor protests to the contrary and clear emphasis on the task of education, *Amoris laetitia* falls in line with the established trajectory by conceiving of parenthood primarily as an extension of sexual ethics, wherein procreation and complementarity remain definitive.

CONCLUSION

The first two chapters of this book traced developments in modern magisterial teaching that led to the prominence of a certain framework for Catholic thinking about the family in general and parenthood in particular. This chapter has sketched the present intellectual context by considering recent scholarship that advances theological dialogue on a number of related concerns. It has also considered Pope Francis's attempts to both reiterate the commitments of his predecessors while moving Catholicism toward a more open dialogue with the needs of the world and how this has exposed problematic tensions in the prevailing Catholic framework for parenthood. This framework consists in a preoccupation with sexual ethics and gender norms that is then extended through sacramental marriage to include the social dimensions of family life as well as the vocation of parenthood itself. This pattern has become so pervasive that its influence can be seen even in scholars who are critical of both the methodology and conclusions of the Magisterium in this and related areas. The prevalence of such a framework restricts Catholic imagination in relation to the full range of considerations related to parenthood and detracts attention from many of its most important dimensions, which are rooted in both individual human capacities and the Christian vocation.

Subsequent chapters now turn to establishing foundations for a more adequate alternative. Along with recent popes and numerous theologians, I believe a moral account of parenthood begins with anthropological commitments. As such, this effort requires a willingness to move discourse toward considerations of parental identity and the human capacities that lie beyond the presently decisive influences of sexual ethics and gender norms. Such disentanglement aims at creating a greater opportunity for concerted theological anthropological reflection that can frame parenthood in broader dimensions. Consequently, decisive moral questions may be reoriented toward the conditions necessary for parental capabilities to manifest themselves in stable, long-term relational commitments.

NOTES

1. Several scholars have offered more developed accounts of the history and development of the field than is possible here. Among others, see Keenan, *History*; Kelly, *Contemporary Catholic Health Care Ethics*, chap. 10; Salzman and Lawler, *Sexual Person*, chaps. 2 and 3; and Curran, *Development*, chap. 3.
2. Writing before Vatican II, Emmanuel Mounier described personalism as more than an attitude but less unified than a system. It was, in his opinion, a philosophy that can be employed by and mapped on to a variety of worldviews. Mounier, *Personalism*, xvi.
3. Charles Curran was integral in drafting a statement of faithful dissent to *Humanae vitae* only hours after the English translation was made available. Ultimately, many theologians signed this statement, but Curran's contentions with Rome had just begun. In 1979 he

was dismissed from the faculty of the Catholic University of America for his positions, and in 1986 he was informed through a letter from the Congregation for the Doctrine of the Faith that he was no longer considered suitable or eligible to teach Catholic theology. Curran's status as an intellectual and the vagaries of the path that led to this discipline exacerbated the growing intellectual divide. In 1993, John Paul II's encyclical *Veritatis splendor* attempted to quell movements toward proportionalism while clarifying fundamental moral commitments that can sustain both a personalist moral perspective and objective evaluations of particular acts apart from considerations of circumstances and subjective intentions. This dampened the overt pursuit of proportionalism, even as its proponents argued that the encyclical did not accurately characterize their position, which they held to be rooted in an accurate interpretation of Thomas Aquinas. The encyclical's rationale remains contested. For a brief but sophisticated comparison of the methodological divide between revisionists and traditionalists, see Salzman, *What Are They Saying?*

4. See Cole, "Introduction," 35–65.
5. Traina, *Feminist Ethics*, 176.
6. Both the College Theology Society and the Catholic Theological Society of America have made regular attempts to dialogue with the US bishops, whereas groups like New Wine New Wineskins, which gathers young Catholic moral theologians, create space for dialogue among academics of differing views.
7. Catholic theologians today range from queer theorists to neo-Thomists and include emerging voices from Africa, Asia, and beyond. See Keenan, *Catholic Theological Ethics Past, Present, and Future*; and Keenan, *Catholic Theological Ethics in the World Church*. The Catholics and Cultures project also documents the diversity of Catholicism globally, which far outstrips the diversities represented in Western academic theology alone; see www.catholicsandcultures.org/.
8. This common starting point does not guarantee common conclusions. As Christina Traina observes, "countless anthropological and ethical decisions intercede between a personalist starting point and concrete judgments." Traina, *Feminist Ethics*, 109.
9. Significant foundational texts in these fields include Gutiérrez, *Theology* (1971); Cone, *Black Theology* (1970); and Ruether, *Sexism* (1983).
10. See, Brown, *Body*; Salzman and Lawler, *Sexual Ethics*, 50; Farley, *Just Love*, 223; and Cahill, *Sex*, 160.
11. See Pope Paul VI, *Humanae vitae*, sec. 4; Congregation for the Doctrine of the Faith, *Persona humana*, sec. 3; John Paul II, *Veritatis splendor*, secs. 47–54; and *Catechism of the Catholic Church*, 2331–2400. This latter assertion has been challenged and reaffirmed repeatedly in recent history. E.g., see Congregation for the Doctrine of the Faith, *Persona humana*, sec. 9; and Curran, "Masturbation," 95–109.
12. John Paul II, *Familiaris consortio*, sec. 34.
13. Cahill, *Sex*, 203.
14. Weaver, *Acting Person*, 74.
15. Salzman and Lawler, *Sexual Ethics*, 52. By contrast, William May strongly supported the personalist method of recent popes. The disagreement centers largely on how narrowly the "object" of an act may be defined. May charges that revisionists (particularly McCormick, "proportionalists," and the drafters of the Papal Birth Control Commission's Majority Report) have reconceived the object of the act too broadly, such that their arguments are distortions of the Catholic moral tradition. In contrast, revisionists claim that

in *Humanae vitae* and in the writings of John Paul II, the object of the act, though paying lip service to personalism, remains narrowly bound to physical acts. See May, "Moral Theologians.'"

16. John Paul II, *Veritatis splendor*, sec. 80.
17. Salzman and Lawler, *Sexual Ethics*, 52.
18. Gudorf, *Body*, 30.
19. Physicalism never held sway over the entire moral tradition but focused primarily on matters of sexual ethics where the ends of certain physical acts could be clearly established.
20. "Revisionism has made historical consciousness a foundational point of its ethical theory. It is, in a sense, the sine qua non of revisionism. . . . As an ethical theory grounded in historical consciousness, revisionism, by definition, is somewhat contingent." Salzman, *What Are They Saying?* 58–59.
21. Cahill, *Sex*, 54.
22. Salzman, *Method*, xii.
23. Cahill, "Same-Sex Marriage," 148.
24. "Experience" in this context denotes reflection on historical developments, dialogue with the increasing scope of human knowledge, and concern for the lived experiences of the faithful.
25. Cahill, *Sex*, 69.
26. Committee on Doctrine, US Conference of Catholic Bishops, "Inadequacies." See also James Alison's argument that religious explanations often function as excuses for not engaging with advancing knowledge. Alison, *On Being Liked*, chap. 4.
27. Traina, *Feminist Ethics*, 324.
28. Similar lines of criticism have been advanced by numerous scholars. E.g., Ann Patrick Ware has proposed that the methodology at work in some magisterial teachings suffers from modern-day Docetism, characterized by a presentation of "the Church" "as a disembodied concept, speaking an eternal truth arrived at in some mysterious and infallible way." David Kelly identified a similar pattern, which he termed "ecclesiastical positivism." See Ware, "Vatican Letter," 28; and Kelly, *Contemporary Catholic Health Care*, 97.
29. Susan Frank Parsons traces the concept of "gender" in modern academic parlance from its origins in the emerging field of biology in the nineteenth century. Biology offered to explain the fundamentals of life, thus grounding gender "in the realities of the physical world." Parsons adds that gender eventually became a "self-critical category," which challenged the "natural" foundations being uncovered. Parsons, *Ethics*, 19.
30. Although magisterial documents tend to reference physical sex or gender at birth, the physiological realties of human gender are complex. Physical sex can be understood according to genetic, chemical, neurological, or internal or external physiological realities. The clearest magisterial referent for physical sex appears to be external genitalia or phenotypical sex. Matters would be more complex if magisterial documents thoroughly engaged existing knowledge of human sexual diversities even at the phenotypical level.
31. "The late-twentieth-century popes, at least Pius XII through John Paul II, have strongly argued that one's maleness or femaleness is an essential part of who one is. The characteristic form of expressing this belief has been instructions to women that they are essentially different from men, and they must take care not to become like men, which would be a betrayal of their creator and his plan of creation. This is a relatively new teaching that develops in the 19th and 20th centuries within modernism. There is a certain irony here,

in that the same church that condemned modernism changed its own teaching, which had long followed Augustine's (and Jerome's and others') dictate that sexuality did not touch the core of the person." Gudorf, "New Moral Discourse," 54.

32. Gender essentialism underlies both John Paul II's Theology of the Body and the New Feminism. Salzman and Lawler, *Sexual Ethics*, 63.
33. Cahill, *Sex*, 84.
34. Farley, *Just Love*, 1.
35. Salzman and Lawler, *Sexual Ethics*, 63; Traina, *Feminist Ethics*, 109.
36. Congregation for Catholic Education, "'Male and Female,'" sec. 2.
37. On adoption and the Catholic tradition specifically, see Weaver, "Water"; and Weaver, "Adoption."
38. The approximate tally is 173 pages on sacramentology, 146 on sexual ethics, 105 on family, and 75 on parenthood. The works consulted are Lawler and Roberts, *Christian Marriage*; Cahill, *Family*; Scott and Warren, *Perspectives*; Gaillardetz, *Daring Promise*; Lawler, *Marriage*; Rubio, *Christian Theology*; Salzman, Kelly, and O'Keefe, *Marriage*; McCarthy, *Sex*; Bourg, *Where Two or Three Are Gathered*; Hauser, *Marriage*; Curran and Rubio, *Marriage*; Weaver, *Marriage*; Rubio, *Family Ethics*; and Bartel and Grabowski, *Catechism*.
39. This argument is particularly common among defenders and popularizers of John Paul II's thought, which is often characterized as hinging on the correctness of his views of human sexuality. See, e.g., West, *Good News*, 17.
40. Farley, *Just Love*, 288–90.
41. Farley, 293–94.
42. Darlene Fozard Weaver has similarly criticized Margaret Farley for her limited use of explicitly theological arguments on these issues. See Weaver, *Acting Person*, 17.
43. Salzman and Lawler, *Sexual Ethics*, 174.
44. May's work is influenced by his participation in the development of New Natural Law, a realist moral methodology that revises Thomism with the aim of conceptually uniting the teachings of the Magisterium around basic human goods.
45. May, Lawler, and Boyle, *Catholic Sexual Ethics*, 26. The authors reject the notion of "dissent" from established teaching so as to reserve the territory proper to theology to open questions related to established teaching. Withholding or suspending assent is permissible in certain circumstances where a clearer understanding is being sought; see 43n2.
46. May, Lawler, and Boyle, 91–93.
47. May, Lawler, and Boyle, 236–37. Like John Paul II, they further argue that Natural Family Planning in no way impedes this willingness; see p. 241.
48. See Lawler and Roberts, *Christian Marriage*, chaps. 4 and 5.
49. Laura Kelly Fanucci's compact and accessible book *Everyday Sacrament* narrates her experiences of parenthood in relation to the sacraments. In staying focused on her honest experiences of parenthood, the book avoids many of the controversial questions in the field while revealing insights about the sacraments and their pattern in the life course. Fanucci, *Everyday Sacrament*.
50. The text devotes roughly equal space to marriage and sexuality as it does to parenting and family life. The social dimensions of the family receive about half as much space as each of these. Although page numbers alone are an imprecise measure, by this count it is the most balanced text presented here.
51. Examples of such questions include, "If a couple adopts a child, is that child really theirs?"; "Does the church have anything to say about being a 'Stay-at-home dad'?"; "How do I

balance work, family, and lifestyle?"; and "Should I get my child a smartphone or other electronic device?" On questions such as these, the responses appear nearly evenly split between authoritative, magisterial documents and less authoritative homilies or addresses. Sections dealing more directly with gender, sexuality, and theology of marriage draw more extensively from more authoritative sources.

52. Topics for further reading include: "Church documents"; "lights and shadows" (addressing social and cultural concerns); "dating and relationships"; "marriage preparation, weddings"; "the Theology of the Body"; "marriage: theology, liturgy, law"; "marriage enrichment"; "Catholic sexual teaching and moral issues"; "NFP and fertility resources"; and "formation in chastity, parenting." The last topic is particularly telling because parenting itself is absent. Notably, though books by popularizers of the Theology of the Body, including Janet Smith and Scott Hahn, are cited multiple times, Julie Hanlon Rubio's significant book *Family Ethics* does not appear in this list.
53. Cahill, *Sex*, 160, 210.
54. Bourg, *Where Two or Three Are Gathered*, 14.
55. Bourg, 18.
56. Rubio, *Family Ethics*, 84.
57. Sullivan-Dunbar, *Human Dependency*.
58. Hinze, "Catholics," 255.
59. McCarthy, *Sex*, 22.
60. McCarthy, 34.
61. McCarthy, 43.
62. McCarthy, 47.
63. McCarthy, 64.
64. McCarthy, 44–45.
65. Meilaender, *Not by Nature*, 11, 21.
66. Meilaender, 21, 84, 96.
67. Farley, *Just Love*, 290.
68. Farley, 227.
69. Gaillardetz, *Daring Promise*, 103.
70. McCarthy, *Sex*, 240.
71. Rubio, *Family Ethics*, 119; Rubio, *Christian Theology*, 144.
72. McCarthy, *Sex*, 123.
73. McCarthy, 141.
74. McCarthy, 160.
75. McCarthy, 177. McCarthy admits that though his identity as a man certainly affects the way he parents, his siblings also say his parenting style is like that of his mother.
76. McCarthy, *Sex*, 111.
77. Cahill, *Family*, 91.
78. Cahill, 50.
79. Rubio, *Family Ethics*, 67.
80. Rubio, *Christian Theology*, 21.
81. Rubio, *Family Ethics*, 77.
82. Bourg, *Where Two or Three Are Gathered*, 54.
83. Bourg, 57.
84. Bourg, 61.

85. *Familiar consortio* directly exacerbates this confusion by presenting marriage as a sacramental linkage of the domestic church to the Church universal while neglecting to reference baptism. Pope John Paul II, *Familiaris consortio*, sec. 21.
86. Bourg, *Where Two or Three Are Gathered*, 78.
87. Bourg, 83–85. Bourg's conclusion in this chapter is exceedingly optimistic as he reads Vatican II as highly continuous with the preceding tradition and offers very generous interpretations of John Paul II.
88. Bourg, 28.
89. Cahill, *Family*, 50.
90. Post, "Adoption," 152.
91. Rubio, *Family Ethics*, 97.
92. Rubio, 148.
93. Rubio, 149.
94. Cahill, *Family*, 16.
95. Cahill, 29.
96. Elsewhere, Cahill treats the topic more thoroughly, yet she remains committed to the importance of biological kinship and concerned about the social influences that create the need for adoption. In *Theological Bio-Ethics* her positive theological supports for adoption are all cited from other authors. See Cahill, *Theological Bio-Ethics*, chap. 6.
97. Cahill, *Sex*, 244.
98. Cahill, 210.
99. Cahill, 210.
100. Meilaender, *Not by Nature*, 11.
101. Meilaender, 32.
102. Meilaender, 33.
103. Meilaender, 58. Meilaender warns against viewing children as possessions to which individuals are entitled, but he selectively employs this critique against behavior and family patterns that he views as undesirable. The fact that children were overtly viewed as possessions by many biological families throughout much of Western Christian history is of evidently little significance to his concerns.
104. Meilaender, 74.
105. Cahill, *Family*, 6.
106. Cahill, 134.
107. Cahill, 4.
108. McCarthy, *Sex*, 4.
109. McCarthy, 2.
110. McCarthy, 101.
111. McCarthy, 141.
112. John Paul II, *Familiaris consortio*, sec. 27; Francis, *Amoris laetitia*.
113. Meilaender, *Not by Nature*, 98.
114. Carmona, "Mixed-Status Families."
115. Flores, "Latina/o Families."
116. Roche, *Schools*, 6.
117. Roche, 8.
118. Rubio, *Family Ethics*, 18.
119. Rubio, 25.

120. Rubio, 30.
121. Rubio sees John Paul II's work as significant on this point: "At each point in his description of the ideal family, the Pope implies that families are about more than themselves. They are communities of love, but not inwardly focused. They serve life by giving birth, physically and spiritually. They serve society, especially the poorest members. They are the church in their home and as such contribute to the ecclesial mission. The Pope's emphasis on the social responsibilities of the family implies that Christian parenting requires something different of parents than focusing on the family. The genius of Catholic teaching on the family is that it refuses to limit families by telling them to just take care of their own. It calls into question any ethic of parenting that centers on the duty of parents to sacrifice for their children. The Pope's definition of family seems to require instead that parents serve their children and the world." Rubio, *Christian Theology*, 107.
122. Rubio, *Family Ethics*, 44.
123. Rubio, 39.
124. Rubio, 30.
125. Cahill, *Family*, 4.
126. Cahill, xii.
127. Cahill, 122.
128. Cahill, 134.
129. Francis, *Evangelii gaudium*, sec. 3.
130. See Holy See Press Office, *Synodus Episcoporum Bulletin*; and Synod of Bishops, *Relatio synodi.*
131. Francis, *Amoris laetitia*, sec. 57.
132. Francis, secs. 61–65, 73–75.
133. Francis, sec. 52.
134. Francis, sec. 292.
135. Francis, sec. 251.
136. Synod of Bishops, "*Relatio post disceptationem*," sec. 17–20.
137. Francis, *Amoris laetitia*, sec. 178. Unlike Farley, the document does not tie this concept of fruitfulness to a revised understanding of procreation.
138. Francis, sec. 181.
139. Francis, secs. 48, 187.
140. Francis, secs. 2–4.
141. Francis, sec. 180.
142. Francis, secs. 82, 179, 181.
143. Francis, sec. 52.
144. Francis, sec. 56.
145. Francis, sec. 173.
146. Hoon Choi, "Beyond 'Helping Out,'" 74.
147. Francis, *Amoris laetitia*, sec. 286.
148. Among others, see Rubio, *Family Ethics*, 84.
149. Francis, *Amoris laetitia*, sec. 197.
150. Francis, sec. 56. Under Pope Francis, magisterial criticisms have reached a new high in that gender theory is now characterized as a dangerous ideology that threatens to disrupt the foundations of society while sowing confusion in the world. Unfortunately, magisterial documents have called for dialogue while grossly misrepresenting both the diversity

and complexity of contemporary academic theories of gender. See Congregation for Catholic Education, "Male and Female."

151. Traina, "How Gendered?" 86; Congregation for Catholic Education, "'Male and Female,'" sec. 4.
152. Francis, *Amoris laetitia,* sec. 286.
153. Francis, sec. 85.

PART II

Toward an Expanded Vision of Parenthood

Part I of this book critically reviewed the modern history of magisterial teaching and recent scholarship on the family while arguing that the prevailing Catholic framework for parenthood is restricted by its tendency to route considerations of parenthood through disputed topics of sexual ethics and gender. The framework's emphasis on structural norms further privilege the private, biological nuclear family while distracting from familial diversities. As a result, Catholic conceptions of parenthood tend to demonstrate limited concern for the realities of caregiving and the adult capabilities that sustain these. Likewise, conceptions of the family struggle to consistently address lived familial experiences because magisterial sources tend to only selectively include experience as a source of confirmation while revisionist theologians tend to incorporate experience with limited theological reflection. However, many aspects of both modern magisterial teaching and contemporary scholarship suggest alternative perspectives on the family and parenthood, even as these are marginalized by the dominant tendency to theologically approach parenthood via the prioritized issues of sex, gender, and family structure.

The task of this book now shifts to developing a stronger theological-anthropological account of parenthood *as parenthood*. Although many sources could be explored in such an undertaking, Catholic theology is compelled to look to the tradition of the faith itself as a primary resource for reflection. As the preceding chapters have made clear, the present state of Catholic discourse on parenthood owes much to the Magisterium's responses to social developments during recent centuries. These responses privileged certain aspects of the larger tradition over others and increasingly came to limit the scope of thought on parenthood through protracted theological disagreements and ongoing objections to social developments. The historical and theological tradition itself still provides a wealth of unclaimed, overlooked, and underrepresented resources for a more expansive view of parenthood.

The first step in this constructive task is investigating why certain aspects of the tradition have been more clearly received into contemporary Catholic thought than others, and to what extent they can be balanced by recovering aspects of parenthood that have been lost or underutilized in contemporary discourse. Contemporary experience also raises historically unique questions that the tradition neither encountered nor imagined that call for new interpretations of the tradition. In this, the moral tradition's willingness to learn from the breadth of modern scholarship across disciplinary fields is a key resource for discerning faithful possibilities. The scope of human knowledge today has expanded beyond what our ancestors in the faith could have ever imagined. Consequently, theological reflection must proceed dialogically between interpreting the fundamental truths expressed throughout the tradition and discerning truths offered by diverse contemporary perspectives and fields of knowledge as it engages contemporary challenges that are both with and without clear historical precedent.[1]

A critically appreciative approach to the tradition and contemporary experience guides part II of this book as it reviews diverse sources to consider how they might contribute to expanding the Catholic theological imagination vis-à-vis parenthood. Subsequent chapters will argue for more expansive theological-anthropological foundations by exploring alternatives to the prevailing framework within the tradition, including larger dimensions of kinship beyond the private, biological nuclear family; diversities in Christian history that may provide a wider vision of parenthood; and trajectories within Catholic Social Teaching that point to more extensive grounds for conceiving of parenthood.

In considering an expanded framework for parenthood, it is helpful to distinguish two historical bodies of teaching—Catholic teaching on the family, and Catholic Social Teaching (CST)—and to note their differences in application. As seen in previous chapters, modern Catholic teaching on the family and modern CST each find their proximate origins in the writings of Pope Leo XIII in the late nineteenth century, and they have grown in tandem ever since. Major encyclicals were added by Pius XI, less formal but still significant developments took place in each under Pius XII, major conceptual transitions occurred through the influence of Vatican II, and John Paul II's prolific writing left a legacy that continues to guide developments.[2]

Often, these sister traditions have converged within the same documents; elsewhere, they have advanced separately. As these codeveloping bodies of teachings move toward the midpoint of their second century, the peculiarities of the late-modern, Eurocentric assumptions at their foundations have become increasingly strained. Yet, despite their parallel and shared histories, CST has displayed greater flexibility in relation to its foundational social context than has Catholic teaching on the family.

The interpretation and development of principles in CST have generally remained open to changing social conditions and evolving theological insight, allowing CST to meaningfully address historical realities while also being open to adaptation. This dynamic capacity is due in no small part to CST's unwillingness to be bound to specific political, social, or economic structures. Catholic teaching on the family, however, is grounded in a particular family structure, which in turn is rooted in concrete sexual ethical norms, a particular theology of marriage, and relatively limited gendered norms. Despite the parallel historical development of these bodies of teaching, each fueled in response to the challenges of the modern world, their differentiated grounding in principles versus structural norms has proven consequential for their ongoing development and application. Interestingly, both CST and Catholic teaching on the family view their objects as society at differing levels. As such, CST's ability to utilize principles that can admit to diverse applications versus Catholic family teaching's structural approach that cannot are due to the society of the family's proximity to absolute dictates in Catholic sexual moral teaching. In other words, the society of the family and larger society appear to be treated very differently because family teaching is often used as a bulwark around sexual teaching.

Catholic teaching on the family also assumes an appearance of inevitability that is further strengthened by its ability to obscure the interpretative decisions upon which it is built, such as its basis in structural norms rather than principles. Alternative possibilities remain, but these are rarely addressed openly in a body of teaching that is bound to absolute norms, which themselves are wrapped up in questions of the exercise of magisterial authority itself. Consequently, what is often taken as the Catholic Church's singular approach to the family is not inevitable.[3]

NOTES

1. Vatican II, *Gaudium et spes*, sec. 33, 36.
2. Leo XIII's encyclicals *Arcanum Divinae sapientiae* of 1880 and *Rerum novarum* of 1891 mark the modern origins of Catholic teaching on the family and Catholic Social

Teaching, respectively. Pius XI authored the encyclicals *Divini illius magistri* on education in 1929, *Casti connubii* on marriage in 1930, and *Quadragesimo anno* on social concerns in 1931. Pius XII contributed to both bodies of teaching primarily through speeches, audiences, and radio addresses. John XXIII addressed the social roles of women and men in his encyclicals on Catholic Social Teaching while *Gaudium et Spes* of Vatican II addressed both social issues and issues related to the family. Likewise, both Catholic Social Teaching and Catholic teaching on the family were influenced by the shift to personalism in moral methodology within and following Vatican II. Paul VI contributed to Catholic Social Teaching through *Populorum Progressio* of 1967 and *Octagesimo Adveniens* of 1971 as well as the controversial encyclical on marriage and the regulation of births, *Humanae vitae* of 1968. The separation of family and social teaching is more pronounced in Paul VI with his written contributions to Catholic Social Teaching being decidedly more significant. John Paul II and Francis again show more balanced attention to both areas.

3. John W. Martens points out that the Catholic and Orthodox traditions have taken differing approaches to marriage while not understanding each other as heretical. This is because each understands the needs for interpretation of scripture within the community and recognizes various interpretive options. See Martins, "A Scriptural look at Jesus' Teachings on Marriage and Divorce."

CHAPTER 4

Repositioning Family and Parenthood

This chapter begins the process of unearthing a more robust anthropology of parenthood from beneath the present labyrinth of anxieties surrounding gender essentialism, sexual ethics, and doctrines of marriage. It is not that these topics are insignificant. Rather, the privileged attention to these matters has obscured realities of parenthood and encouraged a narrow account of parenthood that is hampered in its response to the full range of contemporary concerns.

To create space for broader accounts of parenthood, this chapter begins by exploring both the conflation and distinction of marriage and family within contemporary magisterial teaching. It argues, in accord with contemporary magisterial teaching, that the family ought to be conceived as both a society in itself and as a foundation for larger societies. In taking this fact seriously, however, it rejects the common tendency of magisterial thought to apply doctrines of marriage to family systems as if the existence of a familial society were only a pastoral consideration of no significant doctrinal account.

The chapter then challenges the tendency of magisterial documents to associate irregular family forms more strongly with personal moral failings than with the influence of larger social and economic forces that have historically shaped family systems. In addition, it questions the prevailing ideological commitment to private, biological nuclear families that guide these considerations. In questioning the priority of structure in evaluations of the family, this chapter argues for a dynamic commitment to stabilizing familial bonds of support and affection across social conditions. In so doing, Catholic Social Teaching provides a paradigm for responding to a changing world while maintaining principled moral commitments.

STARTING WITH SEX

The family, based naturally in reproductive marriages, has been a cornerstone of the Catholic theology of the family throughout the modern era. The modern Catholic paradigm behind this commitment follows a tightly choreographed script, in which sex, gender, and biological reproduction create an essential natural foundation upon which grace may build a truly Christian family, witnessed in part in more extended social commitments. Yet Catholic theology also differs from a strict naturalism in its willingness to both abrogate kinship claims attached to biological relatedness and to construct kin obligations through a new kinship in Christ. Chapter 6 more fully explores the negotiated nature of kinship within the historical Christian tradition. For now, it is sufficient to recognize that biblical assertions of God's fidelity joined with a commitment to the unity of all believers in Christ substantiate a theological conviction that all human relationships, no matter how natural or idealized, are fundamentally based in communion with God and others.[1] This theological reality, not biological reproduction, holds priority of place in Christian interpretations of kinship, despite the characteristic Catholic commitment to the goodness of the created order. Although God's creation is good, it provides a context for, not a limit on, the workings of God's grace.

Throughout recent decades, the ecclesial hierarchy has repeatedly defended the exclusive norm of heterosexual marriage based in the natural capacity for reproduction as the social and theological foundation of the family. Despite this effort to emphasize a normative natural family structure, authoritative Catholic documents continue to periodically acknowledge that true Christian parenthood is displayed in its fullest in the supranatural commitments of caregivers to the good of dependents, regardless of a biological relationship. Unfortunately, as Emma Jane Harris states succinctly, such compelling truths of the Christian faith are often "obfuscated by anxieties about sex."[2]

Social revisions of sexual norms in the modern West are undoubtedly a primary driving force in the Catholic hierarchy's resolve to clarify moral teaching on sexuality, gender, marriage, and the family. But reiterations of the tradition within a new context are also necessarily reinterpretations of this tradition. The new context itself shapes the selection and presentation of traditional sources, even when no significant interpretive efforts are being made. In the context of the modern era, Catholicism's anxieties and preoccupations related to changing Western social norms about sex and gender became the primary contextual basis for teaching on marriage and the family. This has led to privileging sexual norms and gender identity as fundamental entry points into reflections on marriage, the family, and ultimately parenthood.

Within the modern Catholic response, noncontraceptive, heterosexual, married, and monogamous sexual intercourse attests to and sustains the interpersonal union between spouses that provides the foundation for the family.[3] Each of these qualifying features of a morally appropriate sexual relationship is a potential point of contestation that must be passed through before the subsequent considerations of the family itself are given significant attention. This is clearly evidenced by the preoccupation with these norms, which is seen not only in magisterial teaching but also among scholars and in popular Catholic resources. The history of these norms being contested has fueled arguments within the realm of sexual ethics, which logically precedes considerations of the family under the prevailing framework, eventually coming to substitute for reflections on family life and parenthood.[4]

Conversely, it might be argued that sacramental marriage, not a preoccupation with sexual norms, is the entry point for Catholic thinking about the family. This view has purchase insofar as sacramental marriage is often presented as the foundation of family life. However, tracking the actual points of contention in Catholic teaching makes this view less forceful. Family systems without sacramentally married caregivers—such as families headed by single, widowed, or divorced parents—are frequently the subject of moral concern in Catholic sources. Typically, this is due to the challenges that such "irregular" family forms may confront. However, these family patterns and caregiving arrangements do not receive the uniquely emphatic moral concern that is provoked when a sexual relationship is involved. Same-sex, nonmarried and cohabitating, and divorced and remarried partnerships have been the subject of much more concerted moral attention than any of the caregiving arrangements noted above that do not involve a sexual relationship among caregivers.[5] Consequently, while sacramental marriage does provide a conceptual foundation for the family that substantively contributes to the prevailing private, biological nuclear ideal, deviation from this foundation only initiates a unique moral emphasis when a sexual relationship among caregivers is involved. In contrast, institutional caregiving arrangements have been all but ignored in magisterial documents, despite their long history within the Catholic tradition.

Sacramental marriage does play an important role in buffering moral concern for violations of sexual norms by extending the benefit of the doubt to partners within these relationships, especially at the pastoral level. Rarely are sacramentally married Catholics subject to public questions about their fidelity, use of contraceptives, or the validity of the interpersonal unity fostered by their sexual encounters. Such is not true for nonmarital sexual relationships, which are defined as always immoral and inherently lustful and selfish.[6] Consequently, it seems that although sacramental marriage is often identified as the foundation of family life, its absence is regarded as a regretful but tolerable reality of some families. Violations of sexual norms that are not buffered by sacramental marriage, however, provoke more serious moral condemnations, alongside declarations that some cannot lead to, and others cannot coexist with, authentic family life.[7]

One illustration of how this privileging of sexual ethics affects actual families comes in the recent global (but largely Western) Catholic disputes over receiving Holy Communion for the divorced and remarried during preparations for the 2014 and 2015 synods on the family. The "problem" dictated by the dominant frame of the remarried receiving communion is the objective impediment constituted by the continuation of a sexual relationship between the partners in the second marriage. The remedy, therefore, is to end the sexual relationship in order to alleviate the irregular situation—ideally, if possible and if the first marriage is judged to be valid, by reconciliation with the first spouse. In some circumstances, continuation of the second marriage may be permitted as long as sexual intimacy is ended and the partnership does not cause scandal.[8] Under such conditions, reception of communion could resume, typically in private so as not to cause scandal.[9]

John Paul II's *Familiar consortio* articulates this option but closes the possibility of communion to all remarried couples that remain sexually active. Although he admits gradations of culpability, the objective nature of the relationship based on sexual activity is the decisive factor. This judgment is reconsidered in Francis's *Amoris laetitia*. Building on John Paul II's acknowledgment of contingencies based on experiential realities, Francis draws the logical conclusion that not all individuals in such situations may actually be culpable for objective sin. If this is the case, then the standard restriction of communion for individuals living in a state of mortal sin would be lifted. Such a situation could arise when an individual is either constrained in such a way that his or her consent to the ongoing sexual relationship is limited or if that person does not fully understand Catholic teaching.[10] In either scenario, a mortal sin is not possible, despite the objective evil, due to a lack of freedom or a lack of understanding. The second example also permits concern for the good of children of the second marriage as a contributing circumstance. That is, an individual might judge that the harm caused to the children and the existing family's stability is of greater moral value than the good that would come from ending the sexual relationship. Because *Amoris laetitia* explicitly states that it is unwilling to alter canonical norms,[11] it seems that such a judgment is wrong precisely because it fails to accept the "the values inherent in the norm," that is, the absolute prioritization of sexual immorality in such situations that overcomes even traditional norms for mortal sin.[12]

The relevant point is that by present standards, the same ideals hold with or without the presence of children within the second marriage. Children of the second marriage certainly complicate matters in discerning the appropriate pastoral response to the irregular situation and give additional support to the conclusion that ending the second marriage is not pastorally appropriate. However, the actual existence of children does not change the fundamental problem being identified as an illicit sexual relationship.

A similar judgment also characterizes norms for the pastoral care of polygamous converts to Catholicism. Here, the irregular situation arises through the presence of sexual relationships with multiple spouses. The accepted solution is to bind the converted husband to one wife with whom his marriage will be permanent.[13] This decision normalizes a monogamous marriage and ends the irregular situation. Here again, the actual presence of children does not produce a change in doctrinal perspective, although it once again calls for more careful pastoral responses to assure support and stability in the aftermath of these marital separations. In both situations, the conceptual framework of the doctrinal issues prioritizes sexual transgressions over the society of the family itself.

This identification of sexual sin as the driving doctrinal issue in these situations has its primary scriptural foundation in Mark 10, Luke 16, and Matthew 19.[14] Although Jesus is very clear about the importance of marital fidelity, the reason the presence of children is regarded as a pastoral and not a doctrinal question rests on an interpretive choice that may not be inherent in the text itself. Within the relevant Gospel texts, tension arises out of the husband's control of the certificate of divorce, while the presence of children is nowhere suggested.[15] The absence of children is, in fact, a likely contextual motivation for divorce, to be understood alongside Jesus's rejection of divorce out of concern for the vulnerability of women. The divorced wife would likely be left in a tenuous social situation as cast off, having lost her virginity and with her fertility in question.[16] Consequently, we cannot assume from a historical context that the situation of divorce being presented necessarily includes the dissolution of a family. We might even presume otherwise.

This likely absence of children in the situation Jesus is addressing is significant because modern Catholic teaching distinguishes between a marriage and a family based on the presence of children. Not all marriages are families. Rather, families emerge from marriages, whether through biological reproduction or adoption, as the distinctive fruition of marital love evidenced in the presence of children, which creates a community of solidarity.[17] This distinction between marriage and family allows John Paul II to affirm the dignity and value of marriage independent of the creation of a family while also stressing the good of procreation as fundamental to family life.

Yet this nuance seems to disappear in Catholic doctrine when Jesus's teaching on divorce is applied directly to family separation. If marriages become families through the fecundity of the relationship, then an answer to marital separation cannot apply unreservedly for family separation. But rather than acknowledging the significance of a society having been created from what was a marriage alone, doctrinal issues direct attention to the illicit sexual relationship. This distinction is of somewhat limited consequence when there is no second marriage in question, but it becomes significantly more meaningful when a second marriage itself has become a family. In these circumstances, such as the two scenarios noted above, the dissolution of the illicit sexual relationship is given priority such that the additional reality that a family system may also be dissolved *is not considered relevant* from a doctrinal point of view. Jesus's words speak to the indissolubility of marriage, not to the dissolubility of families, and Catholic teaching itself seems to privilege families over marriage as their unique fruition that categorically changes their reality. However, present doctrinal responses ignore this distinction so as to treat marriage and family as doctrinally indecipherable when questions of sexual sin are involved.

As Christina Traina argues, the act of moral reasoning is itself a moral act because moral reasoning is always shot through with various commitments and values.[18] Recognizing the tension between the insistence on a particular interpretation of scripture to support a doctrinal judgment, even when this stands in tension with other doctrinal commitments, calls attention to the possible tensions in the values that drive particular moral judgments. By restricting the singular priority of sexual activity in favor of taking the good of family as a concrete society seriously, alternative possibilities for doctrinal understanding could be created. The conditions for this possibility arise within magisterial documents themselves and their commitment to the value of the family, yet at present these convictions do not appear evenly extended across all circumstances.[19]

Pope Francis's apostolic exhortation, *Amoris laetitia*, tentatively moves toward exploring a higher level of consistency in this area. In keeping with previous teaching, the document frames the primary problem of divorce and remarriage as adultery. Nevertheless, *Amoris laetitia* delicately acknowledges a distinction between marriage and family by recognizing, in the context of the experience of pastoral care, that some functioning family systems stem from irregular marriages and must be considered a moral good.[20] This observation violates the neatly scripted progression from marriage to sex to family in the present Catholic framework, which also invalidates the good of all sexual encounters beyond marriage. Hence, it becomes difficult to reconcile how sexual expression can be so central to marriage and family life in one context, while categorically immoral sexual acts can still lead to at least partially functioning families in another. This acknowledgment further requires greater discernment in reconciling the good of the family from a second marriage with the objective immorality of sexual activity within the second marriage. *Amoris laetitia* does not place the family and the illicit sexual relationship on the same level, as the doctrinal emphasis on illicit sex still carries greatest weight, but it recognizes the family itself as a good that must be considered during the process of seeking a remedy to this irregularity, rather than merely a complication to be worked out at the pastoral level.

Further development along this trajectory could move toward evenly weighting the good of protecting stable family systems once established. The critical question would then shift from "Who ought to be permitted to have sex with whom?" to "What functions of family systems do we most value and how ought we foster, support, and encourage these in response to undesirable factors related to adult sexual practices?" The current starting point in sex unfortunately results in a conflict between sexual norms and family well-being, in which the latter is consistently subjected to judgments regarding the former. Moreover, it calls into question the legitimacy and standing of some functioning family systems while undermining the supposed goods of the sexual act for sustaining partnerships and family stability.

GENDERING PARENTHOOD

The emphasis placed on parental gender and the ideals that support this also require scrutiny. As outlined in chapters 1 and 2, changes in modern Western social norms provoked responses in Catholic teaching that initially rejected but ultimately came to a restrained acceptance of women's participation in the public sphere. These changes in women's social roles were the latest step in a longer history of evolving ideals for womanhood that marked the transitions from preindustrial through postindustrial Western society. However, the origins of modern Catholic Social Teaching and Catholic teaching on the family in the decades after the European Industrial Revolution cemented particular modernist ideals of gender roles. Both bodies of teaching evidence their indebtedness to Victorian and romantic influences by emphasizing the discontinuity between the male public sphere and the female private sphere. Unlike earlier insistence on divine law, as Christine Firer Hinze observes, contemporary magisterial teaching allows room for flexibility in its gendered norms for social participation, as these are presented in service to "larger sociomoral purposes."[21]

Nonetheless, contemporary norms for parenthood have aligned on gendered ideals that firmly position women as naturally suited for nurturing childcare and domestic life, while men are regarded primarily as leaders and providers. Gemma Tulud Cruz notes how the complementarity of the Vatican teachings undercuts actual male and female experience and prohibits real imagination and engagement with the family. She writes: "The myopic and binary preoccupation with gender roles in theological and secular literature, which tends toward women and motherhood, has lamentably entrenched positions on gender issues, resulting in the impoverishment of perspectives on parenthood. . . . Assumptions about the complementarity of the sexes often lurk beneath the surface in family ethics and bolster uneven burdens for the work of social reproduction and caregiving rather than calling forth intergenerational solidarity marked by shared responsibility and adequate compensation."[22]

From such a view, "parenthood" seems to be conceptualized primarily as a collective term that encompassed the two essentially distinct realities of motherhood and fatherhood. This usage follows historical developments but was not, and is not, inevitable. The complexities of Christian history demonstrate that parenthood is often full of exceptions. Grandparents, elder siblings, relatives, and other caregivers of various sorts have functioned as parents for countless children, and many households did not experience neat divides between a father's leadership and provision and a mother's responsiveness and nurture, either for a lack of such parents or for diversities in social, economic, and domestic situations.

The present Western social context witnesses further complications in this gendered schema. Rather than conceiving of "parenthood" as a collective term for the underlying realities of motherhood and fatherhood, contemporary parents are increasingly likely to conceive of parenthood as a singular reality within which fatherhood and motherhood serve largely as designations based on gender. As co-parenting has increasingly become the ideal, belief in an absolute distinction between motherhood and fatherhood has become less convincing. The difference in these two conceptions of parenthood, as a collective term or a singular reality, hinges on what is invested with greatest prominence: the differences between motherhood and fatherhood, or the similarities across parental experiences. As co-parenting increases, at least as an ideal, parents are more likely to recognize both the common realities of parenting and the differences that gender can make. Although gender differences are still a reality, contemporary parents often compare their "parenting style" or other aspects of parental practice with their spouse or parents of a different sex just as easily as they compare their mothering or fathering style with peers of the same gender. Such a willingness in itself undermines the late modern concern for strict divisions of parental function based on gender.

However, co-parenting is not necessarily a "nongendered" reality. This term refers to the relatively equal sharing of parental responsibilities; but due to the historical association of motherhood with parenthood in its fullest, co-parenting does more to challenge expectations of fatherhood than motherhood. This imbalance is attested to in men's greater willingness to self-identify as co-parents than their female counterparts.[23] Such unequal self-identification likely results from much lower social standards of parental involvement for men than women as well as men's own failures to equitably share, and thereby come to understand, the tasks mothers commonly assume within families. But though this difference is true generally, women's responses also differ significantly according to their income and parental practices. Higher-earning mothers with spouses who are significantly involved in parenting tend to conceive of themselves more as co-parents.[24]

Recent popes have significantly revised the earlier rigidity of teachings on gender, but they continue to emphasize women's central place in family life while conceiving of mothers as primary caregivers. In the late nineteenth and early twentieth centuries, Catholicism recognized new shifts in gender roles, both within and beyond the household. But Catholic leadership was not ideologically well positioned to respond critically and thoughtfully to these developments. Years of reactionary anti-Modernism and the dominance of a classicist worldview encouraged Catholic leaders to readily assert as absolute the Western cultural norms that happened to mark conservative ideals of that particular moment in history. This resulted in a legacy of framing motherhood and fatherhood as distinctively different realities, based on an essentialist vision of gender that translates sexual differences into behavioral norms. Although magisterial documents made movements toward greater social equality for women, beginning in earnest from the mid–twentieth century, the consequences of this earlier trajectory at the foundations of both Catholic teaching on the family and Catholic Social Teaching still linger.

Part of the reason for the continued emphasis on parental gender roles may be the increased attention paid to the marital union itself in the last century. Owing in no small part to the rise of personalism in the last century, the spousal relationship today assumes increased importance as the center of emotional support, identity, fulfillment, and stability.[25] Anthony Gittens writes, "Part of the reason for the perceived crisis in the institutions of marriage and family seems to be the increased emphasis on the isolated individuation of the conjugal pair, and the privatization of marriage itself. This has largely replaced more traditional emphases both on the integration and socialization of the parties and on the social and moral sanctions intended to emphasize social responsibility rather than individual rights and choices."[26] This increased emphasis on the spousal pair is not the result of ideology alone. It also is due to changes in long-term historical realities. For example, low mortality rates in the developed societies of the contemporary West help make this perspective possible. Historically, the odds of both parents surviving to see all their children reach adulthood were relatively slim. In contrast, parents in the West today can typically expect both partners to see their grandchildren, and increasingly their great-grandchildren. These factors have also extended lifelong marriages, which now contain a larger portion of years spent without children in the household. Sustaining such marriages seems to require increased attention to the quality of the spousal relationship itself, even as attention to the social dimensions of Christian marriage remains necessary. Regarding parenthood, too much focus on the parental pair neglects the very real influences other adults can have on children,[27] while a privatized conception of the family stands in tension with the more communal and socially engaged vision that informs aspects of Catholic Social Teaching.[28]

The post–Vatican II emphasis on the interpersonal spousal relationship centered largely on the concept of gender complementarity, which thereby arose as a central conceptual tool for considerations of parenthood as well. Complementarity saw a meteoric rise in Catholic thought throughout John Paul II's papacy and is now a key concept in the Magisterium's articulation of the centrality of the male–female sexual relationship for founding marriage and the family.[29] This rapid acceptance is due to the term's usefulness in affirming the equality of the genders while also maintaining an essentialist view of gender, upon which differentiated interpretations of social and domestic gender roles can be based.[30] Any criticism of the modern magisterial conception of parenthood requires addressing this relatively new but remarkably influential concept.

Despite its recent influence, the term "complementarity" itself is often employed loosely and admits to a plurality of meanings. Todd Salzman and Michael Lawler argue that these applications fall into two basic categories, which they label "biological" and "personal" complementarity. They further subdivide each category; biological complementarity includes "heterogenital" and "reproductive" complementarity, while personal complementarity includes "communion," "affective," and "parental" complementarity.[31] Salzman and Lawler also detect a hierarchy among these conceptions, and they argue that hetero-genital complementarity is ultimately determinative for moral considerations.[32] Given what has been argued throughout previous chapters, it is not surprising to find that this concept—with its broad application in the realms of marriage, family, and sexual ethics—seems to be ultimately tethered to sexual issues. Moreover, the looseness in complementarity's application and ultimate grounding in physical gender is influenced by the strategic place it holds in supporting contested aspects of Catholic teaching. This is not to claim that the concept itself is invalid; it is abundantly clear that humans are relational beings who form, find meaning in, and, in a very real way, discover ourselves through complementary relationships. However, complementarity's usefulness in protecting certain sexual and gender norms has taken precedence over clarifications of the term's actual content.

Historical shifts and changing social conditions have also made the recovery of complementarity in a more gender-egalitarian mode possible. Christine Gudorf attributes the present prominence of complementary gendered parental roles to the rise of the "two-sex" gender paradigm and its romanticized conceptions of the family, which has associated women with domestic roles and motherhood with love, warmth, and nurture.[33] When the previously accepted understanding of male and female as superior and inferior forms of humanity became unacceptable, the distinctions between male and female gained significance. The earlier hierarchy relied on relative degrees of perfection sustaining male superiority. As an ideal of equality took its place, the new two-sex paradigm made gender distinctions less obvious such that differentiated propensities, virtues, and social and familial roles were highlighted throughout the modern era to sustain this division. By the mid–twentieth century, these had waned somewhat in importance on the social level, but they remained powerfully influential in considerations of family life. Christie Neuger contends that recent Catholic conceptions of the family have relied upon scholarship, specifically Talcott Parsons's functionalist sociological model, which was heavily influenced by the 1950s American context:

> Women, by nature, have the expressive roles. The family is their emotional domain and they are responsible for the nurturance and care of family members. Men, by nature, have the instrumental roles and they provide the structural support for the family and bridge the gap between the private/domestic world and the public world. According to Parsons, deviation from these natural roles creates dysfunction and

> instability for families. Thus, it is important for all of society to support this role division for the sake of the greater good.[34]

Significant arguments in contemporary magisterial teaching hinge on parental gender complementarity and posit some degree of essential functional difference in the capabilities of mothers and fathers.[35]

Changing social realities continue to challenge the idea of predetermined parental roles based on gender. Nonessentialist views of parenthood now emphasize diversity and flexibility in parental functions and are based upon research that exposes the "instability of difference and sameness" in human gender.[36] Considering the implications of this view for lived reality, Susan Frank Parsons writes: "Gender theory is questioning what has been taken to be a primary ground of ethics during modernism. To believe ethics is founded in our biology that those biological realities form a given human nature which expresses itself in differing social systems and makes itself powerfully manifest in the perilous life of the individual person, is part of our modern intellectual inheritance in the West."[37] Such nongendered views of parenthood also promote negotiated parental roles that allow flexibility in arrangements for earning income and care of children. Based on recent neuroscientific research, which demonstrates considerable adaptability across genders, Christina Traina argues that "there is not sex-linked proclivity" to parenthood, but instead, "attuned parenting is natural to human beings generally."[38]

Although this scientific support is new, groundbreaking work in the 1980s mapped important disagreements among advocates for changing parental ideals. The feminist philosopher Sara Ruddick has been an influential advocate of nongendered, function-based conceptions of parenthood. She argues that "mothering" is defined by a distinctive mode of thoughtfulness that gives rise to a unique discipline. That is, through the functional practice of mothering itself, individual behavior builds a habit of responding to the needs of others.[39] This adaptive pattern of behavior, rather than essential female attributes, defines motherhood for Ruddick. Moreover, she contends, "the work or practice of mothering is distinct from the identity of the mother. Mothering may be performed by anyone who commits him- or herself to the demands of maternal practice."[40] In contrast to Ruddick, bell hooks rejects approaches that romanticize the idea of the maternal. Both want to support equal parental roles across genders, but hooks pushes instead for a much-needed expansion of the masculine parental identity to the point of sameness with mothering. She is less optimistic that individuals will cross lines among gendered self-concepts: "Telling a boy acting out the role of a caring parent with his dolls that he is being maternal will not change the idea that women are better suited to parenting; it will reinforce it. Saying to a boy that he is behaving like a good father . . . would teach him a vision of effective parenting, of fatherhood, that is the same as motherhood."[41]

Though such egalitarian visions of shared parenting have been influential, social acceptance has outpaced lived realties in the United States, especially as measured by paternal involvement. Glenda Wall and Stephanie Arnold write that "American fatherhood appears to have undergone more changes in culture than in conduct. For this reason, the general public may conceive of fathers as being more involved and nurturing than they truly are. Subsequent research has certainly borne out the fact that although the conduct of fathers has changed somewhat, it is still mothers who bear the vast majority of responsibility for young children."[42] Some argue that this inequality is more enduring within the home because legislation does not directly affect the domestic sphere; others draw attention to social forces that inhibit mutuality in domestic work.[43] For its part, modern Catholic teaching has done quite little to support equality in actual parental practices. Women continue to be strongly associated with primary parenting, while fatherhood plays a supporting role.

The sociologist Andrea Doucet claims that, in practice, men are not as welcomed into nontraditional roles as social support appears to indicate. Men are much more inhibited and viewed with greater suspicion in communal settings including children or when expressing interest in the children of others.[44] Moreover, primary caregiver fathers must contend with the reality of social environments that "often assume men's incompetence in caregiving."[45] In a similar manner, Wall and Arnold reason that changes in fatherhood have been "undermined by images and text that position fathers as part-time, secondary, less competent parents with fewer parenting responsibilities and greater breadwinning responsibilities than mothers."[46] They conclude that magazines and other sources of parenting advice are so focused on mothers that they inhibit diversity in practice.[47] Once again, hooks surmises that as long as the mother–child relationship remains socially held to a unique and superior status, childcare will be defined as women's domain. She adds: "Even the childless woman is considered more suited to raise children than the male parent because she is seen as an inherently caring nurturer."[48]

Despite social disincentives, research suggests a relationship between equitably sharing domestic labor and childcare and reduces behavioral distinctions between motherhood and fatherhood. Summarizing a similar conclusion by the sociologist Scott L. Coltrane, Julie Hanlon Rubio writes: "Coltrane found that the more parents shared childcare, the less distinguishable Mom and Dad became. Instead of mothering and fathering, he found parenting. Coltrane believes that as men and women continue to share the work of family life, the roles will continue to converge. The new father will truly emerge, and he will look an awful lot like the new mother, who will, in due course, have adjusted her parenting to reflect her new lifestyle."[49] Studies also show similarities between the dispositions of single fathers and employed mothers, suggesting that the activity of parenting itself may shape personality expression and help fathers become more nurturing and build intimacy with their child.[50]

We are increasingly learning, as Traina summarizes, that "biology itself is contextual, not determinative."[51] One study has shown that the birth of a child can lower testosterone in fathers; a physiological change in response to caregiving behavior that could assist fathers in adapting to responsive childcare.[52] Recent research has also revealed similar increases in oxytocin in mothers after childbirth and in care-providing fathers. This chemical is linked to increases in pair bonding and commitment. Moreover, the actual shape of the brain is affected by parenthood through an enlargement of the amygdala, a region associated with planning and caution. This enlargement is typically characteristic of mothers, but it can be just as pronounced in men who take on primary responsibilities in caregiving. As such, it appears that the social influence of acts of parental caregiving is responsible for not only physiological response but also lasting neurological change. Interestingly, this may be driven by both direct parental involvement and interactions with co-parents.[53]

This increasing knowledge of plasticity in brains and behaviors across gender is timely as continued growth in women's educational achievement suggests that the growth in male involvement in childrearing is likely to continue. In spite of a significant gender wage gap, female partners are increasingly likely to find themselves with the greatest household earning potential. In addition to economic incentives, male caregiving could accelerate more rapidly as generational changes further renegotiate gendered norms. If these trends hold, the Magisterium's preferred patterns of conceptualizing parenthood will become increasingly distanced from the experiences of growing numbers of Catholic parents in the Western world.

Nonetheless, men's crawl toward equitable participation in childrearing and its rewriting of previously set gender norms is only one trajectory in changing social realities, as numerous masculinity movements have also arisen in both religious and secular contexts in attempts to reclaim "traditional" or "biblical" manhood.[54] In a less organized manner, reactions against the blurring of gendered domains can also be found in individual reactions to shifting roles. Doucet's extensive research on primary caregiver fathers reveals that these men often emphasize their own masculinity and do so according to traditional conceptions of gender. Despite fulfilling "mothering" functions, they appear determined "to distinguish themselves *as men,* as heterosexual males, and as fathers, *not* as mothers; . . . they must actively work to dispel the idea that they might be gay, un-masculine, or not men."[55]

Women are similarly influenced by social perceptions in their parental experiences. Potentially as a result of dissonance between their own experiences and widespread social conceptions about motherhood, American mothers are largely ambivalent about their experiences of motherhood. Only one in four report that their experience has been mostly positive, while one in five report that it has been mostly negative. Dissatisfied and ambivalent mothers also often report limited involvement by their husbands as a factor.[56] Although women retain the majority of domestic duties, roughly 71 percent of American mothers work outside the home. Most report doing so out of financial need, but most also say they would continue their employment if money were not an issue.[57] For women, work outside the home is associated with increased marital power and an equitable division of household labor, which could enhance marital and parental satisfaction.[58] But these effects vary across racial differences. African American and Hispanic women have historically been employed fulltime at higher rates than Whites, and they therefore have deeper social histories of balancing work and motherhood.[59] Because of the types of employment traditionally available to women of color, African Americans and Hispanics may tend to balance the toil of menial or demeaning work against seeking greater fulfillment in family interactions outside working hours.[60] These realties make a difference in working mothers' relationships with their children. For White mothers, sensitivity toward their children tends to be reduced when early grade school children experience extensive time in childcare, whereas the sensitivity of African American and Hispanic mothers tends to increase. For all mothers, both employed and not, greater time spent interacting with children during nonwork hours had positive effects on sensitivity.[61]

Experiences of parenthood are multidimensional in relation to gender. Western society is entering an era when a strict distinction between the constitutive and necessary practices of motherhood and fatherhood is becoming untenable, even as this distinction still carries significant social weight and shapes individual parental experiences. In this context, a wholesale disowning of motherhood and fatherhood for the sake of the panhuman experience of parenthood would fail to reflect common differences and prove greatly damaging to the self-understanding of many parents. Nonetheless, as the gendered scripts provided by religious and social communities are increasingly misaligned from the lived experiences of parental practices, individuals will also continue to feel the dissonance this creates. The Catholic Church's participation in favoring and advancing a particular set of ideals also influences the possibilities for fulfillment that Catholic parents might experience throughout these changes. Alternative reactions to increasing dissonance have emerged in various forms, and this is likely to continue as long as social developments remain perceptible within relatively short periods of history.

The manner in which individuals are exposed to gender expectations throughout their upbringing also influences adaptability to new parental experiences. Rigid gender roles that limit the way children are socialized into their own human capacities may have an especially profound negative impact on young boys.[62] David James argues that such childrearing practices narrow conceptions of masculinity and "tend to foster a boy's alienation from himself and from others."[63] Christine Gudorf also acknowledges the limitations this creates "for child nurturance or for the emotional self-disclosure necessary for the close friendships and mutual, intimate marriages which become more necessary in modern society as more traditional forms of community and intimacy disintegrate under the influence of mobility and urban anonymity."[64] Further, the clinical psychologist and Jesuit priest John Cecero writes that rigid senses of masculinity create difficulty in accepting aspects of the self that are traditionally labeled as feminine and thereby limit adult sexual maturity. He continues, "In empirical studies with dependency styles, men are far less likely than women to endorse the need for emotional warmth, support, and nurturance on self-report measures; but on projective measures—where they don't realize what they are endorsing—they are just as dependent.[65] This inability to recognize healthy dependency may also impair "healthy spiritual awareness and practice."[66] As such, strong socialization for well-defined gender roles within a social context requiring adult adaptability appears to have limited theological and pastoral value, inasmuch as it may suppress capacities for individuality, friendship, marital health, and religiosity.

In sum, parenthood may be conceptualized as either a singular or a dual reality. From one perspective, motherhood and fatherhood appear distinct and complementary. From the other, parenthood is a foundational term that is labeled either motherhood or fatherhood depending upon which gender is being referenced. From the first perspective, the lack of a mother or a father constitutes an absence of complementarity and thereby a deficiency in a child's parental resources such that a child with two mothers or two fathers still lacks a full and authentic experience of parenthood. From the second perspective, parental function is central, such that a child experiences deficiency in parental resources when the available caregiver or caregivers cannot or do not adequately respond to the child's needs. The first perspective is most influential within modern Catholic Social Teaching and Catholic teaching on the family, as these present parenthood as an essentially gendered reality. Nonetheless, these sources are hesitant to precisely name the gendered functions of male and female caregivers, aside from vague references to the importance of male-masculine and female-feminine parental role models and a firm association of motherhood with nurturing care.

This avoidance distances contemporary magisterial teaching from the rigidities of earlier perspectives and permits relatively greater room for diverse experiences of parenthood. However, as households continue to change relative to the increasingly egalitarian expectations of parental involvement and women's increasing economic potential within the household, even this more restrained commitment to parental gender essentialism will continue to falter. The ongoing negotiations of parental functions influenced by changing social pressures will continue to shrink the range of parental functions that are considered within the competence of only one gender. Because motherhood encompasses a much larger field of parental competencies, this renegotiation will largely take the form of expanding the terrain of fatherhood and merging it with traditionally motherly practices. Whether this leads men to embrace the label of mothering, the perception that parental practices are based in individual capabilities rather than gendered traits is likely to increase. As this trend progresses, Catholic magisterial teaching will face even greater difficulties in defending the essentialist theory of gender that supports its prevailing conception of parenthood. Catholic teaching may continue its advocacy for traditional norms even as their grounding in experience further erodes, or it may begin to reorder patterns of thought around parenthood so as to more clearly consider the common human capabilities that are increasingly evident as the foundation for caregiving. Recent documents point in both directions, although the former option presently holds the upper hand. As chapter 3 demonstrated, Pope Francis's *Amoris laetitia* does not clearly demonstrate how gendered differences matter on a practical level; yet, like earlier teachings, it remains insistent on their centrality. Pursuing the latter option entails revisions to conceptual supports for current defenses of sacramental marriage and sexual ethical norms but also points toward a recovery of the idea of Christian parenthood as a vocation grounded in baptismal identity.

PRIORITIZING STRUCTURE

A third option for reconsidering the framing of parenthood within the contemporary Catholic teaching again relates to the inconsistency with which the family is considered a society. On one hand, the family is described as the fundamental cell of society and is defined by its functioning as a society. Yet on the other hand, teaching on issues pertaining to the family only occasionally utilize the methods of Catholic social ethics. Although Catholic Social Teaching can make firm moral claims, it most notably differs from moral theology in general, and sexual ethics in particular, in its hesitance to apply objective judgments to particular situations without careful considerations of context. By tightly framing family issues with essential structures, governed by approved sexual relationships and focused on gendered parental identities, thinking about the family as a social unit acquiesces to simplistic cause-and-effect reasoning with limited attention to context. Hence, contemporary teaching designates the familial society as a *unique type* of society for which moral questions are *not* approached through the typical methods of Catholic social thought. In addition to this apparent inconsistency, this approach also results in a willingness to frame deviations from acceptable family structures as driven by ideologically distorted individual choices rather than as shaped by the social and economic forces within which families are situated. As Sandra Sullivan-Dunbar writes, this failure to seriously account for families as social and economic units serves to "insulate the family from Catholic Social Thought and reduce the abilities to concretely advance the common good and human flourishing."[67]

An example of this prioritization of ideological commitments is seen in the US Conference of Catholic Bishops' 2009 pastoral letter "Marriage, Love, and Life in the Divine Plan," which acknowledges social factors as practical challenges to marriage but defines the fundamental issue facing marriage as morally insufficient ideas "directed at the very meaning and purposes of marriage," including contraception, same-sex unions, divorce, and cohabitation.[68] Parallel arguments are pronounced in the 2015 volume *Christ's New Homeland: Africa*, through which several leading African prelates attempted to influence the 2015 synod on the family. In each, the Catholic protest against corrosive ideologies follows the outlines of a typical Christian declension narrative of rebellion, decline, and return: (1) Disruptive ideologies have arisen in our time, if not out of nowhere or from the devil himself, then from the wrongheaded pridefulness of a fallen and anti-Christian world. (2) These ideas distance us from an earlier unspoiled tradition. And (3) now is the chosen time when Christians must decisively act to reclaim our values.

Typical targets of this critique include ideologies of sex and sexuality, said to stem from the sexual revolution and, more recently, gender theory.[69] Importantly, the Catholic criticism leaves these ideologies historically rootless so as to allow a romantic remembrance of a displaced past. This enables

Western Catholics to mourn the loss of Christian hegemony and the African bishops to broadly portray the West as "a secularized and godless society" that is now infringing upon traditional values.[70] But changing theories on sex and gender within Western society can no more be abstracted from their historical and cultural roots in suffrage, civil rights, feminism, the peace movement, and the like, than knowledge of traditional African societies can be abstracted from the legacies of colonialism. The work of historians such as Stephanie Coontz have revealed how little our idealized memories of the cultural past correspond to the actual historical realities of Western families across time.[71] Similarly, the Asian feminist theologian Kwok Pui-lan argues that colonization always makes the precolonized past opaque: "It is not really possible to recover an uncorrupted or undefiled Asian national or cultural identity that predates the arrival of Western influences. One of the traumatic characteristics of the 'colonial experience' is that one does not feel at home even in one's own homeland."[72] In each situation, an idealized past is leveraged against a caricature of contemporary realities without due attention to the curated memory of that past or the historical origins of present realities.

More forcefully insisting that families really are societies may mitigate this preoccupation with ideology and idealistic engagement with the past. It would also create space for critical moral questions that are presently trapped in a lacuna between the admittance of families as social systems and the limited willingness to apply social ethical patterns of analysis to the challenges families face. Various exploitations of women's labor are matters of pressing moral concern that have significant effects on the lives of women and their families. Catherine Osborne, for example, has argued that inattention to the sociological realities of the family has permitted migrant domestic care workers to be overlooked by the Magisterium's pattern of ending social ethical considerations at the doorstep of the family.[73] As Sullivan-Dunbar observes, the magisterial commitment to an essentialist theory of gender keeps concern for women's labor restricted by a persistent anxiety that it may be detracting from women's responsibilities in the home.[74] Thus, a hesitance to support women in their actual economic struggles is reinforced by a desire to affirm the unique responsibilities of their gender such that conditions that directly affect families are often underrepresented.

Sullivan-Dunbar has also used Joan Tronto's concept of "moral boundaries" to describe how some topics tend to fall beyond the horizons of ethical concern because of how the moral terrain itself is articulated. Sullivan-Dunbar describes moral boundaries as "conceptual schemas that separate arenas of human life seen as properly the subject of moral debate from those seen as nonmoral. These boundaries determine what will be counted as a moral question and what kind of moral theories will respond to those questions."[75] Such boundaries are neither deliberate nor morally neutral. They reflect the interests and values of those articulating the moral domain and consequently tend to replicate their social privilege. For instance, Kathryn Getek Soltis argues that the lack of moral concern for the cross-generational effects of aggressive incarceration policies is due to a view that parenting is essentially private and thus emphasizes individual responsibilities and blinds itself to systematic failures.[76] Such boundaries at work in magisterial teaching help to explain why particular challenges that families, and particularly women, face are so rarely central to moral reflection on the family.

Shifting toward a greater utilization of social ethical approaches in considerations of the family would require an expansion of moral concerns as well as a more consistent consideration of families as they are positioned within larger social systems.[77] Magisterial teaching already points to important contextual detriments to family well-being, such as poverty, war, a lack of economic opportunity, and racial discrimination (present and historical).[78] A more systematic rethinking of the family could extend these questions beyond mitigating factors that disrupt a structural norm to shaping factors within which diverse family systems are negotiated.

Along with Catholic Social Teaching, academics across disciplines are pointing to the corrosive effects of unregulated capitalism on stable family systems. Particularly in the United States, the current neoliberal incarnation of free market capitalism encourages individual greed while commodifying virtually everything from pleasure to time. Moreover, its pressure pushes toward competition for the lowest possible labor costs while demanding the flexibility and disposability of its labor force.[79] In the absence of effective regulation and decisive political will, this has given rise to high rates of inequality and the corrosion of important conditions for stable family life.[80]

The sociologist Patricia Hill Collins goes so far as to argue that the ideology of the traditional family itself operates as a tool of oppression within a network of systemic injustice that disadvantages women, African Americans, homosexuals, and other groups. Collins writes: "Defined as a natural or biological arrangement based on heterosexual attraction, instead this monolithic family type is actually supported by government policy. It is organized not around a biological core, but a state-sanctioned, heterosexual marriage that confers legitimacy not only on the family structure itself but on children born in this family."[81] Collins highlights the complexity of systemic injustices to show how diverse circumstances and identities can lead to differing social realities with unique social advantages and disadvantages.[82] Importantly, this network is not arbitrary; instead, it advantages those who by various racial, economic, and social standards fit the ideal type while punishing those who do not.[83]

In the postwar liberalism that prevailed from the end of World War II into the 1970s, the US economy more clearly supported familial stability through support for welfare, homeownership, stable union jobs, and the like. These policies were driven by a belief in the American Dream that promised any gifted and hardworking individual the chance to attain a respectable livelihood, regardless of their social starting point. But such policies operated on a collective agreement that certain groups should not have access, or equal access, to benefits. The racist practices within the system ultimately led to an unsustainable internal contradiction in which its ideology of equality could not be squared with its dependence on exclusion. With the demise of postwar liberalism, neoliberalism once again promised the American Dream while reincarnating systematic inequality under a new guise. Rather than race, the economic losers were explained through their own moral failings. Consequently, as Collins observes, welfare policies became more punitive just as African Americans won the right to be included in the formerly White system.[84]

Adam Kotsko argues that in the mid–twentieth century, the dismantling of state-sanctioned economic protections was spurred by placing blame on the impoverished themselves. Cultural tropes, such as the welfare queen, emerged and despite being obviously internally contradictory, maintained significant force because accepting them allowed better-positioned Americans to avoid recognizing the much larger contradictions at the heart of the American economic and political system.[85] According to Kotsko, neoliberalism was born through the theological-come-political motif of "demonization," whereby the freedom of individuals constitutes a trap. Kotsko writes that "all significant concepts of the modern theory of the market are secularized providential concepts."[86] This analogy hinges on the making of Satan in the Christian tradition, in which this angel assumes blame for a "free" rebellion against the same God upon whom the angel is absolutely and utterly dependent. By drawing attention to the supposed freedom of the individual, perpetual and inescapable blame for their own suffering can be placed upon them while blocking attention to the larger systems of power, authority, and, ultimately, victim-making. The truly demonic side of this system is its ability to hide systematic victimization via public policy in plain sight, within historically Christian nations through the unnamed appropriation of theological thought patterns.

The simplest and most effective means for carrying inequality across generations is by supporting some family units and destabilizing others. Within the prevailing economic system, a number of mechanisms for destabilizing family systems disproportionately target racial minorities. Perhaps the clearest in terms of the active breakdown of social support systems for minorities groups are high rates of incarceration,[87] and the disproportionately aggressive foster care system.[88] Each of these is fueled by widely accepted, but statistically bogus, myths of higher rates of drug use and parental neglect among people of color.[89]

The same systems support social and economic winners, which helps explain why the institution of marriage in the United States has become increasingly centered on only the wealthy and well educated.[90] Among the relatively few beneficiaries of neoliberalism, stable family systems are essential carriers of private wealth accumulation.[91] The most important dynamic in this moralistic rereading of economic systems is that the wealthy and middle-class white Americans, who stand as the paradigm of the elect, do not lose ground to the demonized groups whose members are justly condemned. Kotsko writes that "the providential hand of the market rewards the deserving. . . . And if reality does not match up with those beliefs, then so much the worse for reality."[92] This view would be utterly absurd if it were not so effectively demonstrable in the continual reshaping of political and economic rules to reaffirm winners and remarginalize losers. Unfortunately, the present Catholic commitment to ideology and personal morality as the shaping force of family systems restricts the possibility of a thorough Catholic response.

The expansion of a global economic system, led and profoundly shaped by US neoliberal ideology, has spread the system of predestined winners and demonized losers around the globe. Asia is often taken as the paradigm of new economic success within the growing world economy, but as Kwok Pui-lan writes, "while Asian businessmen take pride in the Asian economic miracle, . . . the plight of Asian women workers has largely been ignored. One of the major reasons for the competitiveness of the Asian products in the global market is the availability of cheap labor, much of which comes from the increased participation of Asian women in the workforce. Women are employed mostly in dead-end, low-skilled, or semiskilled manufacturing jobs, in retail and in the service sector."[93] Likewise, Astrid Lobo Gajiwala writes of the dehumanizing conditions of poverty in India marked by the exploitation and dehumanization of women within a country with one of the world's fastest-growing economies.[94]

Considering how economic need has displaced family members across international boundaries, Agnes Brazal describes the plight of families separated through economic migration in the Philippines. Increasingly, mothers are leaving their families to find employment abroad, creating geographically separated families while cultural forces exacerbate women's anxieties and men's discomfort with assuming nontraditional paternal roles.[95] And Gemma Tulud Cruz considers the rise of "transnational motherhood" as a consequence of the gendered realities of migration today. Such mothers "reconstitute mothering by providing acts of care from afar and overcompensating for their physical absence through more regular communication and gift-giving practices since they cannot easily visit their family back home."[96] She continues, "Transnational family life in the age of (feminized) global migration challenges dominant discourses, which generally frame gender relations within households or families and ignore how physical separation and state policies influence family politics and the political economy of emotions."[97]

Cruz argues for a new vision of the family that is less reliant on particular roles and structure but instead attends to the complexity of families shaped and misshaped by a host of factors, including government policy and economic forces. She finds support for her vision in the actions of Jesus on the cross: "In the final interaction between Jesus and a family member (John 19:26–27, when Jesus told Mary, 'Woman, here is your son,' and to the Beloved Disciple, 'Here is your mother') at the cross, a new family comes into being. Family of birth gives way to family of creation. It is specifically at the cross that this family is created, and it is our relationship to Jesus that forms our filial, maternal fraternal, and sisterly bonds."[98]

Speaking from her experience of the plurality of family forms in South Africa, Nontondo Hadebe observes that

> when contextual factors are not integrated, the result is a moralistic and judgmental theology that targets actions and condemns the individuals responsible. . . . This theological approach creates a crisis of belief for the people of God and a crisis of identity for the Church, and betrays her mission to the world, which, in the words of *Gaudium et spes,* is to respond to "the joys and hopes, the griefs and the anxieties of the people of this age, especially those who are poor or in any way afflicted."[99]

To commit fully to appreciating the family *as a society* requires more concerted moral attention to how disruptive social forces shape and destabilize family systems. As societies, families arise out of unique social contexts in response to various desires, needs, and possibilities negotiated within that larger context. Greater attention to this reality would promote a more nuanced response to the social challenges facing families in the contemporary world beyond particular ideological trends.

CONCLUSION

The three issues noted above are intended to illustrate how some of the strongest planks in the contemporary Catholic framework for parenthood are indebted to peculiarities of Catholic teaching on the family that may not be essential or inevitable. Contemporary Catholic teaching on the family routes concern through sexual ethics by interpreting sexual norms as decisive for both marital and familial norms, by framing parenthood as an essentially gendered reality, and by inconsistent moral concern for families as social units. Although theological commitments give rise to these aspects of contemporary teaching, they were also formulated within a particular social and historical context that shaped both the themes and breadth of magisterial thought. Consequently, distinctive features of the contemporary framework are due to particular interpretative choices about the reception and reaffirmation of the tradition in response to such issues.

As argued in previous chapters, the particular reactionary concerns of the Magisterium, which are aimed at both significant social changes and divisions within Catholicism itself, positioned Catholic teaching to emphasize certain controversial issues. This has resulted in a restricted foundation for conceptualizing parenthood that is largely restrained by overextended concerns about sexual ethics and gender. During this same time, developments in Catholic Social Teaching also acknowledged the importance of families as social systems that give rise to and are called to transform the larger society. These two perspectives, despite parallel lines of development, have not been integrated as tightly as might be hoped. This lack of intentional consistency and concerted dialogue across Catholic Social Teaching and Catholic teaching on the family itself provide opportunities for reconsidering how the tradition of Catholic thought on parenthood might be received in the present.

Rather than focusing on the sexual relationship of parental partners, taking seriously the magisterial assertion that marriage and family are not synonymous provides space for rethinking doctrinal conclusions. Likewise, placing concern for gendered parental roles in a larger historical context allows for a more inclusive perspective on both the rise of modern gender ideals and the reactions of the papacy to their decline. Modern studies of parental behavior and adaptability further verify the temporality of these particular gendered ideals. From this vantage point, Catholic parenthood can be reconceived as a vocation based within the Christian baptismal identity that calls all to loving relationships and service to those in need. Finally, taking the idea of the family as a society seriously allows the unique concern for family structure to be placed in dialogue with Catholic Social Teaching's methodological preference for principled discernment over absolute norms. As such, the potential for a larger Catholic theology of parenthood already rests within modern magisterial teaching, despite the limited attention these possibilities have been given.

Contemporary scholarship continues to expand the scope of human knowledge, while theology is called to respond meaningfully to these developments. New insights into the adaptability of human persons certainly unsettles claims based on strong versions of gender essentialism. Rather than viewing these as threats to an immutable moral edifice, a firm commitment to the goodness of God's creation should call theologians into honest and careful dialogue with those who have had such insights. Likewise, the reception of tradition itself requires a concerted look at both its breadth and depth. Chapter 5 turns to these considerations as it explores the fuller dimensions of Christian kinship beyond the private, biological nuclear family.

NOTES

1. Cf. Ps. 27:10, Isa. 49:15, Gal. 3:28, etc.
2. Harris, "Conscience," 103.
3. These conditions specify the necessary conditions for licit intercourse within sexual relationships. The norms for nonsexual relationships are less rigid because not having sex is rarely considered problematic in the Catholic moral tradition.
4. Cahill, "Catholic Families," 58.
5. Modern magisterial teaching includes several reflections on the special needs of single, widowed, and divorced parents while cohabitating and same-sex relationships have been primary subjects of several documents. For the former see John Paul II, *Familiaris consortio*, secs. 71, 77; and Francis, *Amoris laetitia*, secs. 49, 197, 252. For the latter, see Congregation for the Doctrine of the Faith, "Some Considerations"; Pontifical Council for the Family, "Family"; Congregation for the Doctrine of the Faith, "Considerations"; and US Conference of Catholic Bishops, "Between Man and Woman."
6. John Paul II, *Familiaris consortio*, sec. 81; Francis, *Amoris laetitia*, sec. 52; Synod of Bishops, *Relatio post disceptationem*, secs. 17–20.
7. Francis, *Amoris laetitia*, sec. 52.
8. "Reconciliation in the sacrament of Penance which would open the way to the Eucharist, can only be granted to [remarried persons with a valid first marriage] who, repenting of having broken the sign of the Covenant and of fidelity to Christ, are sincerely ready to undertake a way of life that is no longer in contradiction to the indissolubility of marriage. This means, in practice, that when, for serious reasons, such as for example the children's upbringing, a man and a woman cannot satisfy the obligation to separate, they 'take on themselves the duty to live in complete continence, that is, by abstinence from the acts proper to married couples.'" John Paul II, *Familiaris consortio*, sec. 84. See also Francis, *Amoris laetitia*, sec. 329.

9. Pontifical Council for Legislative Texts, "On the Admissibility to the Sacred Communion," sec. 2.
10. Francis, *Amoris laetitia*, sec. 301.
11. Francis, sec. 300.
12. Francis, sec. 301.
13. The husband is typically obligated to choose his first wife, given the Catholic Church's commitment to the validity of natural marriages. However, cultural practices and pressures often outweigh religious injunctions such that a convert whose marriage to only his first wife is religiously recognized may still have obligations to former spouses, such as financial support or an obligation to provide her with children. Alternatively, men may be asked to swear to end sexual interactions with the former wives who remain in their household. From a religious perspective, such wives are free to remarry, although again cultural custom shapes this possibility as well. Although motherhood, children, and family are important values across the continent, variations in customs and understandings of family and marriage abound across Africa. See Hillman, *Polygamy Reconsidered.* Many thanks to Father John Kirby, Dr. George Worgul, and Father John Odeyemi for providing insight on this issue.
14. I am avoiding the practice of annulment, which is also laden with interpretative options based on the Gospels. Commenting on the exception for *porneia* added in the Gospel of Matthew, John W. Martens writes: "I believe this exception clause was first concerned with marriages which ought not to have been contracted due to degrees of consanguinity outlawed by Leviticus and maintained later by the rabbis and does not concern adultery, though this is much disputed. What we can say is that current Catholic Church teaching on annulments has moved much beyond any scholar's interpretation of what *porneia* meant to the Matthean community in the first century, that is, technically incestuous marriages, adultery, or other sexual sins, to include numerous emotional and psychological conditions and situations." Martens, "Scriptural Look," para. 3. Likewise, David Cloutier has questioned the precise meaning of "and" in the phrase "anyone who divorces his wife *and* marries another" found in each synoptic Gospel and interrupted by the *porneia* clause in Matthew. The linkage can imply various meanings including "then at some later point in time" as well as "in order to." The Catholic tradition has chosen the former option. Interestingly, John Paul II's notes and laments that the second option is a daily experience in the modern world; John Paul II, *Familiaris consortio*, sec. 84. 1 Cor. 7:11 may support the former reading, but Jesus's apparent concern for the vulnerable position faced by women under male-only no-fault divorce suggests the charge of adultery, among the most serious offences of the time, is being used to strengthen women's standing within a patriarchal legal structure. This may suggest the latter option is a preferable interpretation. Cloutier, "*Humanae vitae*"; Harvey, *Companion*, 157.
15. Mark 10:2–12, Luke 16:18, Matt. 19:3–12. Cf. 1 Cor. 7:1–17; Paul's statement here is absolutely clear: "A wife should not separate from her husband—and if she does separate she must either remain single or become reconciled to her husband—and a husband should not divorce his wife" (*New American Bible, Revised Edition*). However, Paul's apocalyptic expectations evident in the remainder of the chapter raise questions about his usefulness on the relation of marriage to family. Even in these relatively lengthy reflections on states of life, he gives no attention to procreation and its consequences for Christian life. His advice is instead directed toward preserving sexual continence in close proximity to the end times. Although Paul employs language of children and childhood

frequently, he only makes one reference to actual children, in which they appear as something of an afterthought. Aasgaard, "Paul," 140.

16. By the third century, rabbinic Judaism, through the Mishnah, established that a legal obligation to procreate applied only to men. It further dictated norms for divorcing infertile women in order to allow men to fulfill this obligation.
17. John Paul II, *Familiaris consortio*, sec. 14.
18. Traina, *Feminist Ethics*, 299.
19. Prioritizing concern for the evil of illicit sex over the good of family unity is also influenced by Catholicism's tendency to prioritize sin over virtue in moral teaching. Attempts to overcome this bias have been ongoing in Catholic moral theology. The growth of Liberation Theology likewise brought greater awareness to sins of omission that exacerbate social injustices.
20. Francis, *Amoris laetitia*, sec. 78.
21. Hinze, "Catholics," 251.
22. Cruz, "It Takes a Global Village," 220–21.
23. "The relative representation of one's parental self and one's partner in arranging and planning narratives may denote the extent to which the parental self, at a superordinate level, is a 'self-as-sole-executive-parent' as compared with a 'self-as-coexecutive-parent.'" Pleck and Stueve, "Narrative Approach," 84.
24. Pleck and Stueve, 103.
25. McCarthy, *Sex*, 4.
26. Gittins, "In Search," 169.
27. Although multiple adults fulfilling parental roles within children's lives may have positive effects on a child's support network, it may also lead to uncertainty in understanding the relations of these different parental relationships or introduce conflict among caregivers. There is a role for "nurturing outsiders" who may be particularly important during adolescence, when children often push against parental influence and seek trusted nonparental adults for support. Consequently, it is important to acknowledge that extended spheres of support remain important even if the parental functions are expanded to include more direct caregivers. See Schwartz, "Connective Complexity," 81.
28. Bourg, *Where Two or Three Are Gathered*, 14.
29. Salzman and Lawler, *Sexual Person*, 85.
30. See John Paul II, *Familiaris consortio*, sec. 24.
31. Salzman and Lawler, *Sexual Person*, 141.
32. Salzman and Lawler, 149.
33. Gudorf, "Western Religion," 289.
34. Neuger, "Gender Narratives," 71.
35. Jung, "God Sets the Lonely," 117.
36. Ellison, *Making Love Just*, 20.
37. Parsons, *Ethics*, 23.
38. Traina, "How Gendered?" 85.
39. The research cited by Traina confirms Ruddick's argument. Traina writes, "There is truth to the claim that primary caretaking mothers tend to be more attuned and responsive than secondary caretaking fathers and even to the claim that these mothers' brains work differently: caretaking activities showed up in the women's amygdalae, where emotions are processed, rather than in the sociocognitive centers of their brains, where their male partners processed the same activities. But research suggests that this difference is a

matter not of genetics but of brain plasticity, of the brain wiring itself for the work it is asked to do." Traina, "How Gendered?" 84.

40. Ruddick, "On 'Maternal Thinking,'" 306.
41. hooks, "Revolutionary Parenting," 139.
42. Wall and Arnold, "How Involved?" 510.
43. Anderson, "Between Rhetoric and Reality," 72.
44. Doucet, "'It's Just Not Good for a Man,'" 84, 91.
45. Doucet, 84.
46. Wall and Arnold, "How Involved?" 511.
47. Wall and Arnold, 512.
48. hooks, "Revolutionary Parenting," 137.
49. Rubio, *Family Ethics,* 136.
50. Research on single-father families is inconsistent. Some studies show similar effects on children compared with single-mother families; others show stronger child outcomes. Improved child outcomes among children in single-father families may be due to single fathers tending to be older and more likely to have been previously married than single mothers. The lack of research on single fatherhood is in part due to a tendency to focus on the impact of fathers in dual-parent families as opposed to single-mother families. Krueger et al., "Family Structure," 2, 6.
51. Traina, "How Gendered?" 84.
52. See Gettler et al., "Longitudinal Evidence," 16194–99.
53. Feldman and Bakermans-Kranenburg, "Oxytocin," 15.
54. The common challenge faced in such efforts is presenting "traditional" masculine norms that are highly dependent on particular social contexts while also negotiating as "manly" new experiences of fatherhood that younger generations of men may bring. Such movements play a vital role in supporting self-identity and self-care of many men today but are not typically sensitive to the full complexities of the ideals of "manhood" they seek to claim.
55. Doucet, "'It's Just Not Good," 88. A similar phenomenon has been documented among men who work in traditionally female occupations. Hoon Choi sites a study showing that three-quarters of men in caring professions did not actively seek out the jobs but instead came to them through opportunity. Choi, "Beyond 'Helping Out,'" 74n5. See also Williams and Villemez, "Seekers," 75.
56. Wilcox, "State," 53. Among adoptive parents, rates of satisfaction are significantly higher. See Assistant Secretary for Planning and Evaluation, "Children."
57. Wilcox, "State," 141.
58. Aulette, *Changing American Families,* 150. Women who out-earn their husbands continue to see increases in marital power, but the trend in shared labor drops significantly at this point. This suggests that men who are out-earned by their wives tend to devote increased attention to work outside the home. See Glauber, "Race," 11.
59. bell hooks writes that the early women's liberation movement reflected the ambitions of its White, educated, middle-class participants. This included arguments that motherhood confined women to the home away from careers and public pursuits. "Had Black women voiced their views on motherhood, it would not have been named a serious obstacle to our freedom as women. Racism, availability of jobs, lack of skills or education and a number of other issues would have been at the top of the list—but not motherhood." hooks, "Revolutionary Parenting," 133.

60. bell hooks explains the differing trends between White and Black women's perspectives on the need for liberation. "Many Black women were saying 'we want to have more time to share with family, we want to leave the world of alienated work.' Many White women's liberationists were saying 'we are tired of being emotionally and economically dependent; we want to be liberated to enter the world of work.'" hooks, "Revolutionary Parenting," 134.
61. Huston, Bobbitt, and Bently, "Time Spent," 626.
62. James, "Integration," 290.
63. James, 290.
64. Gudorf, "Western Religion," 290.
65. Cecero, "Toward Christian Sexual Maturity," 38.
66. Cecero, 38.
67. Sullivan-Dunbar, "Valuing Family Care," 151.
68. US Conference of Catholic Bishops, "Marriage," sec. 17.
69. The recent statement on gender theory from the Vatican begins with a proclamation of a crisis and subsequently fills out the traditional elements of a declension narrative. See Congregation for Catholic Education, "'Male and Female.'"
70. African Pastors, *Christ's New Homeland*, 23.
71. See Coontz, *Marriage*.
72. Pui-lan, *Introducing Asian Feminist Theology*, 18.
73. See Osborne, "Migrant Domestic Careworkers."
74. Sullivan-Dunbar, "Valuing Family Care," 158.
75. Sullivan-Dunbar, *Human Dependency*, 139–40.
76. Soltis, "Family Relationships," 168.
77. Benedict XVI demonstrates a measured sophistication in relating individual freedom to social structures in his encyclical *Spe salvi*. Like Catholic Social Teaching, this balances acknowledgment that structures alone do not fully constrain human freedom with the reality that human freedom operates largely within and in response to social structures. See Benedict XVI, *Spe salvi*, sec. 25.
78. See John Paul II, *Familiaris consortio*; John Paul II, *Gratissimam sane*; and National Conference of Catholic Bishops, "Economic Justice."
79. Kotsko, *Neoliberalism's Demons*, 6.
80. Kotsko, 34.
81. Collins, *Black Feminist Thought*, 47.
82. Collins, 18.
83. Collins, 71.
84. Collins, *Black Sexual Politics*, 132.
85. Kotsko's comparison of the welfare queen to the witch of the colonial era is intriguing because it suggests parallels in the theological and political regulation of social order via demonization across time. Kotsko, *Neoliberalism's Demons*, 78.
86. Kotsko, 80.
87. Collins, *Black Feminist Thought*, 77.
88. Rivaux et al., "Intersection," 165. Cooper's description of the foster system as a "billion-dollar, publicly funded bureaucracy" that sustains and fosters racial disparities is aptly applied to the prison system as well; see p. 216.
89. Kotsko, *Neoliberalism's Demons*, 92.
90. Wilcox, "State," 69.

91. Kotsko, *Neoliberalism's Demons*, 71.
92. Kotsko, 113.
93. Pui-lan, *Introducing Asian Feminist Theology*, 15.
94. Gajiwala, "Challenging Families," 141.
95. Brazal, "Maternal Migration," 151.
96. Cruz, "It Takes a Global Village," 214.
97. Cruz, 218.
98. Cruz, 218.
99. Hadebe, "Reading the Signs," 149.

CHAPTER 5

Rethinking Family Diversity

Having considered interpretive options within the contemporary magisterial framing of the family, this chapter turns to the need for greater attention to the actual diversities and complexities of family life. Despite the influence of gender and sexual ethical norms in Catholic conceptions of parenthood, compelling explanations of their necessary and exclusive connection to parenthood can be elusive.[1] The Congregation for the Doctrine of the Faith's 2003 document, "Considerations Regarding Proposals to Give Legal recognition to Unions between Homosexual Persons," provides one of the most concise magisterial summaries of these connections in its opposition to same-sex unions:

> The Church's teaching on marriage and on the complementarity of the sexes reiterates a truth that is evident to right reason and recognized as such by all the major cultures of the world. Marriage is not just any relationship between human beings. It was established by the Creator with its own nature, essential properties and purpose. No ideology can erase from the human spirit the certainty that marriage exists solely between a man and a woman, who by mutual personal gift, proper and exclusive to themselves, tend toward the communion of their persons. In this way, they mutually perfect each other, in order to cooperate with God in the procreation and upbringing of new human lives.[2]

This presentation gestures to the natural law and common human reason but immediately follows this with specifically Catholic ways of framing marriage and the family. Consequently, its theist, monogamous, and individual-voluntarist commitments stand in contrast to diversities in marriage practices historically and cross-culturally, despite the broad view of the opening lines. The view of marriage described is, in fact, specific to the contemporary Catholic personalist commitments and articulation of the ends of marriage. With no transition between the claim of common knowledge and the presentation of theologically charged concepts, the argument stretches its own credibility as it associates a relatively recent Catholic theological framework with inherent natural realities.

Contemporary magisterial teaching largely relies on gender complementarity to connect the various elements of its conception of the family. This centralizes attention on the parental pair while pushing considerations of family life and the childrearing to the periphery. As seen in the statement of the Congregation for the Doctrine of the Faith (CDF) above, the life of the family itself is relegated to an afterthought that is more or less assumed secure so long as the primary moral issues related to gender, marriage, and sexual relations are properly ordered. As seen in chapter 3, revisionist theologians have made more use of social scientific data as a means of engaging the actual diversities and complexities of family life, and they commonly employ this research to argue that parental abilities can and do exist beyond the biological nuclear family. Unfortunately, such arguments also tend to offer thin theological explanations in their preoccupation with justifying moral judgments about adult sexual relationships that diverge from those of the Magisterium. Hence, contemporary Catholicism is left with an insufficient moral-theological vision of parenthood. On one hand, there is a magisterial vision that is hesitant to engage the full diversities of family experiences for the sake of a tightly coherent moral-theological vision. When magisterial documents do engage experience, they tend to utilize it for confirmation, while challenging evidence is disregarded or presented as an aspect of sin. On the other hand, revisionist theological perspectives critically engage research on diversities and complexities but seldom place this within a robust theological-anthropological vision of parenthood.

In response, this chapter engages research from the social sciences to assess the veracity of moral theological claims related to parenthood and children's well-being.[3] It contends that, although the biological, nuclear family is statistically linked to favorable child outcomes, available data are nonetheless complex and problematize universal claims. Moreover, acknowledging the general benefits of a particular family structure is distinct from the claim that other family forms are either untenable or categorically inferior.[4] Family forms must be evaluated with attention to their diversities and the various social contexts in which actual families are embedded. When social scientific data are given this scrutiny, biological kinship, parental gender, and family structure, each fails to be categorically determinative for child well-being. Instead, external factors (e.g., social and economic forces), parental abilities, and family function emerge as significant. Therefore, a conception of parenthood centered on child well-being can neither be derived from a structural model of family alone nor built on statistical data alone. Instead, such an account must attend to the functioning of family systems and the capabilities of adult caregivers in view of Christian social and anthropological commitments.

This methodological commitment to constructing parenthood around capabilities and function guides the engagement with social scientific data. Catholic moral theology is rightly directed toward human flourishing, such that studies of human well-being legitimately support or challenge moral theological claims.[5] The Magisterium occasionally acknowledges the value of these sources, but the form of natural law reasoning commonly employed tends to privilege certain modes of reason and established tradition so as to avoid or supersede potentially conflicting evidence on contested issues.[6]

This chapter takes a fundamental conviction of natural law reasoning, that moral knowledge can be arrived at through engagement with the created order, as sufficient validation for substantively engaging experiential evidence.[7] Through this methodological commitment, child well-being can be employed as a norm for theological conceptions of parenthood that are centered on adult capabilities and family function.[8] Such a moral commitment cannot stop at simple association but must explore why particular capabilities and functions tend to yield desirable outcomes. In this regard, due caution must be observed to refrain from assuming particular conceptions of children's needs without attending to studies of actual children. This is particularly important given that significant changes have occurred in cultural conceptions of children and childhood throughout Western history.[9] The New Testament's commitment to criticizing prevailing structures of social control when these do not serve the interests of those in need might be taken as a critical guide in considering present realities.[10]

The concept of child well-being itself proceeds from normative judgments about desirable human qualities. Although some of these are quite basic (physical health, educational achievement, psychological adjustment, etc.), others are more closely bound to religious commitments (social altruism, moral development, development of an inner spiritual life, etc.).[11] All such criteria are necessarily based on normative judgments, the former including goods that are typically expressed in terms of human rights, and the latter in terms of values. This complexity in the notion of well-being calls attention to the reality that the Catholic vision of human flourishing is significantly broader than the interests of most social-scientific inquiries. As such, an adequate theological engagement with this research must examine these findings fully and carefully while nonetheless looking to integrate them within a larger moral-theological framework.

Magisterial teaching and social scientific research tend to find general agreement while more specific claims that rely upon greater measures of interpretation are often contested. For example, both point to a similar array of detrimental factors for family well-being. Poverty, racial discrimination (present and historical), gender discrimination, and unstable family structures are interconnected realities that cumulatively have profoundly negative consequences for children.[12] The only risk factor consistently identified in modern magisterial teaching that is not strongly supported by research on child well-being is same-sex parenthood. At the level of interpretation, however, the Magisterium's suggestion of a causal influence from traditional marriage to stability is less supported by the evidence.[13] The danger here is that the Magisterium's intention to support well-being, when extolled uncritically, may effectively lend moral support to those who are already socially and economically advantaged while identifying deviations from the biological, nuclear norm as moral failings without due recognition of contributing factors (a pattern identified in the previous chapter). Reality is not so stark. Neither marriage itself nor socioeconomic factors fully account for all data alone.[14] Moreover, the methodological tools proper to the social sciences are designed to measure social data at the collective level and can neither fully account for nor precisely predict individual variation. Accordingly, even as magisterial teaching requires greater moral engagement with the significant social and economic influences that shape family formation and functioning, moral concern at the individual level cannot thereby be abandoned. To consider the shape of an ongoing moral engagement that is aware of both broad influences and individual variations, a closer examination of factors supporting the operative biological, nuclear ideal is required.

Although recognizing that long-term stable families are associated with traditional marriage, families formed through or including adoption also tend to have strong outcomes. Care for nonbiological children has a long history in Christianity, and families formed through adoption are at times praised in modern magisterial teaching. However, the general emphasis on biological kinship and resolve to link the good of procreation exclusively with biological reproduction raise questions about the place of adoptive families in contemporary Catholic thought. Especially since *Humanae vitae,* the energy committed to magisterial defenses of the procreative end of sex and marriage has created clear biases toward biological parenthood. Nonetheless, there is reason to believe that many adoptive parents are in fact models of "the true meaning of parenthood" and therefore ought to play a more significant role in our theological conceptions of parenthood and the family.[15]

THE BIOLOGICAL NUCLEAR FAMILY

The biological, nuclear family centered on heterosexual marriage with clearly defined parental gender roles is in decline across the West. When not overtly targeting the decline of sexual morals, concern over this breakdown often includes the argument that this structural form (i.e., the traditional family), promotes children's healthy development in ways other family forms cannot.[16] Social scientific evidence indicates that children who live in stable households with their married biological parents do, in fact, tend to fare better on average across basic measures of well-being.[17]

Although the nuclear family, with a father in the labor force and a mother in the home with children, remains an influential ideal, it was only briefly the majority family structure among American families. Throughout the early twentieth century, nuclear families rose until peaking in 1965 at about 55 percent of households and have since declined rapidly. Today about 22 percent of American children live in such households, while dual-earner and single-parent families account for three-quarters of the remainder.[18] Rates of divorce peaked in the 1980s, and the divorce rate per capita has likewise dropped ever since. This recent decline in divorce corresponds to a dropping marriage rate such that the proportion of divorce to marriages has held mostly steady over the past three decades.[19] It appears that the high divorce rate of the late twentieth century influenced a negative perception of marriage among that generation's children. When they entered adulthood, the children of the 1970s and 1980s nearly doubled rates of cohabitation.[20] Adult children of divorced parents tend to have weaker commitments to lifelong marriage, less marital satisfaction, and a reduced likelihood of being married.[21] Fully one-fifth of children of divorced parents feel that they are destined to repeat their parents' experiences.[22] In general, more Americans desire to become parents than are confident in the possibility of a stable marriage.[23] Nonetheless, at least two-thirds of children who experience divorce adjust successfully and, under limited circumstances such as high-conflict marriages, divorces can be beneficial to children's well-being.[24] Declining social stigma may also be lessening the negative impact of divorced, single, and nonmarried parenting, while numerous needs traditionally met by the family or extended family can now be fulfilled through the state or market.[25]

Americans today are inclined to believe that rewarding parental experiences can exist beyond a stable parental partnership, despite research indicating that married parents have significant advantages in happiness and mental health.[26] Over 40 percent of nonmarried cohabitating couples have children; yet, on average, child well-being in households with cohabitating parents resembles single-parent households more closely than married parent households.[27] Parental relationships among cohabitating couples also tend to be significantly less stable than those of married couples.[28] Fully 95 percent of cohabitating couples with children consider marriage at least a 50/50 prospect for their future, yet only 9 percent marry within a year of childbirth. The majority will eventually end their relationship.[29] As a result, roughly 90 percent of children living with cohabitating parents will experience the end of their parent's relationship.[30]

Individuals living in less stable socioeconomic contexts tend to have less stable pathways to family formation.[31] Marriage is not a cure-all for such factors, although the long-term commitment it fosters seems to have a positive influence. Willingness to marry is itself a weak predictor of long-term relational stability compared with factors such as income, education, age at marriage, and timing of first birth relative to marriage.[32] Risk factors for divorce are also predictive of cohabitation, which suggests that couples tend to avoid marriage when destabilizing factors are present.[33] Conversely, couples that are engaged before cohabitating show no negative correlation in marital longevity. As such, it appears that a couple's understanding of their relationship is a strong predictor of long-term stability because couples tend to choose the commitments that fit their realities. Such understandings are influenced by social contexts that work either for or against long-term, stable commitments. Partnerships undertaken without long-term commitments are more common when external supports for such a commitment are lacking, and the partnerships themselves tend to exacerbate these disadvantages.[34] In contrast, partnerships like marriage that are undertaken with an expectation of a long-term commitment tend to take place where external supports for such a commitment are available and tend to increase these advantages. Accordingly, as W. Bradford Wilcox laments, "marriage is progressively becoming the preserve of the well-educated."[35]

Summarizing research on the effects of family structure for children's well-being, Kristin Anderson Moore concludes that "a family headed by two biological parents in a low-conflict marriage" is most conducive to child well-being compared with "children in single-parent families, children born to unmarried mothers, and children in stepfamilies or cohabiting relationships."[36] Children who live with biological married parents show the greatest emotional, behavioral, and psychological well-being, as well as educational and economic outcomes.[37] One study that intentionally targeted a wide variety of family forms showed disadvantages for all nonmarital family structures relative to marriage across measures of health and dental care, access to health care, and school attendance and performance.[38] Problems related to psychological health are also associated with family structure and have increased dramatically over recent decades as marriage has declined and family structures have diversified.[39]

The influence of children on their parents also appears to vary with family structure. Children tend to stress adult partnerships generally but positively influence individual parental well-being by showing empathy to parents, creating responsibility and commitment, and promoting emotional expression, especially through the opportunity to experience socially approved childlike play.[40] Marriage is again associated with the greatest overall adult benefits.[41] Moreover, commitment to children may be a significant factor in the long-term health of marriages, with large families tending to reap the greatest benefits in marital satisfaction.[42] However, this finding may be largely accounted for through selection effects. That is, "particular types of couples end up having large numbers of children, remain married to one another, and also enjoy cultural, social, and relational strengths that more than offset the challenges of parenting a large family."[43] Religious motivations are a common driver of self-selection for large families. This helps explain why religious mothers of four or more children are significantly more likely to report being "very happy" with their marriage, while nonreligious mothers with large families show no significant difference compared with nonreligious mothers with fewer children.[44]

Selection effects also appear to influence the benefits associated with the traditional family's division of gender roles. Spouses who report satisfaction with traditionally divided gender roles are also more likely to have brought these expectations into their marriages. Although marriage tends to be good for both men and women on a number of measures, including income and health, the benefits for men are much more pronounced.[45] Married fathers benefit from both greater divisions of household labor as well as preferential social treatment compared with their unmarried peers.[46]

Upon reviewing the profound influence of such external factors, the effect of marriage itself on parental, child, and familial well-being becomes difficult to determine. Moreover, marriage in the United States today correlates to socioeconomic advantages, such as income and education, that also enhance measurable well-being. Consequently, enumerating the benefits of marriage can easily turn into enumerating the benefits of being well positioned in social, educational, racial, economic, and even religious systems that advantage some and disadvantage others.

NONBIOLOGICAL FAMILIES

Adoptive families, foster families, and stepfamilies constitute the dominant forms of nonbiological families, but they have divergent outcomes. Adoptive families tend to have very strong outcomes relative to other family structures, but stepfamilies tend to have greater limitations. For example, despite having two parents and greater average financial resources, stepfamilies have child educational outcomes that resemble single-parent households more closely than biological, married households.[47] In contrast, outcomes among adopted children are similar to average outcomes for all American children, despite the selection effects that adoption itself presupposes.[48]

As in biological families, stability remains an important predictor of long-term well-being for nonbiological families. The disadvantages of children in foster care are largely influenced by the degree of instability children experience within the system. One study found instability alone accounted for a 63 percent rise in behavioral problems among foster children.[49] Unfortunately, over a quarter of all children in the foster system never find stable, permanent placements. Those who do tend to be similar to their adoptive peers outside foster care because they are "more likely to be young, have normal baseline behavior, have no prior history with child welfare, and have birth parents without mental health problems."[50] Compared with their peers, adopted children have more conditions that impede educational performance, with those adopted from foster care facing greater educational and emotional challenges. Yet adopted children's parental advantages compensate for these factors when children's well-being is considered comprehensively. This helps explain why adopted children tend to form stronger relationships with their parents compared with their peers while also fairing worse educationally.[51] Adoptees from foster care are more likely to be adopted at older ages and to have suffered neglect or abuse. Their adoptive parents are, on average, less educated, with lower household incomes than those who adopt by other means.[52] In light of the expense of adopting through private agencies, this variance is not surprising.[53]

The most common factor motivating parents who adopt through foster care is their desire to provide a permanent home to a child in need, although factors such as infertility, family expansion, and providing a sibling for an existing child are also common.[54] Although such virtuous motivations are admirable, the parents with the greatest income and educational assets do not tend to adopt the children with the greatest needs. For this reason, Elizabeth Bartholet argues that present adoption practices tend to advantage those with financial resources rather than serve children. Financial assets provide greater opportunities to seek younger, healthier children with fewer initial disadvantages.[55] Although adoption functions through the good intentions of adults, it also fulfills adult desires, which can harbor any number of explicit or implicit prejudices. Consequently, individual motivations for adopting are diverse and morally complex. Although the beneficial role of adoption should be acknowledged, differences in parental motivations and real disparities within present systems raise concern about their promotion of systematic disadvantages. Like the biological nuclear family, the general good of families formed by adoption gives way to greater complexity under further examination.

RACE, CLASS, AND ECONOMICS

American families of all structural types face racial disparities in treatment and opportunity, economic pressures, and systemic social disadvantages. These factors create real distinctions in the ability to form and maintain stable family units and in available resources for parental support. Here again, simplistic causal connections between family structure and child well-being cannot be sustained because social disparities exert considerable influence on the formation, function, and fragmentation of family units. Although families headed by married partners have the highest income on average, family structure itself depends on more than individual choice. Beyond a natural, religious, or ideological reality, the family is, and has always been, a social and economic unit that is responsive to social and economic realities.[56] Given these realities, divergence from the nuclear family form must be viewed within the context of interlocking economic and social forces.

Children constitute the largest single group of poor persons in the United States.[57] In fact, the average American child is "poorer than the average child in 12 of the 14 most developed nations."[58] Only about 10.5 percent of children in stable, two-parent homes live in poverty, compared with over 50 percent in mother-only homes.[59] When the household income of single-mother households is expanded to include those categorized as "near poor" (i.e., living at less than 150 percent of the poverty line), nearly 70 percent fit the category.[60] Among college-educated women, more than nine in ten will be married before the birth of their first child, compared with just 43 percent of those who have never attended college.[61]

Until recently, many studies assumed either married or single-parent households and thereby obscured the presence and diversity of cohabitating partnerships.[62] Research on race and poverty has likewise tended to overlook alternative familial or childrearing arrangements beyond the nuclear family, which may be employed at higher rates among nonwhites.[63] The use of fictive and extended kin among African Americans is commonly cited as an example of a system of familial support that tends to compensate for divergence from the biological nuclear structure, although some research indicates that this is a broader phenomenon that is better defined by lower socioeconomic class.[64] These networks can provide direct caregiving support and assure communal standards of parental care, which may explain why African American children experience maltreatment at lower rates than their white peers when adjusted for income, employment, and urbanization.[65] However, the social and economic shifts of recent decades have fragmented Black communal and familial networks.[66] Meanwhile, decreases in urban male employment, high rates of incarceration, and increasingly punitive social welfare policies have left many Black families facing harsh economic circumstances.[67] Throughout the last half century, once economically homogenous Black communities became more stratified. At the same time, the increasing privatization of American families, led by upper- and middle-class Whites, has left contemporary American families more insular and less communally supported than those in previous generations.[68] In this context, extended and fictive kin networks are simply not a significant reality for many African American children.[69]

Nonetheless, the centrality of mothers as the nexus of support networks has generally remained strong, but this maternal primacy can also be employed as a means of coping with the absence of stable adult relationships and co-parenting.[70] In addition, intergenerational support of single motherhood may be weakening or may have been misconstrued in earlier research. Lower- and middle-income grandparents commonly reported feeling that their efforts to provide their daughters with a better life had been wasted. Moreover, the option to abort is often supported by the parents of single Black mothers, which may later exacerbate intergenerational conflict in caregiving.[71] In response to such conflict, single mothers often seek support in friends of the same age cohort, even as grandparents remain the primary source of co-parental support.[72] The level of conflict within grandparent–parent relationships as well as the physical health of grandparents can also mitigate positive effects.[73] Consequently, the influence of grandparent co-parenting on children's well-being depends largely on the quality of the adult relationship among caregivers.[74] Here again, stability emerges as of singular importance, while familial function and structure interact to support child well-being.[75]

Incarceration, foster care, and migration policies are notable for their roles in systematically destabilizing poor and minority families in the United States. Over recent decades, rates of incarceration in the United States have increased dramatically and are now roughly seven times higher than two generations ago.[76] Between 1991 and 2007, the number of American children with a parent in prison increased by 82 percent.[77] These trends have a strong racial dynamic given that the incarceration rate of African Americans is nearly eight times greater than that of Whites.[78] Over half of all inmates are parents, while almost a quarter of their children are under age five.[79] Black women, most of whom are mothers, constitute the most rapidly growing group among the incarcerated.[80] Adding to the disruption of imprisonment, mothers are also less likely to be visited by their family than are incarcerated fathers. This disparity is due to the greater likelihood of children being removed from their former home after maternal imprisonment, along with the fact that federal prisons for women are fewer and more physically distanced than male facilities.[81]

Incarceration exacerbates long-term instability after release by complicating both reentry into the labor force and losses in access to social safety nets such as housing vouchers.[82] For these and related reasons, high rates of imprisonment tend to reproduce social disadvantages across generations, making children and families themselves hidden victims. These disadvantages skew heavily toward African American and Hispanic families.[83] As Kathryn Getek Soltis writes, "Research suggests that mass imprisonment creates greater social inequality through its impact on children than from its effects on the men and women actually behind the bars."[84] She also observes, "There are particularly strong negative impacts on children's mental and behavioral health, and these are linked with outcomes that continue into adulthood."[85] Incarceration disrupts not only families but also structures of community support, and thereby undermines needed assets for organized resistance against its unequal effects and multigenerational consequences.[86]

The foster care system likewise represents a racially and economically unequal system of family disruption. Tanya Asim Cooper argues that professionals within the foster care system "routinely contend that Native American and African American children are the most at-risk for child abuse and neglect" and apply this belief despite contradictory statistical evidence.[87] She continues:

> Besides being reported, investigated, and removed from their homes more often for suspicions of abuse and neglect, these children are less likely to receive the mental health services they need in foster

> care; are more likely to have fewer visits with their parents and siblings; are less likely to receive services designed to reunify them with their family; are less likely to have contact with their foster care caseworkers; and are more likely to see their parents' rights to maintain a relationship with them terminated.[88]

Despite properly adjusted studies showing lower risk among African American families than similarly positioned Whites, foster care is systematically more aggressive among minority families.[89] This in part because financial incentives reward retaining children within the system but do not similarly reward permanent placement or preventing children's entry altogether. Such perverse incentives suppress the alternative use of family preservation strategies, which involve less disruption for the child and are generally considered cheaper.[90] Cooper concludes that the foster care system works primarily for self-perpetuation as a "billion-dollar, publicly funded bureaucracy" that builds and sustains racial disparities.[91]

Finally, migration policy can also severely disrupt families already facing significant hardships. As Victor Carmona writes, families of mixed legal status "live under the constant threat of deportation that has created a culture of fear that affects individual family members in different ways."[92] This constant worry of separation leaves spouses knowing that they may suddenly be made single parents through government intervention. Thus, Carmona names the US immigration system a structure of sin, inasmuch as it operates with the intention of breaking the natural bonds of affection shared within families.[93] Carmona also argues that this highly damaging system rests on the combinations of an economic desire for cheap labor and a social aversion to give such workers full legal rights. Through this long-standing tension, exploitative migration systems have been repeated and reinvented throughout American history.[94]

SEXUALITY, INCOME, AND ADOPTION

In a much more overt way than those located at other intersections of social disadvantages, families headed by same-sex couples find themselves facing challenges that take on explicitly religious justifications. Social acceptance of homosexuality and same-sex relationships has increased markedly in only a few decades and has led to increased rates of both marriage and adoption.[95] Demographically, same-sex partners are largely similar to their heterosexual peers, but they raise children at lower rates with much greater unevenness across racial and educational differences.[96] African American, Hispanic, and Native American same-sex couples are significantly more likely to be raising children than their White peers.[97] The least educated same-sex couples raise children near the average for all couples (43 percent). But this rate falls sharply for the college educated (10 percent) before reversing again among the highly educated.[98] As a result, same-sex parenthood is common primarily among racial minorities and the less educated, leading to greater average economic disadvantage among children of same-sex parents compared to their peers with different-sex parents.[99] Same-sex couples are also four times more likely to adopt and six times more likely to be involved with foster care.[100] As is true generally, interaction with the foster care system corresponds to lower income, while the White and well-educated have the highest rates of adoption by other means.[101]

When all factors are accounted for, measures of child well-being among same-sex-headed households are very similar to their different-sex peers. Accordingly, advocates of same-sex adoptive parenthood argue that these couples represent a valuable resource of capable adults and stable homes for children caught in the instabilities of the foster care system.[102] However, from the Catholic Magisterium's perspective, the present plight of stable, long-term marriage in Western society is itself linked to moral decay exemplified in public acceptance of same-sex relationships. For example, the US Conference of Catholic Bishops' 2009 pastoral "Marriage, Love, and Life in the Divine Plan" identifies same-sex unions as among the misconstrued ideas about marriage that erode understanding of its very purpose and meaning.[103] The earlier document of the CDF, "Considerations Regarding Proposals to Give Legal Recognition to Unions Between Homosexual Persons," likewise decried growing social acceptance of same-sex partnerships as a corruption of the proper and natural view of marriage.[104] The document explicitly rejects any right to adoption among same-sex couples and claims that this would constitute "doing violence to these children," inasmuch as the context of such children's adoption would not serve their full human development.[105] More recent magisterial documents affirm these positions.[106] Consequently, there is fundamental opposition between those who encourage adoption by same-sex couples as a service for the good of children in need of stable homes and those who support the magisterial teaching that views all such practice as constituting a grave injustice.

As has been argued, the particular framing of the magisterial response must be considered, especially given that the prevailing contemporary framework for parenthood restricts issues largely to sexual ethics and gender norms. Holding the sexual relationships of adults as one aspect of an overall moral appraisal, rather than a singularly decisive feature, and more forcefully asserting the relational goods of the family itself could introduce new possibilities for moral evaluation. This approach was clearly rejected by the head of the CDF, Cardinal Levada, in his 2006 letter to the archbishop of San Francisco absolutely prohibiting participation in adoption by same-sex couples. Yet Levada's aversion to such absolutist reasoning on the same question during his own tenure as archbishop of San Francisco only a few years earlier demonstrates the shallow historical roots of this judgment.[107] Moreover, the rationale for this morally absolutist shift relies upon the prior commitment to interpreting the entire moral nature of same-sex families as contingent upon a sexual relationship.

A shift away from this perspective would require a more robust magisterial engagement with the actual experiences of children living in same-sex-headed households, but this too is complicated by the prevailing framework. Although research shows little evidence of deficits related to generally accepted measures of child well-being, the magisterial perspective rests on normative claims, including the proper moral development of children and right understanding of relationships between the genders. The social sciences are not methodologically aimed at delving into the normative interpretation of data beyond broadly agreeable measures. As such, responsibility rests on the moral-theological perspective to demonstrate how its own assertions about the normative interpretation of right relationships can be sustained in relation to empirical studies of human well-being. Without this willingness, the Catholic moral appeal to natural law and common reason is called into question as the moral-theological vision of "the way things are," and the social scientific data related to "the way things are" would stand in isolation or even contradiction.

The lack of such concerted engagement isolates magisterial authority within its own internal verification. Present magisterial moral argumentation against childrearing by same-sex partners is rational and consistent within its own parameters. However, the reality of healthy, stable same-sex-headed families that do not seem to be detrimental to child well-being clearly challenges these authoritative pronouncements. The selective use of social scientific data according to predetermined normative judgments only widens the gap between moral pronouncement and lived reality. Without a reevaluation of the framework that guides such conclusions, the relevance of authoritative pronouncements will continue to maintain this distance from lived experience.

Beyond the tendency to root moral evaluations of parental capacities in sexual ethical judgments, gender norms also play a key role in the official position of the Catholic Church regarding same-sex parenthood. Owing deeply to the thought of John Paul II, complementarity among adult partners is frequently presented as an essential requirement of childrearing and is posited as a matter of basic justice.[108] Echoing several years of statements by the US Catholic bishops and the CDF, Pope Francis explains that "it is necessary to emphasize the right of children to grow up within a family, with a father and a mother able to create a suitable environment for their development and emotional maturity. Continuing to mature in the relationship, in the complementarity of the masculinity and femininity of a father and a mother, and thus preparing the way for emotional maturity."[109]

Revisionist theologians typically disagree strongly with such arguments and are quick to cite sociological and psychological evidence that children raised by same-sex parents have outcomes comparable to children of heterosexual parents. In response to the CDF's often-repeated 2003 argument against same-sex parenthood, Patricia Beattie Jung writes that "despite the Vatican's assertion that claims to be based on experience, after more than twenty years of scrutiny, not a single research study suggests that children raised by same-sex parents fail to flourish. As early as 1999, reviews of the relevant literature had given clear evidence to the contrary. In fact, ample evidence suggests that normal development among children may be expected among same-sex parents at the same rate as their heterosexual peers."[110] During recent decades, resistance to same-sex parenting has often included worry that children will develop impaired sexual identities, abnormal conceptions of gender roles, or will themselves become homosexual. Moreover, issues have also surfaced for children's mental health, social adjustment, behavior, ability to form social relationships, and risk of sexual abuse.[111] Contemporary evidence clearly contradicts the validity of these anxieties when data are properly adjusted for all factors.[112] Children of gay and lesbian parents do not generally report their parents' sexuality as a significant factor in their parenting capabilities but do report social stigma as a challenge in their upbringing.[113] Openness about their sexuality has been shown to benefit psychological well-being among same-sex parents.[114] As in all families, psychological health and happiness among parents has a positive impact on children.[115]

Consequently, on the issue of parental complementarity, magisterial teaching is confronted with three difficult realities. First, even as clear parental gender roles may have benefits for some parents, they are evidently not necessary for securing broadly accepted measures of child well-being. Second, the insistence on gender complementarity among caregivers as essential does not specify which parental functions are the irreplaceable domain of one gender or arise only between parents of differing genders. In contrast, research on parental practices suggests that parental roles are both adaptable and influenced by societal and cultural expectations as well as individual capabilities and preferences. Third, and perhaps most significantly, magisterial arguments for parental complementarity rely upon an essentially private conception of the family such that the influences of nonparental adults are severely underestimated.[116]

This privatized conception of the family stands in tension with the more communal and socially engaged vision of the family that informs Catholic Social Teaching and undermines the fundamental value of solidarity.[117] The Catholic tradition itself attests to institutional practices of single-sex caregiving in boarding schools, shelters, and orphanages. Moreover, contemporary Catholic teaching advocates for the inclusion of different-sex adult influences when considering the challenges of single parenting. However, the influence of nonparental adults is ignored when teaching pertains to same-sex parenting. Instead, the sexual practices and gendered norms of same-sex partners are found wanting through a narrow contrast to a private, biological nuclear ideal—as if the larger social extensions of the family were of little significance. Although this framing clearly reinforces the Magisterium's moral condemnation of same-sex sexual acts and support for monogamous heterosexual marriage tied to the good of procreation, in a broader perspective, it undermines the Catholic Church's own commitment to the role of the community in supporting families, the social role of the family in open societies, and historical practices of responding to the needs of children by negotiating structures of nonbiological kinship and childrearing.

COMMUNITY AND CHILDREARING

The vision of the family that informs magisterial opposition to same-sex parenthood appeals to natural law and common reason to secure the basis of the family in a male–female parental pair while excluding the larger social contexts of family life from moral reflection. Although heterosexual partnerships are clearly relevant to considerations of natural family patterns, the isolation of these partnerships betrays an ideological commitment to privatization that stands in contrast to broadly observable historical and cultural practices and to the Catholic Church's own moral commitments. Elizabeth Janeway contends that "the idea of an individual having sole responsibility for childrearing is the most unusual pattern of parenting in the world, one that has proved to be unsuccessful because it isolates children and parents from society."[118] Moreover, such isolation excludes children from the benefits of multiple adult role models of both sexes.[119] Several Catholic theologians have likewise noted both the historical contingency of the private nuclear family and the limitations this ideal poses. For example, Lisa Cahill argues that "the extended consanguineous family is more ancient and more universal in social importance than the modern so-called nuclear family, consisting of spouses and children and considered to have been formed through marriage."[120]

The social anthropologist Esther Goody's functional framework for parenthood further clarifies why a singular focus on parental partners fails to capture all pertinent factors in child well-being. For Goody, parenthood itself is the process of fulfilling important tasks related to childrearing. As such, numerous "parental" roles may be assumed by various adults such that the members of the parental pair are rarely the only ones engaged in parenting.[121] Goody's view challenges privatized conceptions of the nuclear family as both factually inaccurate and developmentally unhealthy. Biological parents may be central to many families, but their centrality correlates to the array of parental functions these adults fulfill. As argued above, though the private nuclear norm does strengthen commitment to marriage, it does so as an essentially private, gendered institution while insulating parental responsibility around just two individuals. Goody's view helps to reduce the dichotomy between the parenthood of the parental pair and the participation of other involved adults. In so doing, a functional view of parenthood extends recognition of social supports that can buffer instability on the practical level while calling greater attention to the social nature of the family at the moral-theological level. The importance of nonparent caring adults is recognized in some aspects of magisterial teaching as well as social scientific research that shows children benefit from a network of caring adults both within and beyond their own household.[122]

The social commitments of Catholic teaching regarding the family seem to support the basic insights of Goody's framework. Yet this commitment to community and social participation is undermined internally by the sexual ethical and gender essentialist issues that drive contemporary thinking on parenthood.[123] Although Catholic teaching rightfully defends the importance of parental rights and responsibilities in caring for their children and directing family affairs, presentations of parental partners as their children's *only* significant adult influences undermines the more expansive vision of the family held within the larger Catholic moral perspective. This concentration on the parental pair alone is seen most clearly in the claimed necessity of parental gender complementarity.

Importantly, magisterial and revisionist sources agree that the family does not operate for itself but is an outwardly directed social institution aimed at benefiting the common good.[124] Nonetheless, the family's role in advancing the common good remains an underappreciated element of Catholic teaching that is obscured by the prevailing bias toward gender and sexual ethical questions.[125] Calling greater attention to the social dimension of the family necessarily diminishes the centrality placed upon the parental pair alone and detracts attention from the bulwark of teaching on gender and sexual ethics that has been contentiously maintained in recent decades. One cannot uphold a vision of the family as a socially engaged and supported entity while simultaneously claiming that parents are the only meaningful models of masculinity and femininity. Relationships beyond the nuclear family are either significant or they are not.

At a pastoral level, this ambiguity influences inconsistent responses to the reality of same-sex parenting. In recent years, some homosexual individuals have been refused communion and fired from Catholic parishes and schools.[126] Same-sex couples have also been denied baptism for their children and refused admittance into Catholic schools.[127] These incidents raise serious concerns because they constitute a refusal to offer communal support for individuals, partners, and children on the grounds that presumed sexual behavior cannot be tolerated within Catholic communities or organizations. If families are essentially privatized units that may influence but are not essentially bound to one another, then removing immoral aberrations from the collective is defensible. But this view would not recognize the full Catholic vision of the family presented within magisterial teaching. Accepting that Catholic families are obligated to serve each other and the common good on the basis of their shared baptism and shared humanity makes isolating families headed by same-sex parents from the resources of the community more difficult to defend. Because relationships with adults other than their parents have an impact on children's well-being, giving children of same-sex couples the opportunity to form such relationships with faithful adults through Catholic schools and parish life seems not only defensible but necessary.

Balancing concerns for family structure with attention to parental function may also encourage broader moral perspectives on the family and parenthood. Anthony Gittins suggests such a framework in arguing for replacing the present "extensional" approach with an "intensional" approach to the family.[128] The former begins by defining what the family is and then considers its function, and thereby tends to exclude diversities in family form. In contrast, an intensional approach would "first specify common characteristics such as adequate structure; the support, protection, dignity, and fulfillment of members; the intention of stability and endurance; and the relation to the wider world." This approach would look to include all interpersonal arrangements along the specified parameters; even as some could still be judged preferable.[129] In this, Goody's articulation of familial attributes proves valuable because it parallels the social duties of parenthood articulated in modern Catholic teaching.

CONCLUSION

Some family structures tend toward stability but can have these benefits mitigated by functional deficits. Other family structures tend toward instability but can have these deficits mitigated by functional assets. In general, the increasing privatization of American families combined with social and economic forces creates conditions for increased familial instability. Lacking social buffers, such as extended kin support and strong social ties, such insular families are more prone to disruption by parental conflict, job insecurity, alcoholism, and many other factors, including personal parental capabilities. Within this environment, nuclear families based in marriage are better positioned than are single-parent and cohabitating households due to the mutual support of spouses and the long-term commitments that tend to accompany marriage. At the same time, those who marry also tend to have individual assets and dispositions that are best suited to maintain familial stability in this environment, such as higher-than-average income and education. But it is a mistake to call attention to the virtues of such family structures while ignoring the social and economic conditions that help create their relatively strong outcomes. Even single parents, who are most vulnerable to such disruptions, can effectively buffer against instability when external conditions permit social supports, extended kin networks, and co-parenting arrangements.

The increasing privatization of the family makes all families vulnerable to disruption by minimizing the bonds of social support that can be vital to families and individual family members in disruptive circumstances. Although nuclear families feel these vulnerabilities the least, this only signals that this family form is better adapted for a social context that is hostile to lasting extended social bonds. In this context, attention to the decline of stable marriages and the nuclear family is warranted but should be viewed within the historical context of larger social and economic factors that exacerbate isolation while disrupting traditional support structures. Ideological trends have certainly contributed to the diversity of contemporary families, but critiques of ideology, especially those centered on sexuality or dispositions toward marriage alone, miss larger ideological realities.

Magisterial writings show awareness of these factors, particularly in the context of extreme poverty, but commonly privilege ideological concerns related to sexual and gender norms.[130] This emphasis limits the ability to offer a theology of parenthood that is meaningfully inclusive of parental function defined by children's well-being. In the face of present research, extended arguments over the significance of gender difference and sexual ethical norms simply do not appear as significant features for evaluating capacities for parenthood based on children's well-being. Moreover, idealization of the biological nuclear family and attendant gender roles can lead to a moral analysis of diverse family forms without giving sufficient attention to the economic and social influences that shape individual realities. Giving more attention to parental functions in response to social pressures could lead to a more nuanced analysis, which would strengthen the Magisterium's own methodological commitments to natural law.

A significant number of valuable principles within Catholic thought are supported by social scientific studies yet remain underappreciated. Prominent among these is the concern for socially engaged families supported by expansive relational networks. However, an emphasis on social engagement and communal relationships beyond the nuclear family stands in tension with the privatized vision of the family that is pivotal in asserting the importance of parental complementarity over and against same-sex parenthood. Acknowledging the wider network of adult influences recognized within Catholic teaching limits the moral weight that concern for parental complementarity alone can bear. Moreover, the goals that the Catholic Church posits for the family have a closer correlation to dispositions and commitments of parents than to a specific family structure and gender roles. Christian parents ought to strive for stability in family life while fostering social commitments. Biological kinship, family structure, parental gender, and other factors influence these goals but are not definitive from the perspective of parental function.[131] When such factors are taken to be definitive, they undermine attention to the actual functioning of families and parents within a larger network of social relations. An adequate theology of parenthood ought to be based in adult capacities to provide care in light of social contexts that variously encourage or discourage the growth of healthy, stabile, and socially engaged families.

NOTES

1. Cahill, "Same-Sex Marriage," 154.
2. Congregation for the Doctrine of the Faith, "Considerations," sec. 4.
3. The "social sciences" throughout this chapter refer primarily to sociology and psychology, though anthropology and history are at times utilized. History is not always considered among the social sciences, yet it often plays an essential role in the research of the

other disciplines. Because research on the family within the American context is politically charged, I have attempted to select a balanced representation of available resources.

4. Here, "form" is used as a general term and refers to any specific type of family (nuclear, stable, wealthy, etc.), "structure" refers to the makeup of a family in terms of its constituents (nuclear, biological, etc.), and "function" refers to the operations of a family (socially oriented, stable, etc.). This use of structure should not be confused with psychological and sociological uses of "structuralism."
5. Salzman, *What Are They Saying?* 11. The relationships between the social sciences and moral theology have been explored by a number of authors. Among others, see Lawler, *What Is*; and Browning, *Christian Ethics*.
6. For a critique of this use of social scientific information in magisterial teaching see Pope, "Scientific and Natural Law," 89–126.
7. Salzman and Lawler, *Sexual Person*, 7.
8. This use of "function" should not be confused with psychological or sociological "functionalism," even though some overlap may exist. In both psychology and sociology, functionalism refers to perspectives that evaluate behavior based on needs and lacks a teleological orientation that can view behavior as seeking theological goods.
9. See Ariès, *Centuries*; and Cunningham, *Children*.
10. Ruether, "Christianity," 95.
11. It is also important to acknowledge that some of the human goods associated with child well-being that appear basic have not always been so and are not always valued cross-culturally. Education for all children, not just males or the affluent, is one such example.
12. See John Paul II, *Familiaris consortio*; John Paul II, *Gratissimam sane*; and US Conference of Catholic Bishops, "Economic Justice."
13. "A committed, permanent, faithful relationship of husband and wife is the root of a family. It strengthens all the members, provides best for the needs of children, and causes the Church of the home to be an effective sign of Christ in the world." US Conference of Catholic Bishops, *Follow the Way*.
14. Center for Marriage and Families, "Research Brief 1," 1–2.
15. John Paul II, *Familiaris consortio*, sec. 14.
16. See Pontifical Council for the Family, "Family," sec. I.2.
17. For an intentionally secular argument on the importance of traditional marriage related to childrearing, see Giris, George, and Anderson, "What Is Marriage?" 245–87.
18. Aulette, *Changing American Families*, 33.
19. Clarke-Stewart and Brentano, *Divorce*, 106.
20. Popenoe, "American Family," no. 1.
21. Clarke-Stewart and Brentano, *Divorce*, 128.
22. Clarke-Stewart and Brentano, 109.
23. Crane and Heaton, *Handbook*, 123.
24. Clarke-Stewart and Brentano, *Divorce*, 129.
25. Popenoe, "American Family," nos. 4, 13.
26. Wilcox, Waite, and Roberts, "Marriage," 4; Brodzinski and Evan B. Donaldson Adoption Institute, "Expanding Resources," 6.
27. Wilcox, "State," 3.
28. England and Edin, *Unmarried Couples*, 139.
29. Crane and Heaton, *Handbook*, 457ff.
30. Crane and Heaton, 457; see also Clarke-Stewart and Brentano, *Divorce*, 106.

31. Krueger, "Family Structure," 6.
32. The reduction in the likelihood of divorce for these factors is as follows: income above the median = 30, high education = 25, over age twenty-five at marriage = 24, and at least seven months between marriage and birth of first child = 24 points. Intact families of origin and religious affiliation follow after these at 14 points each. Wilcox, "State," 73.
33. US Department of Health and Human Services, "Marriage," 1–12.
34. Aulette, *Changing American Families*, 128.
35. Wilcox, "State," 69.
36. Moore, "Marriage," 2. This particular study does not consider same-sex or adoptive parenting.
37. Moore, "Research Brief," n9.
38. Krueger, "Family Structure," 1.
39. Popenoe, "American Family," 3.
40. Aulette, *Changing American Families*, 359.
41. Wilcox, "State," x.
42. Moore, "What Is 'Healthy Marriage'?" 1.
43. Moore, 53.
44. Moore, 55.
45. Harvard Men's Health Watch, "Marriage."
46. Glauber, "Race," 24.
47. Center for Marriage and Families, "Research Brief 1," 5.
48. Bramlett, "National Survey," 6.
49. Rubin, "Impact," 336.
50. Rubin.
51. Bramlett, "National Survey," 8.
52. Vandivere and Malm, *Adoption USA*, 10.
53. According to the US Department of Health and Human Services, more than half of adoptions from foster care cost no money, and only about 15 percent cost more than $5,000. The cost of private adoptions ranges significantly, with 22 percent at no cost and 33 percent at more than $10,000. International adoptions are the most expensive, with 93 percent costing more than $10,000. Vandivere and Malm, *Adoption USA*, 43.
54. Vandivere and Malm, 11.
55. Bartholet, *Family Bonds*, 73–74.
56. Krueger, "Family Structure," 6.
57. Aulette, *Changing American Families*, 85, 369.
58. Crane and Heaton, *Handbook*, 311.
59. Aulette, *Changing American Families*, 368. Of individuals age eighteen to forty-six years, those who are married with or without children report being "very happy" at the highest rate (50 percent for women and 39 percent for men across both categories), while cohabitating individuals without children and single parents report being "very happy" at the lowest rate (22 percent and 25 percent for men and 24 percent and 13 percent for women, respectively). Wilcox, "State," 10.
60. Crane and Heaton, *Handbook*, 133.
61. New Oxford Notes, "Future," 13.
62. Aulette, *Changing American Families*, 128.
63. Aulette, 127.

64. See Gerstel, "Rethinking," 1–20; Sarkisian, Gerena, and Gerstel, "Extended Family," 40–54.
65. Collins, *Black Feminist Thought*, 133.
66. Collins, 59–61.
67. Collins, 133.
68. Collins contends that this privatization directly correlates with objectification and commodification of children under the framework of a consumer asset. This produces an underlying concept of parents as owners of their children who are alone responsible for the care of their private property (i.e., children). See Collins, 182.
69. Collins, 183.
70. Collins, 161.
71. Collins, 189.
72. Shoulberg, "Role," 259.
73. The study did not focus on African American families and had respondents who roughly represented the racial demography of the United States at large: 61 percent White, 15 percent Black, 19 percent Mexican/Hispanic, and 6 percent other. See Krueger, "Family Structure," 6. Even among married couples, residential grandparents do not appear to have a strong positive impact on child outcomes.
74. Shoulberg, "Role," 259.
75. Stability generally refers to low-conflict families without divorce, separation, or other significant shifts that affect caregiving arrangements. When such disruptions occur, stability characterizes family systems that adapt readily and diminish secondary effects. I am grateful to Dr. Craig Ford for pointing out that while stability may be good for children in general, for many LGBTIQ persons, family stability mixed with social, religious, and/or moral rigidity has caused significant harm.
76. Crane and Heaton, *Handbook*, 269.
77. Roberts, "Prison," 1481.
78. Angela Davis, quoted by Collins, *Black Feminist Thought*, 77.
79. Soltis, "Family Relationships," 165.
80. Roberts, "Prison," 1480.
81. Roberts, 1496. Roberts adds, "Even telephone calls to prison, which are typically saddled with exorbitant fees and charges, may be too expensive for regular communication."
82. Crane and Heaton, *Handbook*, 277.
83. Roberts, "Prison," 1481.
84. Soltis, "Family Relationships," 166.
85. Soltis, 165.
86. Roberts, "Prison," 1483.
87. Cooper, "Racial Bias," 217.
88. Cooper, 243.
89. Cooper, 217n3. See also Rivaux, "Intersection," 165.
90. Cooper, "Racial Bias," 260, 264.
91. Cooper, 216.
92. Carmona, "Mixed-Status Families, Solidarity, and *Lo Cotidiano*," 205.
93. Carmona, 207.
94. Carmona, "Mixed-Status Families and Brokenness," 159. See also Collier and Strain with Catholic Relief Services, *Global Migration*.

95. Gates, "Same-Sex and Different-Sex Couples," 2; See also Lofquist, "Same-Sex Couple Households."
96. Gates, "Same-Sex and Different-Sex Couples," 3.
97. Gates, "Family Focus," F3.
98. Gates.
99. Gates, F4.
100. Gates, "LGBT Parenting," 2.
101. Gates, "Family Focus," F3.
102. Brodzinski, "Expanding Resources," 5.
103. US Conference of Catholic Bishops, "Marriage," sec. 17.
104. Congregation for the Doctrine of the Faith, "Considerations," sec. 4.
105. Congregation for the Doctrine of the Faith, sec. 7.
106. Francis, *Amoris laetitia*, sec. 251.
107. "Catholic Charities."
108. See US Conference of Catholic Bishops, "Frequently Asked Questions."
109. "Every Child Has a Right."
110. Jung, "God Sets the Lonely," 128.
111. American Psychological Association, *Lesbian and Gay Parenting*, 8.
112. American Psychological Association, 7–8. See also Brodzinski, "Expanding Resources," 13.
113. American Psychological Association, *Lesbian and Gay Parenting*, 14; Fairtlough, "Growing Up," 521–28.
114. American Psychological Association, *Lesbian and Gay Parenting*, 13.
115. Brodzinski, "Expanding Resources," 5.
116. Although multiple adults fulfilling parental roles within children's lives may have positive impacts on that child's support network, it also may lead to uncertainty in understanding the relations of these different parental relationships for children as well as conflict among multiple caregivers. Furthermore, when extended kin function in parental roles, they are removed from the role of "nurturing outsider," which may be particularly important during adolescence when children push against parental influence and may seek safe nonparental adults for support. Consequently, it is important to acknowledge that extended spheres of support remain important even if the parental functions are expanded to include more direct caregivers. See Schwartz, "Connective Complexity," 81.
117. See Cloutier, "Wanting 'the Best.'"
118. hooks, "Revolutionary Parenting," 143.
119. Janeway, *Cross Sections*, 1982; cited by hooks, "Revolutionary Parenting," 143.
120. Cahill, *Family*, xi.
121. Jussen, *Spiritual Kinship*, 24.
122. Murphy, "Caring Adults," 4.
123. E.g., John Paul II encouraged families to welcome in the elderly but did not acknowledge the important role of grandparents for childcare both historically and among many today. See John Paul II, *Familiaris consortio*, sec. 27.
124. John Paul II, sec. 72.
125. Julie Hanlon Rubio, drawing heavily upon the writings of John Paul II, has argued this point well. Rubio, *Christian Theology*, 186–88.
126. Among others, see Paulson, "Gay Marriages"; and Borestein, "DC Archdiocese."
127. See Anonymous, "Sins," 10–15.
128. Gittins, "In Search," 178.

CHAPTER 6

Reconsidering Kinship throughout History

rgued in previous chapters, opportunities exist within magisterial teach- for engaging alternative interpretive options, asserting certain aspects e tradition more forcefully, and creating greater consistency across the body of teachings related to the family and parenthood while engaging rience more consistently. This chapter turns to a larger historical view of tradition in order to point to resources that could further augment the ailing framework for parenthood. Contemporary magisterial documents to reference historical figures, ideas, or events primarily to demonstrate inuity and do not generally rely upon extensive critical research. In rast, revisionist theologians tend to call attention to historical develop- t, diversity, and the cultural roots of religious ideals.[1] More traditional- eologians also employ critical methods but emphasize continuity and istency throughout historical developments. For their part, feminist logians have uncovered gendered hierarchies and ideologies that have omen's voices silent, lost, or muted within the patriarchal legacies of the tion.[2] Each of these approaches offers insight into how parenthood has understood throughout Christian history, yet each also tends to repli- the concerns of its authors, most of whom have tended to undervalue thood as a theological consideration in its own right.

his chapter first addresses the concept of kinship and then reviews tian history with attention to diverse conceptions of family, children, parenthood. This exploration aims to demonstrate that presently influ- views of kinship are limited in comparison with the broader histori- hristian tradition. The primacy of the private, biological nuclear family n conceptions of parenthood is questioned in light of diverse caregiv- ractices and their theological supports. Recognizing this diversity does egate the value of the biologically based family unit but does challenge

129. Gittins, 178. Gittins does not offer a theological intensional d
repeats the revisionist tendency to articulate social and psycho
well-being while remaining largely ambiguous on the theolog

130. On the inclusion of poverty as a significant factor in familial s
laetitia, secs. 49, 294; US Conference of Catholic Bishops, "E
Paul II, *Familiaris consortio.*

131. Interestingly, "Gay men more often reported they were spec
ents because of their sexual orientation than did lesbians (3
in the majority of these cases, the men indicated the birthmot
her child's 'only mother.'" Brodzinski, "Expanding Resources

biological kinship's prominence as it has been employed in service to upholding sexual ethical and gendered norms, which limits wider reception of tradition.

MAKING KINSHIP

Historical resources suggest that Christian conceptions of kinship are not inherently tied to biological relatedness. Instead, Christians have created kinship by recognizing some underlying reality (biological relation, baptism, need, etc.) that gives rise to specific interpersonal obligations through moral interpretations of its significance. The presence of kin obligations apart from biological relatedness is commonly termed "fictive kinship," a problematic and value-laden term that suggests a dichotomy between real and imagined kinship. *All kinship is imagined. All kinship is interpreted.* Kinship is a way of ordering the world, not a genetic necessity.[3] Kinship entails a set of obligations and ways of acting that differentiate kin from nonkin.[4] Biological relatedness is a dominant underlying reality in many interpretations of kinship, but biological facts still yield considerable diversity across various understandings of kin obligations.[5] Moreover, strong kin obligations remain common without biological relatedness, such as the juridical recognition of adopted parenthood or relations through marriage.

Some have argued that care for biological kin is an important element of evolutionary adaptation. By focusing on the transmission of individual genes, the protection of biological children can be seen as an extension of self-interest in the form of one's own genetic survival.[6] This view suggests that biological kinship is a basic natural reality arising from the evolutionary inheritance of the human species. However, such a view leads to an easy determinism that obscures larger population genetics, sexual and social selection, and behavioral adaptability. Presently, sociobiology is divided on the question of whether individual genes or those of the social group are most influential in adaptive behaviors. When the long-term survival of groups is prioritized over that of individuals, the evolutionary basis for extending kin obligations beyond biological children alone becomes more obvious.[7] For instance, the prevalence of homosexual and other nonbiologically reproductive individuals within a social group may be explained as an adaptive means of increasing support for children within a group. Such potential social assets are missed when concerns are restricted to individuals and their actions alone. The balance of sociobiological forces wrought through evolution is certainly complex and likely dynamic. Reductionist appeals to "natural" behaviors based in these sciences mischaracterize the complexity of human persons and the fields of research themselves. Tempered by concern for the plethora of forces shaping individual and social behavior, hope of conclusive scientific support for a single "natural kinship" becomes vanishingly small. Even if such unlikely support could be sustained, it would still require a moral interpretation of these basic facts, adding layers of complexity.[8]

Bernard Jussen acknowledges that contemporary historians, like most anthropologists, have learned to decouple kinship from biological relatedness. Jussen writes, the "difficulty lies in the tightrope walk involved in retaining some connection between biology and kinship while conceiving of kinship as a *mental* system used to structure social relations of *all kinds*" (emphasis in the original).[9] As a mental system, kinship is an interpretation of obligations owed within a particular relationship or set of relationships. Such interpretations are not fully uncoupled from biological relatedness and dominant cultural norms can make certain interpretations appear given. Yet, Jussen argues, nonbiological kinship is a key aspect of the Christian tradition that has grounded social understanding and caregiving support. Since the early Middle Ages, Christian parents have commonly allied themselves with several sets of godparents and confirmation sponsors, thereby extending their familial networks. The various stages of baptism alone required multiple sponsors such that a single baptism could produce up to sixteen new kin relations, each prohibited from marriage to the baptized individual on account of this relationship. Through this kin-making, Jussen concludes, "a couple could easily acquire twenty to thirty spiritual cofathers and comothers."[10]

The challenge at present lies in addressing the biases that associate "real" kinship with biological relatedness and centralize the biological nuclear family as the true form of Christian family. Such biological bias relegates other forms of kinship to mere metaphor, even as nonbiological kinship has been central to historical Christian theological commitments. Christianity differs markedly from a strict biological naturalism in its willingness to both extend nonbiological kinship claims as well as abrogate the claims of biological kinship. Kinship in the Christian tradition is based upon recognition of the most fundamental human relationship as children of a common Creator.[11] The sacrament of baptism acknowledges and celebrates this fundamental identity while calling individuals into participation in the life of the Church. As such, universal human kinship and kinship in Christ through baptism are essential theological convictions that direct the self-understanding and mission of Christian communities. These forms of fictive kinship are no less real or significant than biological kinship. Like all forms of kinship, these fundamental Christian understandings arise as interpretations of conditions that Christians take to be essential to the faith—namely, God's acts of creation and redemption.

Christian kinship is neither more relativist nor more fictional than other patterns of kinship. The evangelical reality of a new kinship in Christ, celebrated in Christian baptism, simply limits both the extent and exclusiveness of biological kinship. Herbert Anderson observes that, in baptism, parents recognize "their children are not their children, for they belong to God who has called them into existence and calls them into service of the world."[12] From a theological perspective, baptism displaces biological parenthood in two important ways: by redefining both who the child belongs to and the boundaries of the child's family. Christian kinship recognizes that the realities of shared humanity and shared baptism run deeper than biological relatedness. Biological relatedness retains theological significance, particularly in the willingness of parents to cooperate with the Creator in bringing new life into the world.[13] Nonetheless, the manner in which humans cooperate with God in biological procreation must be viewed within the larger theological context of God's creative and redemptive grace.

Biblical assertions of God's fidelity as superior to biological ties, joined with commitment to the unity of all believers in Christ, substantiate the theological conviction that all human relationships are fundamentally based in communion with God and others.[14] This reality is not inherently conflictual with biological kin commitments, even as moral claims may at times conflict. Yet natural law arguments have tended to dominate interpretations of the norms of biological relatedness, even as the identity given in baptism can and has been employed to frame these norms. This broader Christian kinship in Christ is more commonly employed to explain extended or irregular kin obligations. This does not suggest a natural primacy of biological kinship so much as a bias toward naturalistic interpretations. The presumption that "real" kinship, and thus "real families," only arise through biological procreation not only unfairly dismisses the social scientific evidence that adoptive families can function as well as biological families but also misinterprets Christian commitments.

No modern magisterial document explicitly claims the necessity of biological kinship for real or true Christian families; in fact, some statements in praise of adoption flatly reject this point of view. Nonetheless, the way adoption so often arises as an exception to the biological norm, or simply as an alternative to immoral means in assisted reproduction, betrays the biological bias of contemporary thinking. Correcting this requires wresting conceptions of family from the primary influences of sexual ethics and gender norms so as to balance the implications of biological relatedness with the evangelical commitments of the faith.

SCRIPTURE AND ANCIENT MEDITERRANEAN CULTURE

Neither the ancient Roman nor Jewish worlds held a direct equivalent for the contemporary idea of the family. The Roman household was multigenerational, extended beyond biological kin, and functioned largely as an economic unit. In Ancient Hebrew, the terms "father's house" and "clan" are the nearest equivalents as they define close and extended biological relations.[15] Of the later Jewish context, Adriana Destro and Mauro Pesce write, "In first-century Galilee, . . . we do not find the 'family' but the household (οίκος), a group that lives together and makes a 'living together.' . . . The focus on households implies attention not only to primary kinship ties but also to communal existence and work, property and power that bind kin and nonkin people."[16]

Throughout the Hebrew Scriptures, God is identified with care for the orphan and widow. In the New Testament, care for the orphan remains an important act of piety,[17] Jesus relativizes kin allegiances, and the metaphor of adoption functions centrally within Pauline soteriology.[18] During the New Testament's composition, a growing identity as kin united by faith through baptism made adopted siblings out of Christian communities.

Kinship in the Hebrew Scriptures is strongly associated with biological relatedness, even as mechanisms for accepting foreigners into the community and assuring care for children in need were also provided.[19] In ancient Israel, Children could be raised by adoptive parents, but their distinction from biological children was preserved. Adopted children were not typically regarded as heirs, and later Jewish law made exceptions for adopted children in mourning the death of adoptive parents and permitted marriage among nonbiological brothers and sisters.[20] When Israel fell under the jurisdiction of the Roman Empire, the more sophisticated Roman legal tradition on adoption had little influence on Jewish law.[21] Adoption as a means of fully integrating a child into a new family was quite literally a foreign concept in ancient Israel.[22]

Diverse caregiving patterns were practiced, but the nearest parallels to legal adoption occurred within families where children were raised by close relatives. In these cases, familial identity, not legal recognition, secured their position and inheritance. This makes both Jesus's propensity for redrawing the lines of kin obligations as well as Paul's use of adoption as a theological concept worthy of attention given that they constitute disruptions of practice.

The New Testament differs from the Hebrew Scriptures in the extensive influence that Greco-Roman society then held within Jewish experience. Although the modern Western concept of adoption joins humanitarian concern for a child's well-being with the legal creation of familial ties, the ancient Jewish world had the former but reserved the latter for biological relations. In contrast, Roman adoption law primarily dealt with creating legal heirs. As such, consenting adult males were common adoptees.[23] When minors were adopted, their level of need, the existence of living relatives, and their own consent were of little consequence. Although this history is largely the story of the upper class, it is clear that at least in Roman legal practice, families were based in but not limited by biological relatedness. Male heads of households had the right to adopt and use this power to set the boundaries of their family.[24]

The ideal household of the Greco-Roman upper class was built on a two-parent family with their children, possibly their children's families, their slaves, and their slaves' families.[25] Substantial differences in age at marriage produced young wives who could outlive their husbands by decades. Meanwhile, childbirth posed a substantial risk that produced many widowers and subsequent remarriages. High mortality rates at all ages assured variations in family form. By early adulthood, most people would have lost their paterfamilias, and many would have lost parents much earlier "At the age of five, the probability of having a father alive was perhaps 88 percent, but by the age of ten this had reduced to about 75 percent, and by the age of fifteen it was about 63 percent. Corresponding figures for mothers were 91, 81, and 72 percent."[26]

Given such variation, rather than a clear nuclear ideal, households were ordered hierarchically based on gender, age, and class.[27] The eldest patrilineal male, the paterfamilias, stood as lord and insurer of good order over all within the household. Wives could hold positions of considerable authority within the family; especially when they controlled a portion of the household's wealth, which a widow might administer for decades after her husband's death.[28] Although physical separations in public and private spaces within the home served to shelter female family members from outside attention, such divisions did not reflect a conceptual differentiation of public-economic and private-familial spheres as came to prominence in more recent Western history.[29] Instead, women's space in the Greco-Roman household was central to economic production.[30] Moreover, Roman mothers of well-to-do families often did not devote themselves to nurturing small children as wet nurses, and other domestic servants assumed most of these tasks.[31] As children grew, their direct oversight transitioned from household servants, to teachers, to custodians while parents exercised a supervisory role.[32] Roman moralists often protested the widespread practice of assigning the care of infants to the lowest rung on the domestic hierarchy, but such arrangements were probably driven by maternal mortality as much as cultural convention.[33] Nonetheless, mothers consistently held a central relational role within the family that helped solidify kin relationships and familial cohesion.[34]

Unlike the flow of authority from the top down, shame moved in both directions. This required paternal supervision of those of lower status (i.e., women, children, and servants) because their misconduct could mar the honor of male kin.[35] At times, and in theory, the authority of the paterfamilias extended even over the lives of those under his care, but circumstances tended to mitigate the exercise of this power. Most men had relatively few years as paterfamilias; for those who did live to an advanced age, adult sons, though still technically under their father's rule, often held separate residences. In practice, newborn infants alone had their lives at the mercy of their father's will. Undesired infants of any class might be exposed (i.e., abandoned in a public space), while the children of slaves were sold freely.[36] Exposed children could die, but they were also taken into slavery, pressed into physical labor or prostitution, or even intentionally mutilated for begging. Some exposed children were also taken in by families, even families of higher classes. To complicate matters, some biological parents subsequently petitioned for the recovery of the children they had exposed.[37]

Burial customs suggest that infants and young children, whose deaths were common, were regarded with much less emotional attachment than adolescents.[38] Still, Roman parents also formed strong emotional bonds with their children, and the deaths of young children were occasionally mourned deeply.[39] The overarching view was that children were primarily a thing to be developed, such that their value depended largely on the willingness of parents to invest in shaping them into respectable adult citizens.[40] Although marriage was understood as being *for* children, the significant investment required for rearing any particular child encouraged limiting family size. As Suzanne Dixon writes, there are many "sober, casual references to the economic and emotional burdens of child-rearing," which indicate "that parenthood was not universally viewed as desirable."[41] The inverse correlation of wealth and family size held as true for first-century Romans as it does today. Family limitation is not generally about devaluing children. Rather, it is associated with "strong sentimental attachment to children and a serious view of the parental role."[42] Among the upper classes, increased economic and social obligations as well as the costs of educating and preparing heirs could increase parental obligations beyond available resources. Near the turn of the first century CE, low fertility rates among the upper class even motivated legislation aimed at reducing celibacy, childlessness, and adultery so as to increase legitimate heirs.[43]

In contrast to Greco-Roman culture, first-century Jewish culture contained much stronger obligations to rear children. Jewish men could be legally compelled to marry, while the status of Jewish wives was tied to the number and gender of their children.[44] The Abrahamic covenant's central connection to offspring gave childbearing religious significance and may have assured relatively better treatment of children within Jewish communities.[45] The concept of children as gifts from God both influenced belief in infertility as divine punishment and provided an understanding of children's inherent value.[46]

New Testament perspectives on the family generally align along two distinct trends. The first is a conditioned acceptance of the hierarchal and patriarchal family structures that prevailed in Greco-Roman society. This accommodationist trend is exemplified most clearly in the household codes of Ephesians and Colossians and eventually came to dominate post–New Testament theological development. The second perspective is far more hostile to culturally supported familial obligations and finds its clearest supports in the Synoptic Gospels. At its greatest extent, Lisa Sowle Cahill claims, Jesus's dichotomy of discipleship and family demands "that family relations be completely repudiated and abandoned."[47] Likewise, Julie Hanlon Rubio observes that Mark 3: 31–35 "proposes a new radical moral standard that threatens the most basic family loyalties and engenders the most difficult conflicts between family and religious commitment."[48]

Cahill argues that the conflicting voices of the New Testament can be reconciled when understood as a critique of power structures and a call to reprioritized commitments. According to Cahill, the New Testament consistently decenters hierarchical relationships and subverts self-interested concepts of family. In her view, even Jesus's use of the term *abba* was essentially antipatriarchal because calling God "father" challenged the role of the paterfamilias.[49] Key to her interpretation is Mark 10: 29–30, in which Jesus includes fathers among those left behind for the sake of the Gospel yet does not again include fathers among those who will be received back in the kingdom (as are brothers, sisters, mothers, children, houses, and fields). Rubio agrees that this absence indicates that the power culturally associated with fatherhood has no place in the coming kingdom.[50]

If Jesus's words are taken to indicate a subversion of the power of fathers, as Cahill claims, Jesus's perspective on mothers remains more complex. Mothers were subordinate to fathers but could still exercise considerable power within the family. Consequently, the authority of mothers, like that of fathers, could conflict with the Gospel. But Jesus's attitude toward motherhood must also be viewed in light of his relatively high regard for women. Although Jesus did not directly confront the gendered hierarchy of household relationships, he often used descriptions of women that would have been extraordinary in his time and broke with accepted norms of female subservience.[51] Likewise, Jesus distanced himself from the Jewish tendency to value women singularly for their procreative maternal roles. Rubio notes, "[Jesus] places the work of the Gospel above this nurturing work, suggesting that nurturing is not to be the primary form of God's word for women who follow him."[52] In response to Mark 3: 31–35, when Jesus's mother and brothers come to interrupt his ministry, Rubio observes that more gracious possibilities existed for halting this intervention. Yet Jesus used the opportunity "to call the whole nature of the kinship bond into question. He says very plainly that those he has gathered round him are his new family, and he seems to deny all loyalty or duty to his family of origin."[53] Consequently, Jesus's words tended to reduce male authority, decouple female obligations from childrearing, and generally relativize the significance of kin obligations based in biological relatedness.[54]

A century before Jesus, Cicero had written that childhood was a condition unworthy of praise and childishness among adults was entirely undesirable.[55] Even among Jews, Jesus's assertion that the kingdom belongs only to those who receive it like a child was extraordinary. Judith Gundry-Volf argues that Jesus "cast judgment on the adult world because it is not the child's world. . . . He invited the children to come to him not so that he might initiate them in the adult realm but that they might receive what is properly theirs—the reign of God."[56] Rubio observes, "To those who thought of children as objects requiring care and formation, Jesus suggests quite plainly that children have qualities adults ought to develop."[57] Moreover, by holding children in his arms, Jesus may have demonstrated the service required of disciples while subverting cultural expectations of children's value.[58]

Although these perspectives call attention to the culturally radical dimensions of Jesus's interactions with children, it is noteworthy that his engagements are not entirely child-centric. Jesus used children primarily as teaching tools, making his actual interactions with children secondary to the message directed to his adult audience. In addition, Jesus's interactions with children usually come at the request of adults (particularly parents requesting healing for children) or are used within the narrative to reveal and clarify Jesus's own identity.[59] Finally, Jesus's apparent prioritization of children may not relate to any essential quality of childhood or children themselves but could be connected primarily to their powerlessness in society.

Also, though there are internal tensions and areas of uncertainty within the New Testament, its pattern of calling biological kinship into question would have stood in significant discontinuity with prevailing Jewish cultural norms. Nonetheless, Jewish tradition before Jesus had already privileged allegiance to God above familial obligations. Though Jesus's words and actions may have been radical, they were not particularly new.

It is difficult to ascertain the degree to which position itself (i.e., fatherhood, motherhood, and childhood) or cultural interpretations of that position's power are being addressed in these critiques.[60] Moreover, the extent of corollary egalitarian ideals in both Jesus's ministry as well as early Christianity remains a matter of dispute.[61] Whatever resolution one finds preferable, Jesus's apparent rejection of dominant cultural interpretations of familial obligations complicates any attempt to read the New Testament as unilaterally profamily or consistently antifamily. The New Testament perspective recognizes potential conflict between familial obligations and faith commitments yet affirms marriage and the dignity of each family member. Moreover, Jesus's ministry itself relied upon households as places of public gathering and teaching as well as centers for hospitality and rest. As John H. Elliott explains, the Gospels primarily assert that "the new primary allegiance of followers of Jesus is 'the new solidarity which consists of the eschatological family of God.'"[62]

EARLY CHRISTIANITY AND PATRISTICS

After the composition of the New Testament, early Christians continued negotiating their religious ideals with prevailing cultural norms.[63] One telling sign of Christianity's divergence from Greco-Roman culture is the new evaluation Christians made of the practice of adoption.[64] Stephen Post argues that the early Christian willingness to allow children to be raised by nonbiological kin when this suited children's interests demonstrates the prioritization of love over biological kinship.[65] Rubio likewise views the willingness to extend kinship as demarcating Christian families from their Roman and Jewish counterparts. She writes, "We know that Jesus's message included the claim that his real family was a Christian community not his mother and his brothers. We know that others noticed that the Christians sometimes left their biological families for their new Christian families. And we know that the Christians were often seen as unpatriotic and immoral, as family-wreckers, because they sometimes refused to give into what was expected of them."[66] Osiek writes, "the Church was considered more and more to be a family, a 'family of families' that claimed the absolute allegiance that the family of origin had previously commanded."[67]

That early Christians understood their kinship in Christ as fundamental is further borne out by early Christian martyrologies.[68] In the *Passion of Perpetua and Felicity*, an account from the early third century, the imprisoned young mother, Perpetua, listens to the pleas of her pagan father as he urges her to avoid death for the sake of her family—especially himself and her infant son. Perpetua remains resolute in seeking martyrdom.[69] Her pregnant companion, Felicity, rejoices when labor comes early, enabling her to be martyred alongside her fellow prisoners.[70] Biological motherhood and Christian martyrdom stand in tension within these accounts even as martyrdom is clearly presented as the more desirable Christian calling. For these female companions, biological kin, including their own children, are portrayed primarily as impediments to their approaching deaths. The conflict is heightened by the apparent ease of avoiding this demise. The opportunity to confess the faith and face martyrdom clearly supersedes obligations to provide direct care for biological children. Arrangements for the future care of their children are made; however, it is only Perpetua's non-Christian father who expresses concern that a child ought to be raised by his biological mother.[71]

In the Greek account of the *Acts of the Martyrs Carpus, Papylus, and Agathonicê*, Papylus claims to have children but later reveals he is speaking of his fellow Christians.[72] In contrast, his sister, Agathonicê, is a biological mother. She is not among the imprisoned destined for execution, but upon seeing their deaths, she confesses her own identity as a Christian. Non-Christian onlookers urge her to take pity on her children and cease agitating for martyrdom. Agathonicê replies that her children have God to watch over them, then leaps to her death atop the fire that has already consumed her companions.[73] Such enthusiasm for death appears to have crossed a line for some early Christians. A longer Latin account places Agathonicê among the imprisoned from the start, allowing her death to follow the form of an execution rather than the enthusiastic suicide portrayed in the Greek text.

Minimally, these martyrologies demonstrate a tradition of skepticism toward familial obligations within early Christianity while placing concern for biological kinship, particularly motherhood, in the mouths of pagans. Such views stand in marked contrast to 1 Timothy's counsel that women "be saved through childbearing—if they continue in faith, love and holiness with propriety,"[74] as well as the Pastoral Epistles' apparent counsel for greater cultural conformity in domestic affairs.[75] For these female martyrs, biological motherhood appears as a relatively minor consideration in comparison with their commitment to the Christian faith. That they were recognized as examples of faith through stories recorded to inspire later generations of Christians further validates the significance of their views.

The second-century apocryphal text *The Acts of Paul and Thecla* also evidences early Christian willingness to prioritize faith over familial commitments. In this account of Paul's journeys, his female companion, Thecla, leaves her fiancé to join Paul in his missionary work and commits to a life of celibacy.[76] Thecla's decision foreshadows the rise of consecrated virgins and women religious, which challenged prevailing notions of kin obligations in both Greco-Roman and Jewish culture while affording women a means of valuation distinct from their procreative abilities. Such developments were also fueled by a distrust of the body and sexuality. Rosemary Radford Ruether observes that the early centuries of Christianity saw "a gradual synthesis between patriarchy and celibacy."[77] Bearing children not only complicated total commitment to the faith but also, in a religious culture increasingly enamored with celibacy, was a clear sign of having given into the body's sexual appetites.

Christianity grew in prominence during the fourth century, as did the ideal of sexual renunciation. Clerical celibacy had been decreed by regional councils since the late third century and Siricius (334–99), who served as bishop of Rome, advocated for a celibate clergy, among both married and unmarried clerics, as did many of his successors throughout the fifth century.[78] With respect to the religious life, Peter Brown writes, "When Simplicia, a Roman nun, died in middle age, all that needed to be said of her was that 'she took no heed to produce children, treading beneath her feet the body's snares.'"[79] For Ambrose of Milan (340–97), sexuality was evidence of human sinfulness that stood in glaring contrast to Christ's purity.[80] Rejection of the body's desires was intimately tied to service to Christ and freedom from the demands of family. Ambrose held that it was good for parents to encourage vocations of celibacy but more noble when a child is drawn against parental will. He portrayed the pressures and enticements of parents against a life of virginity as mere training for overcoming earthly temptations. Moreover, he counseled the would-be vowed virgin, "conquer family-loyalty first, my girl: if you overcome the household, you overcome the world."[81] Even starker expression is found in the asceticism of Ambrose's contemporary Jerome (347–420), for whom human sexuality formed women and men into perpetual and mutual sources of temptation for each other.[82] Jerome's disdain for all things sexual, which led him to question if even martyrdom could remove the "dirt of marriage,"[83] marked an outer edge that was not embraced by many of his co-religionists, even in an era shaped by fascination with virginal purity.[84]

Considered alongside these near-contemporaries, Augustine of Hippo's (354–430) apprehensive view of human sexuality and limited affirmation of Christian marriage appear as an achievement in moderation. What distinguished Augustine's approach was his conviction that human bodies and their sexual faculties were aspects of God's created order, not consequences of humanity's fall. Earlier authors had written of Adam and Eve as nearly angelic beings devoid of such bodily impediments as genitalia, while many Christians viewed biological reproduction as in conflict with the Gospel. Augustine observed that God had commanded Adam and Eve to procreate before the fall, clearly implying a place for prelapsarian sexuality.[85] In so doing, he reconciled sexual capacities with the goodness of creation and was able to present marriage as a form of friendship fit for the communion of the redeemed.[86] Augustine's perspective removed the apparent conflict between procreation and salvation but, as Brown observes, came at the expense of transferring anxiety inwardly. It was no longer humanity as such that required explanation but the deeply distorted human will. For Augustine and beyond, "The twisted human will, not marriage, not even the sexual drive, was what was new in the human condition after Adam's fall."[87]

Augustine's contemporary in the East, John Chrysostom (347–407), who served as bishop of Constantinople, had once been persuaded that Christian children ought to be raised in monasteries but through pastoral experiences became convinced that the family held the principal responsibility for forming children in faith and morality.[88] Despite the preoccupations of his Western contemporaries, Chrysostom indicates little desire to justify the existence of sexuality or marriage. Instead, he gave these broadly positive interpretations and devoted his greatest attention to the moral problem of greed.[89] Chrysostom understood the family as a center of charity in response to the Christian obligations to proclaim the Gospel and serve the poor. In recognition of this mission parallel to the Church, Chrysostom described the family as the "domestic church." Like the larger Church, the domestic Christian community was based upon the communal nature of salvation, with children being the nearest of social relations. Chrysostom was also acutely aware of the tendency for families to become self-serving and for parents to neglect their Christian duties.[90] In response, he placed so much weight on parental obligations, which he viewed as parallel to Christ's own task for all humanity, that he tied the salvation of parents to the virtues of their children.[91] In his view, parents are artists who carefully sculpt their children so as to restore God's image within them and, as such, are responsible for their work.[92]

THE MIDDLE AGES AND THE REFORMATION

As the Middle Ages progressed, more stable Christian ideals of family life emerged, and households across social strata became increasingly uniform and centered on kin relations.[93] Augustinian notions of original sin, joined with admiration for virginity, informed a low religious valuation of procreation, while a willingness to renounce family and children for the sake of the faith remained a consistent theme in medieval hagiographies.[94] Christian society generally maintained a higher valuation of young children than had been common in Greco-Roman society, while medieval literature offered images of pure and innocent children with "an ability to seize on truths hidden from adults."[95] The practice of exposure continued, but historians disagree on its frequency, both overall and relative to earlier eras.[96] The best historical sources are sermons and legislative codes that provide little evidence of actual prevalence.[97] What is clear, however, is that Christian leaders placed moral concern at an earlier stage than had Greco-Roman society, such that concern for life extended from contraception to abortion to infanticide and child abandonment.[98] These moral considerations were also influenced by an Augustinian understanding of sexuality that justified sexual intercourse only through procreation, such that concern for prenatal life and repulsion at sex for pleasure's sake were inseparably intermingled. In fact, many Christian warnings against contraception within marriage were simply recycled Roman tropes against contraception for the purposes of concealing infidelity.[99] Moreover, such admonitions frequently came from the mouths or pens of celibate male clerics such that the extent of their actual influence on long-accepted patterns of family limitation is very uncertain.

Christian parents almost certainly felt moral conflicts in their practices of family limitation, but the decline of social structures in the postimperial West also likely increased pressures to limit family size. Although their attitudes toward abandonment may not have been markedly different from those of Roman times, two uniquely Christian concerns emerged: greater attention to the conditions that drove parents to abandon children, and a widespread belief that care for orphans was a concrete act of Christian charity.[100] Byzantium established public institutions for care, such as the Orphanotropheion, in the early medieval period.[101] However, Western Europe remained far more agrarian and neither felt the same population pressures nor had the organizational capacities of the more urbanized East until the late medieval period. Instead, monasteries served as social resources for abandoned children. The sixth-century Rule of Saint Benedict offers several directions for childcare (most often concessions made for the young) and gives no indication of this being an exceptional practice.[102] The rules of some other medieval religious communities even required a minimum number of orphans within the community.[103]

The majority of children whose parents could not provide for them found care among kin. Biological relatives could be legally bound to provide such care, a custom dating back to Roman law. The Western Church's growing obsession with consanguinity also led to extensive mapping of kin relations and generally assured that some obligated party would be found.[104] This same concern for consanguinity may have exacerbated the decline of clan structures that had been traditionally supported by endogamous marriages; and in doing so, it reshaped understandings of extended kinship across Western Europe. As traditional kin systems declined, the High Middle Ages initiated a new appreciation of individual freedom over and against family intentions.[105] With respect to parenthood, Anselm of Canterbury (c. 1030–1109) counseled parents to provide children with affection, gentleness, mercy, and similar comforts. Within a century, he became a favored source for preaching on children and childrearing.[106] With respect to children, medieval hagiographic literature alternately "praises absolute filial obedience and rewards independent mindedness."[107]

Medieval Christians saw the position of the Fourth Commandment, to honor mother and father, as a clear sign of its foundational importance as it marks the transition of ordinances directed toward God to those directed toward others. As the first among the list of social commands, it can be presumed as foundational to social morality. Indeed, this command comes before such basic social principles as the prohibition of stealing and killing. Nonetheless, the extent of its import was disputed.[108] John of La Rochelle (c. 1200–1245) argued that the positive phrasing of this commandment demonstrates that giving honor to parents is never wrong.[109] However, La Rochelle also asserted a hierarchy that placed entry into religious life above acquiescence to specific parental demands. There was, he argued, no true conflict, because "the prayers of a vowed religious will, in the long run, do parents more good than providing them with food and drink."[110] His younger contemporary, Thomas Aquinas (c. 1224–74), disagreed and argued that care for ailing parents prohibits acceptance into religious life.

Aquinas supported sweeping parental rights and believed that parents, especially fathers, deserve full credit for their children's success or failure. Parental rights extended to include betrothal or committing a child to a religious order but stopped just short of vows, as he also held adult consent to be essential in such decisions.[111] Foundational to these claims was Aquinas's belief that the work of procreation establishes the natural rights of parents.

Just as the craftsman rightfully owns that which he creates, so too does the parent.[112] Such an approach might have suggested greater maternal rights in proportion to the female reproductive role, but Aquinas instead centralized paternal authority based on a theory of shared substance.[113] Informed by the Aristotelean theory of fetal development, Aquinas understood the male semen as the essential procreative substance.[114] This "seed" required only the protection of a mother's womb to develop into a full human person.[115] Children, in Aquinas's view, are a literal extension of their father, who is thereby naturally invested in their future.[116] Aquinas held that his strong interpretation of parental rights and obligations constituted universal moral law due to it foundations in both nature and reason. Consequently, he twice argued that baptizing a Jewish child against parental will is a greater sin than allowing the child to die unbaptized. Furthermore, he argued that the primary evil of fornication was not sexual sin but the failure to assure the well-being of potential future children. In Aquinas's era, an illegitimate child would not only be deprived of the paternal influence that Aquinas held so central but also faced the possibilities of abandonment and poverty and had no right to inheritance or priestly ordination.[117] Aquinas's argument both reinforced patriarchal authority and solidified paternal duties at a time when the lives of children were quite perilous. Relative political stability, expanding agriculture, a warmer climate, and a host of other factors supported considerable population growth throughout the High and Late Middle Ages. This expansion came at a cost as rates of child mortality may have reached 50 percent during Aquinas's lifetime. These were driven by crude and unsanitary medical practices and "high rates of abandonment, exposure, infanticide, overly harsh beatings, fatal 'trials' of suspected changelings, and suspicious overlaying of children in bed."[118]

Aquinas's view leaves little room for equally strong obligations based in nonbiological kinship in general or nonbiological parenthood in particular.[119] The extent to which Aquinas's assertions reflect actual practice is worth questioning given his own background, which includes years spent in monastic care and rebellion against his family's wishes, as well as diverse practices of caregiving in the medieval world. Beyond the orphaned and abandoned, many children had nonbiological caregivers even while their biological parents remained responsible for them. Such practices reflect the realities of family life and the need for all adults to participate in the family economy. Both mothers and fathers worked fields, tended livestock, slaughtered, harvested, prepared food, produced essential and saleable goods, and operated businesses to support their family. Because sustenance required female work, women were not singularly associated with childcare. Instead, these myriad obligations supported the common assumption that any reasonably capable adult could provide care for children. This belief was experientially proven by the central role that grandparents, siblings, and wet-nurses commonly played in childcare.[120] In addition, children were often sent away for schooling or apprenticeships. In both instances, care providers were selected based on their functional capabilities and the needs of the family and child.

Throughout the Late Middle Ages, Christian piety turned increasingly to the needs of children. By the Reformation era, interest in childrearing had united with a general concern for morality and discipline.[121] Despite the dramatic religious, social, and political changes of the era, the Protestant reformers tended to replicate their Catholic counterparts in their concern for good order, community, and education.[122] Aquinas had seen childhood as an undesirable time when limited rationality reduced children to little more than animals.[123] As such, concerted development through diligent parenthood was required to bring children into the full rational powers of adulthood.[124] Desiderius Erasmus (1466–1536) echoed this concern, writing that "the child that nature has given you is nothing but a shapeless lump, the material is still pliable, capable of assuming any form, and you must so mould it that it takes on the best possible character. If you are negligent, you will rear an animal; but if you apply yourself, you will fashion, if I may use such a bold term, a godlike creature."[125] Both Martin Luther (1483–1546) and Jon Calvin (1509–64) similarly stressed the importance of parental involvement, as well as the wonderful and monstrous possibilities of childhood. This broad agreement on the importance and demandingness of the work of parenting is also evident in abundant comparisons with horticulture and animal husbandry. But concerted parenthood also easily shifted between a tabula rasa view of the child to a decidedly more pessimistic view that imagined all manner of evil desires lurking within the hearts of even the youngest children. The mid–sixteenth century English philosopher Thomas Beccon, for example, writes that "a child in Scripture is a wicked man, as he that is ignorant and not exercised in godliness.'"[126]

Erasmus, like other Renaissance humanists, called attention to "the importance of infancy and early childhood in the development of good Christians and good citizens."[127] He published a series of books and essays on the topic, drawing heavily from classical sources.[128] His greatest concern was that early education not be postponed by either the coddling of female caregivers or the negligence of fathers. This emphasis stemmed from his belief that young children have an innate desire to learn and are capable of absorbing information at a greater rate than in subsequent ages. He encouraged parents to take control of their children's education, and he saw rationality and self-control as instilled in children by the hard work of parents and educators.[129] However, he clearly distinguished himself from those who emphasized original sin, arguing instead that adults are often culpable for corrupting young minds.[130] Further, he was horrified by the practice of beating children and lamented the existence of schools, which were supposed centers of education but were in reality centers of "brutal abuse."[131]

Like Aquinas, Luther was a strong supporter of broad parental rights. He writes that "there is no greater or nobler authority on earth than that of parents over their children, for this authority is both spiritual and temporal."[132] He even asserted a lack of parental consent as grounds for dissolving a marriage.[133] He agreed with Augustine that the very first duty of Christian parents is to have children baptized quickly, and he further described parents as "apostles and bishops" of their children.[134] Like Chrysostom, Luther saw proximity as differentiating the parental vocation from the common vocation of Christians. That is, the obligation to care for children is grounded in them being their parents' nearest neighbors in need.[135] Luther writes,

> Now you tell me, when a father goes ahead and washes diapers or performs some other mean task for his child, and someone ridicules him as an effeminate fool, . . . my dear fellow you tell me, which of the two is more keenly ridiculing the other? God, with all his angels and creatures, is smiling—not because that father's washing diapers, but because he is doing so in Christian faith. Those who sneer at him and see only the task but not the faith are ridiculing God with all his creatures, as the biggest fool on earth.[136]

Although Luther clearly upholds dominant views of gender roles, these are relativized in light of the demands of Christian faith, such that those who ridicule transgressions of gender motivated by Christian charity make themselves the fools.

Luther's view of the family, through the paradigm of neighbor love, also demanded parenthood to extend to all Christians as all are equally compelled by faith to attend to those in need. Notably, his own experience of parenthood included raising several children from among his kin. Like adults, he viewed children as inherent and culpable sinners who are offered salvific grace through baptism.[137] In fact, he supported infant baptism precisely on the grounds that children are incapable of reason and therefore free of its uncertainties.[138] Like adults, the baptized child shares in the conditions necessary for salvation and faithful discipleship. Consequently, Christian children have a duty to bear witness, through Christian service and love, to the salvific grace of baptism.[139]

Calvin's emphasis on the depravity of the human condition led him to argue that "even infants bear their condemnation with them from their mother's womb." Despite not having yet sinned, "they have the seed enclosed within themselves. Indeed, their whole nature is a seed of sin; thus it cannot be but hateful and abominable to God."[140] Yet Calvin also believed that children have active spiritual lives, such that even infants can proclaim God's goodness.[141] Furthermore, he disagreed with Luther and Augustine on the central importance of the ritual of baptism, and instead urged Christian parents to trust that God's mercy would extend salvation to their unbaptized children. Calvin's confidence rested in his commitment to salvation residing entirely in the absolutely free judgment of God.[142]

Despite its domestically conservative bent, the Reformation initiated reappraisals of the Christian home and education. Protestants came to see the family "as a microcosm of the church and the state, both in the sense that in its internal government it should marry those larger institutions, and in the sense that the family should be a nursery of both the church and state."[143] The ideal of the private family also began to emerge during this time, as evidenced by Luther's view of the home as a safe haven for the formation of children in the faith.[144] Within the patriarchal standards of the day, placing this importance on the family also increased emphasis on paternal responsibility. Fathers assumed central importance in managing the family, while mothers were to be virtuous and honorable.[145] By the seventeenth century, the ideal Protestant family was a "little commonwealth" governed by paternal authority and populated with obedient, submissive children. Catholicism lagged but eventually underwent similar developments as Catholic literature gave increasing attention to parental duties, paternal authority, and the domestic sphere as a place of affection requiring a pious mother.[146]

THE MODERN PERIOD

In the late seventeenth century, the leading figure of the Enlightenment, John Locke (1632–1704), was among the first to approach childrearing from a principally secular perspective, choosing to argue through "natural rights" with little reference to Christian scripture.[147] Locke emphasized the importance of teaching children submission to authority, so that as adults they would learn to submit to the authority of their own reason.[148] Both Locke and his near contemporary Thomas Hobbes (1588–1679) argued in favor of human equality and opposed associations of political authority with the patriarchal family. In contrast, Robert Filmer (1588–1653) held that patriarchal headship within the family and monarchal political authority are of a shared kind and mutually supportive. Sandra Sullivan-Dunbar reports that, in Filmer's view, "God had granted Adam absolute political authority in the Garden of Eden, and this authority had been passed down biologically from father to son, such that contemporary monarchs partook in the original grant of authority via 'natural' lines of fatherhood and sonship. In other words, paternal and political forms of authority were identical in essence, based on natural kinship ties, and profoundly hierarchical."[149]

Across the Atlantic, Jonathan Edwards (1703–58) soon came to prominence as a powerful conservative Protestant voice who likewise feared the collapse of traditional patriarchy authority.[150] Not only was paternal authority in decline, but the increasingly industrial economy now also allowed children to relocate far from their parents' home and oversight.[151] Sullivan-Dunbar describes how industrialization brought about a reversal whereby positive recognition of vital social interdependencies was transformed into stigmatization of the "weak," while the worrisome reckless and antisocial issues about independence were transformed into a social virtue to which all should aspire. Views of wage labor likewise shifted from earlier scorn for it as "wage slavery" to recognition of it as a pathway to independence. Inversely, the formerly positive social value of dependence, which was central to good order in patriarchal society, assumed negative associations with those excluded from wage labor.[152]

Against this turning tide, Edwards vigorously reclaimed traditional Protestant doctrines while reveling in descriptions of hellfire. Whereas Augustine had wrestled with the damnation of unbaptized infants before finally conceding to its necessity, and Calvin had avoided the same conclusion by counseling trust in God's sovereignty, Edwards embraced the doctrine and described it as "exceedingly just."[153] Edwards wrote, "As innocent as children seem to us, . . . if they are out of Christ, they are not so in God's sight, but are young vipers, and are infinitely more hateful than vipers."[154] Yet, by centralizing salvation at the expense of any natural rights, Edwards's vision gave a redeemed child the upper hand over unredeemed parents.[155] Thus Edwards relativized the authority of parents even as he lamented and sought to reverse the breakdown of the patriarchal family.

Although Edwards resisted social change in America, back in Europe, the Romantics welcomed it. In direct opposition to Edwards's defense of paternal authority, John-Jacques Rousseau (1712–78) promoted the priority of mothers within the family. Throughout the eighteenth century, romantic ideals mixed with changing social and economic circumstances to solidify childrearing as a distinctly feminine competence. Into the early nineteenth century, both men and women were still assumed to be capable of childcare, at least in a basic sense. By midcentury, these capabilities had come to be understood as the exclusive domain of women.[156] As work moved outside the home, combining economic participation, caregiving, and domestic chores became more difficult. And as children spent more years in formal education and less contributing to the family's economy, men's and women's spheres became increasingly focused on, respectively, economic production and household maintenance. Moreover, with growing life expectancy, elder care also increased, leading to an aggregate increase in caregiving demands.[157]

Still, it is important to keep in mind that such transitions were largely race- and class-based phenomena. As Christina Traina points out, in 1870, while the "angel of the house" feminine ideal was growing, "Black married women were almost eight times as likely to work for pay as White married women" throughout the cities of the northern United States.[158]

As children of the White and financially stable transitioned from economic assets to liabilities, they also gained sentimental value. In the late eighteenth century, popular Christian writing portrayed children as filled with evil intentions, which could only be curbed by severe discipline.[159] By the nineteenth century, the innocence of childhood had gained prominence. As the future cardinal John Henry Newman (1800–1890) wrote, a child has come recently from the hands of God "with all the lessons and thoughts of heaven freshly marked upon him."[160]

In this context, the Protestant theologian Horace Bushnell (1802–76) developed a positive Christian developmental approach to childhood. He famously advised, "the child is to grow up a Christian, never knowing himself as being otherwise."[161] Bushnell emphasized parental involvement, trusted in the "near salvific power of a godly mother," and stressed children's pliability and helplessness in the face of negative adult influences.[162] Bushnell's contemporary Catherine Beecher, the author of the influential book *Religious Training of Childhood,* simply denied the possibility of original sin in children.[163] Such views were initially dismissed among more conservative Evangelicals; but by the end of the nineteenth century, American churches across denominations had "settled into a regular package of weekly Sunday school instruction and family devotions, not dire warnings about infants being consumed by the fires of hell."[164]

This social and historical context would prove informative for Pope Leo XIII as he penned the first modern encyclicals on marriage and the education of children. Here, traditional concerns for parental care mixed with uniquely modern conceptions of femininity, childhood, and the family. Leo's presentation of the family also gives little indication of the diverse and negotiated patterns of childrearing that had continued throughout the modern period and into his own day. Perhaps closest to home was the dramatic action of his immediate predecessor, Pius IX, who in 1958 took a young Jewish child, Edgardo Mortara, into his own care. As an infant, Mortara had been baptized by a Catholic servant who feared he was near death. After the report surfaced, the boy was seized from his Jewish parents. Although Aquinas had argued that a Jewish child should not be baptized against parental consent, the Papal States legally prohibited Christian children from being reared by Jewish parents. Having been made a Christian through baptism, this identity was judged as superseding the natural rights of non-Christian biological parents. Despite international outrage, Mortara was raised under the protection of Pius IX and eventually became a priest.[165] Setting aside the many serious moral questions about Pius's action, it is important to note that though contemporary teaching emphasizes the importance of complimentary gendered, biological, married parents for children's healthy development, *this exact criterion was dismissed* just over 150 years ago in favor of kinship in Christ. As with the early martyrs, it was primarily those outside the Church who cried foul against this violation of biological kinship, while Pius IX remained resolute in his actions.[166]

The long history of orphan care and boarding schools run by religious communities throughout Western Christian history constitutes another form of nonbiological care for children within primarily single-sex settings.[167] As institutionalized care grew in the West from the fifteenth century onward, overcrowding led to high mortality rates.[168] By the mid–eighteenth century, École Française de Rome reports, "death rates at the Milan asylum and in the newer infant orphanages in Paris and Vienna were approaching 80 percent of the babies left in their care."[169] Although these numbers are appalling, Annelies van Heijst reminds that such religious institutions voluntarily shouldered a share of a much larger social problem.[170]

In Heijst's analysis of the Ursulines in Amsterdam from the nineteenth century to the twentieth century, she reports the women assumed a dual self-identification. In relation to the children in their care, they imagined themselves as mothers, within a framework of "true" motherhood based on spiritual love through Christ. This motherhood experienced all the joys and sorrows of biological motherhood but remained unstained by biological or personal attachment. One advertisement for the congregation read: "And now it is precisely the love of God, to whom the religious dedicates her entire life and all her works, that gives you the power to do this beautiful and abundant work. In this work of charity she can make use of her female skills, which are aimed at motherhood, to be used to the child *and yet keep her entire heart free for God*."[171]

Simultaneously they also imagined themselves as children; especially in relation to the male clergy.[172] The child metaphor permeated their entire spirituality and may have assisted the sisters in building solidarity with the unrelated children in their care.[173] Like many religious men and women before them, these women self-selected into caregiving practices driven by a religious commitment to alleviating social needs and for the sake of the children themselves.

In the nineteenth-century United States, crowding in Eastern cities led to the formation of orphan asylums by religious and secular organizations.[174] By the Civil War, major shifts had occurred in American conceptions of children and the family, influenced by thinkers like Bushnell, who extolled the virtues of the family and labeled all other childrearing environments "artificial." Simultaneously, paternal authority was reduced by the growing view that women had a natural capacity for childrearing.[175] But in postbellum American cities, overcrowding of asylums was a growing problem, partially due to successes in reducing child mortality. Charles Loring Brace, influenced by the English practice of "transportation," devised a system of orphan transportation utilizing the rapidly growing railway system to the western frontier.[176] From the mid–nineteenth century to the early twentieth century, "orphan trains" placed more than 200,000 children with families to the West.[177] Several additional Protestant organizations soon replicated Brace's system.

Brace's model married a Protestant work ethic with social charity. Older boys where especially desired by rural families in need of additional laborers. Indenturing remained a common and legally permissible practice in many western states; and because Brace's system relied primarily on verbal contracts, foster parents could obtain indenture after accepting a child.[178] Placed children deserted their homes with relative frequency such that replacing children was a common task. Additionally, because foster parents were not arranged beforehand, children were displayed for public evaluation by potential parents. Farmers in need of laborers were allowed to ask children to perform or scrutinize children's physical features, and children had their nationality, background, and other personal information read aloud.[179] Although they would accept children from Catholic parents, Protestant systems placed them with Protestant families.[180] Moreover, most Protestant systems would not accept Italian and Slavonic children even as the Irish were prized for their ambiguous Northern European features.[181]

In 1866, Catholic bishops gathered in Baltimore lamented how Catholic children were being transported to western homes to be "brought up in ignorance of, and most commonly in hostility to, the religion in which they had been baptized."[182] Segregation from the dominant Protestant culture still constituted an important aspect of the American Catholic identity but required self-sufficiency among Catholics that was stressed by each new wave of immigration.[183] In 1869, the New York Foundling Hospital, which was operated by the Sisters of Charity of Saint Vincent de Paul, began what became the most prominent Catholic system of orphan transportation.[184] In contrast to Brace's system, which did not generally place babies due to the challenges of their transportation (including their potential to cause a ruckus with eager parents at train platforms), the Foundling Hospital preferred infants and young children. Local clergy arranged homes before transportation, and an identification number was then sent to the new parents and stitched to the children's collars.[185]

Even with this level of coordination, children still faced a good deal of physical labor, and not all placements could be sustained.[186] Correspondence reveals that adoptees were often treated unequally in comparison with biological children and were frequently subject to criticism.[187] It is also unclear what information was being shared by the institutions with the parents on either end. Many receiving parents were probably not aware that the majority of children being relocated had at least one living parent and had been surrendered as a result of poverty, inability, unwed motherhood, or broken marriages.[188] Back in the East, institutions avoided acknowledging the true perils of rural farm life, which was liberally idealized.[189]

The orphan train system was also predominantly a White phenomenon. Records from the Foundling and the Children's Aid Society indicate that children of African, Chinese, Slavonic, or Spanish descent were placed at dismally low rates.[190] One infamous episode unfolded in 1904, when a French Catholic priest in Arizona arranged placement of about forty children of Irish descent with working-class Hispanic families.[191] The spectacle so agitated the local White Protestants that a mob soon abducted the children. When the Foundling attempted to reclaim the children, local residents refused to cooperate. The ensuing legal battle ended in the Supreme Court, which upheld the confiscation of the children and overrode the Foundling's claim to guardianship.[192] As in the Mortara case, also on US soil, ethnicity and religion again combined to justify child abduction under a Christian interpretation.

Both Protestant and Catholic orphan train systems relied upon religious responses to social need and operated under the assumption that placing children with Christian strangers served the best interest of the child, even when many had known living parents. Yet denominational and racial divisions reveal the operative limits of this nonbiological Christian kin-making within nineteenth-century America.

The history of African American kin structures provides another unique and noteworthy source for Christian conceptions of kinship beyond these predominantly White histories. African Americans have had to repeatedly respond to family fragmentation caused by weighty and intrusive external forces. Enslaved Africans and their descendants held no control over their family's future within a system that denied rights to marriage and citizenship along with degrading their very status as human persons. Slaves were often bought and sold without serious regard for family units, and sexual contact with female slaves could be coerced by male slaveholders, rendering sexual exclusivity beyond a slave's control.[193] Such liaisons gave rise to many mixed-race children, who typically inherited the social status of their mothers.[194]

In West African cultures, knowledge of one's kinship and lineage had been highly valued, but the repeated disruptions of family units in the lives of slaves led to uncertainty of lasting contact among biological relations as well as control in reproduction itself. Consequently, American slaves redefined kinship as a feature of the enslaved community itself.[195] This sustained a broad kin network despite conditions that undermined particular attachments. Unlike early Christians martyrs and medieval saints, American slaves did not voluntarily disavow biological kin, but in the absence of these bonds similarly responded by utilizing a nonbiological reinterpretation.

With slavery's end, kin networks took on new forms in response to the possibility of stable family units. During the Reconstruction Era and into the early twentieth century, Black women's experiences and issues differed markedly from those of the leaders of the nascent feminist movement, which grew among upper- and middle-class White women. Instead of seeking freedom from domesticity, African American women sought to withdraw from the workforce for the sake of their families. Unlike Whites, the vast majority of Black women had always worked. Now paid employment for Black men provided a chance at motherhood without full-time participation in the workforce. However, the conditions of male employment repeatedly limited this possibility. African American men often received salaries sufficient to sustain a family, but opportunities were limited and they were far more vulnerable to layoffs and unemployment than their White counterparts. This instability led the majority of African American mothers to assume low-paying but steady jobs in service work.[196] As the majority of African American mothers worked full time outside the home through the dawn of the Civil Rights Movement, they continued to rely upon the support of extended kin networks, biological or not. At times, temporary arrangements for childcare led to long-term informal adoption.[197] The impact of this history remains embedded in contemporary African American communities, where grandmothers, aunts, and other women are frequently referred to by maternal names such as "momma."[198] Patricia Hill Collins explains, "Fluid and changing boundaries often distinguish biological mothers from other women who care for children. Biological mothers, or bloodmothers, are expected to care for their children. But African and African American communities have also recognized that vesting one person with full responsibility for mothering a child may not be wise or possible. As a result, 'othermothers'—women who assist blood mothers by sharing mothering responsibilities—traditionally have been central to the institution of Black motherhood."[199]

Throughout, African American conceptions of kinship have proven resilient in response to social conditions that often destroyed the autonomy and privacy of biological families despite the growing Western cultural ideal of private, nuclear families centered on a mother's care and nurture. Biological kinship was not devalued, a fact supported by the former slaves who invested great effort in locating biological kin and the African American mothers who later sought to free themselves from employment in order to be present in the home.[200] Nonetheless, communal forms of nonbiological kinship took root within African American communities and sustained many through difficult circumstances.

CONCLUSION

Although this sketch of history does little justice to the full depth and complexity of the Christian tradition, it has attempted to highlight and explain key historical realities that point to greater diversity than contemporary Catholic conceptions of the family typically acknowledge. Diverse and competing conceptions of kinship, familial obligations, children, and parenthood have emerged and reemerged among Christians across various sociohistorical contexts. For example, conceptions of children have ranged from innate sinners to inert matter in need of concerted parental formation to near-angelic gifts from God. Family limitation has shifted from broadly acceptable patterns of abandonment through exposure to informal care among kin to highly formalized care through institutions or legal adoption.

In response to their faith, Christians have both denied their own parental obligations and willingly accepted parental responsibilities for unrelated children, and at times have even forcefully taken children from other parents. Responsibility for childrearing has shifted from parents to all of society to mothers and fathers within uniquely gendered roles. Parental authority has moved between strong assertions of parental power to its contingency in light of the demands of faith. Paternal authority in particular has been displaced from near-absolute control over children and the household to questioning male competence in household affairs and childrearing in light of women's innate propensity and competence in such matters. Differing accounts of parental obligations have also arisen. For both Chrysostom and Luther, Christian charity and the obligation to serve neighbors in need are important features of the family's cohesion, whereas for Aquinas the family is grounded in the natural bonds of kinship and obligations arising from procreation.

Despite these significant differences, Christians throughout history have largely recognized and attempted to balance both the natural and evangelical dimensions of Christian kinship. Although some have moved to one extreme or the other, most views have negotiated these tensions. Even Aquinas's commitment to natural law, for instance, gave way to a nonbiologically based argument for parental obligations, while Luther's evangelical commitments also acknowledged the family as a "critical order of creation within God's temporal governance."[201] Though kinship based on biological ties has often been central, kinship in the faith has also served as a powerful resource to support and extend practices of care.

The present emphases and patterns of modern Catholic family teaching reflect the historical conditions and moral concerns of its own origins. Throughout history, it is abundantly clear that the moral interests of social and religious leaders have rarely reflected the full dimensions and negotiated complexities of actual family life. Modern family teaching has encouraged a narrow focus on two-parent families, with restricted roles for mothers in particular, despite much more expansive historical precedents. Much in historical Christian practice, modern magisterial teaching, and contemporary Catholic theology suggests a priority of biological kinship. However, functional ways of approaching caregiving based on the needs of families, children, and social conditions have arisen with enough historical consistency to demonstrate the possibility of superseding biological kinship without necessarily devaluing it. Christian kinship—whether arising from biology, baptism, communal identity, or social commitment—is always a theologically interpreted reality. Although the fact of biological relatedness has often held precedence, convictions more central to the Gospel have also provided the fundamental realities from which caregiving practices are explained. As such, parenthood is a reality that is in some sense both given and accepted.

Moreover, the gender roles that characterize contemporary Catholic thought on the family appear as little more than recent innovations against the larger backdrop of history. Although there are sources that support innate characteristics of each gender as well as the unique complementarity of man and woman, there are equally sources that demonstrate how contemporary understandings of gender and complementarity are indebted to their position within history as much as any innate qualities of men and women. The dominance of motherhood in conceptions of parenthood has emerged relatively recently alongside the understanding that only men are naturally suited for wage labor. Also recent is the idea that nonbiological caregiving arrangements are somehow regrettable and "artificial" replications of a more basic biological nuclear pattern.

Without undermining the significance of biological kinship or married partners in parenthood, we must recognize that Christian parenthood relies upon a willingness to form kinship through commitment to the common bond of baptism and recognition of a common human identity as children of God. As such, an anthropological account of parenthood cannot be reduced to gender or sexual behavior but instead is rooted in the common human capacities to recognize the needs of others and respond through a particularly parental form of solidarity. Parenthood, as a theological-anthropological reality, is rooted as much in the common human origin in God as in the common vocation of all Christians given in baptism.

NOTES

1. See Ruether, *Christianity*.
2. Ruether, 5.
3. Marshall Sahlins describes a variety of conditions that lead to kinship across cultures. Beyond marriage and biological relatedness, these include shared land, shared food, and shared memories. Sahlins, *What Kinship Is*, 89.
4. Sahlins, 6–8.
5. Sahlins, 77.
6. Oord, "Morals," 288–89.
7. Monroe, "Explanations," 162.
8. E.g., it may well be argued that humans have a natural tendency toward selfishness. Though this may be true, the fact alone does not sustain the conclusion that humans ought to be selfish. Instead, a moral interpretation that considers both the state of what is and convictions about what ought to be must be undertaken. This differs from a strict naturalist ethic, which attempts to limit but can never fully excise such interpretive judgments. The Christian concept of sin has often played an important explanatory role in accounting for the gap between these realities.
9. Jussen, *Spiritual Kinship*, 17.
10. Jussen, 33.
11. The idea that common human kinship is largely fictive is increasingly being undermined by genetic studies that demonstrate just how closely related the entire human family actually is. All people of European descent share a single common ancestor (i.e., a single

individual appearing in all lineages) only about 600 years ago. All living humans have a common ancestor only about 3,600 years ago. Rutherford, *Brief History*, 161–64.
12. Ostdiek, "More Than a Family Affair," 201.
13. Paul VI, *Humanae vitae*, sec. 8.
14. Ps. 27:10, Isa. 49:15, Gal. 3:28, etc.
15. Dearman, "Family," paras. 1–5.
16. Destro and Pesce, "Fathers," 212.
17. Care for the orphans is described as the mark of true religion in James 1:27. Additional references to the weak or needy may be inferred to include the orphaned or abandoned. See Matt. 6:1–4, Acts 20:35, etc.
18. Rom. 8:15, Gal. 4:4–5, John 14:18.
19. Lev. 19:34; Deut. 10:19, 14:29.
20. Leven, "Jesus," 424.
21. Leven, 429.
22. Dearman, "Family," paras. 1–5.
23. Failinger, "Co-Creating Adoption Law," 267.
24. Leven, "Jesus," 426.
25. Rawson, "Roman Family," 121.
26. Rawson, 127.
27. Dixon, *Roman Mother*, 13.
28. Dixon, 28.
29. Rawson, "Roman Family," 123. See also Osiek, "Pietas," 166–72.
30. Cahill, *Family*, 22.
31. Dixon, *Roman Mother*, 105.
32. Dixon, 142.
33. Dixon, 17.
34. Dixon, 35.
35. The importance of hierarchy in the Greco-Roman family leads Cahill to conclude that it was (and may remain) "the nexus of relationships of social inequalities maintained by structures of precedence and subjugation." Cahill, *Family*, 20.
36. John Boswell argues exposure led to fewer deaths than is often supposed. Rather than "exposure," he suggests "exposition" as a more accurate translation. Others have asserted that exposure was a form of indirect infanticide that was psychologically easier on parents but nonetheless aimed at their death, even if some children were claimed. See Boswell, "*Exposito*," 10–33; and Southon, "Family Planning."
37. Cunningham, *Children*, 22.
38. Cunningham, 23.
39. Dixon, *Roman Mother*, 26.
40. Gundry-Volf, "Least," 31–34.
41. Dixon, *Roman Mother*, 23.
42. Dixon, 23.
43. Dixon, 21.
44. Mackin, "Primitive Christian Understanding," 23, 27.
45. Gundry-Volf, "Least," 35.
46. Failinger, "Co-Creating Adoption Law," 267.
47. Cahill, *Family*, 29.

48. Rubio, *Christian Theology*, 48. Rubio also finds Luke 2:41–52 significant due to the child Jesus's dismissal of his parent's concerns.
49. Cahill, *Family*, 31; See also Matt. 23:9. Whether Jesus's use of *abba* was distinctive or had cultural precedent is a topic of scholarly debate.
50. Rubio, *Christian Theology*, 51.
51. Gudorf, "Western Religion," 286.
52. Rubio, *Christian Theology*, 50. 1 Tim. 2:8–15 appears to stand in significant tension with this perspective.
53. Rubio, *Christian Theology*, 48.
54. Cahill, *Family*, 18.
55. Gundry-Volf, "Least," 32.
56. Gundry-Volf, 60.
57. Rubio, *Christian Theology*, 151.
58. Cahill, *Family*, 30; Mark 10:16.
59. Matt. 21:16.
60. Both assertions can be found in the supporting literature, but it does not seem consistent to argue that Jesus's critique of fathers was aimed at patriarchal social power structures, while his interactions with children relate to their innate qualities.
61. See Elliott, "Jesus Movement," 173–210.
62. Elliott, 200.
63. For the purposes of this research, this history remains focused on the Western spread of Christianity. But this is only a partial story, given that early Christianity spread in all directions. Unfortunately, Western Christianity remains largely unaware of the culturally diverse origins beyond the Roman Empire, through a Eurocentric view that sees Eastern Europe and Southwest Asia and the "East" of Christianity. For many centuries, these regions were instead the Northwest in global perspective. See Jenkins, *Lost History*; Moffett, *History*.
64. Rubio, *Christian Theology*, 54.
65. Post, "Adoption," 152.
66. Rubio, *Christian Theology*, 60.
67. Osiek, "Pietas," 168.
68. Llewellyn and Middleton, "Motherhood."
69. Perpetua, "Martyrdom of Perpetua," 28–29.
70. Perpetua, 33.
71. Perpetua, 28.
72. See D'Angelo, "Roman Imperial Family Values," 142; and Elliott, "Jesus Movement," 200.
73. "Agathonicê."
74. 1 Timothy almost certainly predates both martyriologies, though the dates are disputed. 1 Timothy's admonition that women are to be quiet, submissive, and should not teach men stands in direct opposition to the martyr narratives in which women are central figures whose words and actions are intended to inform and inspire their Christian readers (presumably men included).
75. D'Angelo, "Roman Imperial Family Values," 159.
76. "Acts of Paul and Thecla," 21–25. See also Ruether, "Christianity," 85.
77. Ruether, "Christianity," 86.
78. These Western views technically supported clerical continence, not celibacy, and were concerned with extended periods of abstinence before celebrating sacraments at the

altar, as in the Levite priesthood. But because Christian clergy celebrated sacraments on a regular basis, continence was effectively celibacy regardless of a priest's marital status. See Cholij, "Priestly Celibacy."

79. Brown, *Body*, 343.
80. In Ambrose's words, "how can sensuality recall us to Paradise, when it alone robbed us of its delights?" Brown, *Body*, 361.
81. Ambrose, *Concerning Virginity*, 1.12.63; quoted by Brown, *Body*, 344.
82. Brown, *Body*, 376.
83. Brown, 398.
84. Jerome shocked many Christians with his perspective that "even first marriages were regrettable, if pardonable, capitulations to the flesh, and that second marriages were only one step away from the brothel." Brown, *Body*, 377.
85. Brown, 400.
86. Brown, 402.
87. Brown, 404.
88. Cahill, *Family*, 52.
89. Cahill, 57; Chrysostom, "Address," secs. 12ff.
90. Guroian, "Ecclesial Family," 73.
91. Bunge, "Introduction," 21.
92. Bunge; Chrysostom, "Address," sec. 22.
93. Herlihy, *Medieval Households*, vi.
94. Cunningham, *Children*, 33.
95. Cunningham, 33–35.
96. Dixon, *Roman Mother*, 20; see also Boswell, *Kindness.*
97. Southon, "Family Planning," 70–72.
98. "In 374 the Christian emperors Valentinian, Valens, and Gratian decreed that 'if anyone, man or woman, should commit the sin of killing an infant, that crime should be punishable with death,' an attitude considerably at variance with the Roman law code of the Twelve Tables (fifth century BC), where any child obviously deformed at birth was to be put to death." Cunningham, *Children*, 25.
99. Southon, "Family Planning," 66.
100. Cunningham, *Children*, 25.
101. Miller, *Orphans*, 3.
102. See *The Rule of St. Benedict*, chaps. 22, 30, 36, 37, 39, 40, 63, 64, 70.
103. Miller, *Orphans*, xi.
104. Rome defined an orphan as a child whose father was deceased. Because the household was based on male authority, even if mothers continued to care for their children, it was with the approval of a male guardian. Miller, *Orphans*, 31.
105. Traina, "Person," 107.
106. Cunningham, *Children*, 30.
107. Traina, "Person," 109.
108. Smith, "Who Is My Mother?" 158.
109. Smith, 164.
110. Smith, 160.
111. Traina, "Person," 118.
112. Traina, 107.
113. Traina, 115.

114. This argument further supported the importance of female fidelity, given that confidence in biological paternity is central to a father's investment.
115. A competing but less widely embraced theory of fetal development had been introduced in the later eleventh century. This was based on Galen's argument that both men and women contributed "seed," which was only released when the body was moved to pleasure. This allowed consent to sexual intercourse to be "objectively" determined by pregnancy. The theory was championed in the West by William of Conches and certainly challenged the West's dichotomous view of the good of reproduction and guilt of sexual pleasure, but it also held disastrous implications for victims of rape. William's interlocutors objected on the basis of experience and the view never gained widespread acceptance. Unfortunately, it has had continuing influence throughout history as a means of denying accusations of rape. See Resnick, "Marriage," 361–63.
116. Browning and Witte, "Christianity's Mixed Contributions," 727. Aquinas was building on an argument found in Aristotle and now identified by evolutionary psychology as "kin-altruism," which observes that people tend to invest more in those with whom they are biologically related.
117. Traina, "Person," 116.
118. Traina, 125.
119. Traina, 129.
120. "It has probably been historically accurate to posit that contemporary working mothers with a 40-hour workweek spend more time interacting with their children than their ancestresses did." Gudorf, "Western Religion," 297.
121. Strohl, "Child," 149.
122. Despite significant social changes in this era, gender relations remained remarkably stable. Merry E. Wiesner writes, "Of all the ways in which society was hierarchically arranged—class, age, rank, occupation—gender was regarded as the more 'natural' and therefore the most important to defend." See Strohl, "Child," n3.
123. Traina, "Person," 126.
124. Traina, 130.
125. Cunningham, *Children*, 43.
126. Cunningham, 47.
127. Atkinson, "'Wonderful Affection,'" 231.
128. Cunningham, *Children*, 43.
129. Ozment, *When Fathers Ruled*, 177. See also Strohl, "Child," n52.
130. Cunningham, *Children*, 45.
131. Cunningham, 44.
132. Luther, quoted by Bunge, "Introduction," 21.
133. Strohl, "Child," 155. Luther's perspective was at odds with the long struggle of the medieval Church to make consent central to the ritual of marriage. Notably, both Luther and Aquinas chose their vocations to religious life *against* the wishes of their fathers.
134. Luther, quoted by Cahill, *Family*, 66.
135. Strohl, "Child," 158.
136. Luther, quoted by Strohl, "Child," 140.
137. Strohl, "Child," 141. See also Pitkin, "'Heritage," n16.
138. Luther did not share Aquinas's trust in rationality. Explaining the third article of the creed, he writes, "I believe that by my own reason or strength I cannot believe in Jesus Christ, my Lord, or come to him." Luther, quoted by Strohl, "Child," 143.

139. Strohl, 134.
140. Calvin, quoted by Pitkin, "'Heritage,'" 167.
141. Pitkin, 166.
142. Pitkin, 182.
143. Cunningham, *Children*, 46.
144. Cahill, *Family*, 66.
145. Ruether observes the effect of the Reformers' conviction that "nobody could possibly be celibate and not fall into fornication" was to leave women with only marriage as a viable vocation. Celibate vocations were removed, and singleness has been notoriously suspect throughout Protestant history. Ruether, "Christianity," 88ff.
146. Cunningham, *Children*, 55.
147. Cunningham, 62; Browning and Witte, "Christianity's Mixed Contributions," 729.
148. Cunningham, *Children*, 60.
149. Sullivan-Dunbar, *Human Dependency*, 30.
150. Carp, *Adoption*, 3.
151. Brekus, "Children," 307.
152. Sullivan-Dunbar, *Human Dependency*, 53–55.
153. Edwards, quoted by Brekus, "Children," 303. Before Edwards, in 1662, the American Puritan Michael Wigglesworth had published a popular tale of God's condemnation of sinners, though he added that children were given "the easiest room in Hell." See Brekus, n10.
154. Edwards, quoted by Brekus, 303.
155. Brekus, 312.
156. Allen, *Feminism*, 10.
157. Sullivan-Dunbar, *Human Dependency*, 54.
158. Traina, "How Gendered?" 84.
159. Bendroth, "Horace Bushnell," 357.
160. Newman, quoted by Cunningham, *Children*, 69.
161. Bushnell, quoted by Bendroth, "Horace Bushnell," 350.
162. Bendroth, "Horace Bushnell," 358.
163. Holt, *Orphan Trains*, 12.
164. Bendroth, "Mainline Protestants," 33.
165. Mortara's own memoirs testify to his unwavering gratitude for the pope's intervention, while his theological perspective aligns with the exclusivist soteriological views prevalent in Catholicism during this time. Recent accusations have surfaced alleging that Mortara's memoirs were altered in translation to downplay the anti-Semitic aspects of his thought. See Winfield, "Memoir."
166. Defenders of Pius IX's actions have recently emerged in more traditionalist Catholic circles and tend to revive a dualistic nineteenth-century view of Catholicism in which the salvation of souls is of paramount importance. Although this view also leads to a willingness to abrogate the claims of biological kinship, it proceeds from an entirely different orientation than the present argument. See Momigliano, "Why Some Catholics Defend the Kidnapping."
167. Individual religious women and priests adopting children should also be considered among the diversities of parenthood within the Catholic tradition. Among other examples, see Catholic News Service, "Father George Clements."
168. Miller, *Orphans*, 11.

169. Miller, 9.
170. Heijst, *Models*, 96.
171. Heijst, 55.
172. Heijst, 230.
173. Heijst, 221.
174. Creagh, "Baby Trains," 198.
175. Carp, *Adoption*, 5.
176. The western frontier continually shifted with westward expansion. Originally, Ohio, Indiana, and Illinois were considered frontier destinations. By the early twentieth century, these states were themselves sending children to the American Southwest. As a child, Brace listened to the sermons of Horace Bushnell, who may have been influential in his decision to become a minister. Holt, *Orphan Trains*, 41–42.
177. The system was encouraged by the widespread belief that institutional care and cities themselves were detrimental to children's development. Brace himself remarked that "the best of all asylums for the outcast child is the farmer's home." Kidder, "West by Orphan Train," 33.
178. Holt explains, "In a time when there were few choices in the care of the unfortunate, indenture was a respectable alternative and certainly preferable to the spectacle of impoverished children or young adults trying to eke out a life for themselves. As an accepted custom, the legal mechanics for indenture were carried with westward expansion." The Children's Aid Society did not utilize legal adoption because many of its children were not true orphans. Holt, *Orphan Trains*, 33, 62.
179. Kidder, "West by Orphan Train," 33.
180. Kidder, 32.
181. Despite the evident public nature of these systems, adoption itself was still held secret within many families. Consequently, many sought children whose physical features would not appear out of place within the family.
182. Creagh, "Baby Trains," 202.
183. Creagh, 199.
184. "The Foundling Asylum opened in 1869, the revelation of Sister Mary Irene Fitzgibbon, who became alarmed by the 'lengthened record of infanticide' in the chaotic, postwar city, as well as the number of living babies left on the doorstep of her convent in lower Manhattan." Creagh, "Baby Trains," 200.
185. Creagh, 203.
186. Creagh, 209.
187. Kidder, "West by Orphan Train," 35.
188. In large part, asylums served as support for poor families without the means to care for young children. The majority of asylum children rejoined their families within a few years. Hacsi, *Second Home*, 32.
189. Creagh, "Baby Trains," 207–8.
190. Creagh, 206; Holt, *Orphan Trains*, 73.
191. See Gordon, *Great Arizona Orphan Abduction*.
192. Creagh, "Baby Trains," 206.
193. Historians disagree on the existence, extent, and direct intervention involved in coercive "slave breeding" by slave owners. Suggestions of such realities are clearly an important aspect of northern abolitionist rhetoric, but verification is controversial. See Smithers, "American Abolitionism," 551–70.

194. Individuals inherited the race of their mother, which continued to justify enslavement until an individual was less than one-eighth African descent. Under this system, "quadroons" and "octoroons" were especially prized as slave mistresses for their White masters. In contrast, these individuals also served as valuable public advocates against slavery in the North, as White audiences saw "African slaves" who were indistinguishable from themselves. Collins, *Black Feminist Thought*, 135–36, 144.
195. Collins, 49.
196. Collins, 55.
197. Collins, 179.
198. Schwartz, "Connective Complexity," 91.
199. Collins, *Black Feminist Thought*, 178.
200. Collins, 152.
201. Browning and Witte, "Christianity's Mixed Contributions," 727; Failinger, "Co-Creating Adoption Law," 268.

CHAPTER 7

Rereading Catholic Social Teaching

Previous chapters have destabilized ongoing Catholic emphasis on the private, biological nuclear family that has resulted from the prevailing framework for parenthood's tendency to direct attention to sex and gender. In so doing, they have established lines for a more robust Catholic anthropology of parenthood that can remain based in tradition while more adequately engaging the complexities of contemporary experience. This final chapter sketches an anthropology of parenthood that is consonant with the preceding arguments and utilizes Catholic Social Teaching to suggest possibilities for further articulating such a perspective. Although this anthropology of parenthood is intentionally open to multiple children and co-parents as well as the social vocation of the family to which parenthood is always linked, in its most reduced form, this framework presents parenthood as a form of labor defined by a specific committed relationship that is ordered toward a child's development and well-being.[1] This basic schema contains conditions for articulating the inherently social nature of the family and understanding parenthood as a vocation.

The chapter's further development of this framework draws from John Paul II's encyclical on labor, *Laborem exercens*, and Francis's encyclical on care for creation, *Laudato si'*. Admittedly, these are not typical documents to employ for reflections on parenthood. But, in large part because they are not centrally concerned with the family, they offer anthropological insights from the Magisterium that can offer support for understanding parenthood as relational work based in common human capacities while avoiding the prevailing framework's biases toward sex and gender. This alternative path to conceptualizing parenthood is not aimed at dismissing the importance of sexual ethical norms or the real differences in gendered human experiences. However, it intentionally displaces these issues as definitive framing mechanisms for conceptions of parenthood in order to explore an alternative and potentially more robust anthropological framework.

PARENTHOOD AS LABOR AND RELATIONSHIP

In John Paul II's apostolic exhortation *Redemptoris custos*, Joseph's "authentic human fatherhood" is juridically grounded in his marriage to Mary but morally rooted in his acceptance of the gift of fatherhood.[2] This responsibility within a particular family is presented as Joseph's vocation, which is fulfilled through his "total gift of self, of his life and work" ordered toward God through his family.[3]

John Paul II is very concerned to explain the legitimacy of Joseph's marriage to Mary despite the lack of a sexual relationship. This is driven by both the prevailing framework for parenthood that he himself greatly influenced as well as considerable debate on this question throughout the tradition. Importantly, John Paul II identifies the marriage relationship as the basis for Joseph's juridical fatherhood. Moreover, though he attempts to center Joseph's fatherhood in his marriage, Joseph's commitment and actions provide a parallel, and ultimately more convincing, foundation for his moral status as father.

Although John Paul II's presentation of Joseph's life and personality is thickly influenced by traditional, but biblically unverifiable, ascriptions as well as modern masculine ideals, the pope's reflections nonetheless provide important theological diversity as they take up the topic of parenthood while conscientiously avoiding questions of sexual activity and biological relatedness. Like John Paul II's speech to adoptive parents, such restricted conditions push his theological reflections toward recognizing parenthood's basic human and evangelical realities. In such a view, it becomes more evident that parenthood, theologically considered, is not an extension of sexual ethics or gendered norms but instead consists primarily in relationship and action.

The relational dimension of parenthood differentiates the work of parenting from other forms of labor such that parenthood both participates in the general labor of caregiving while specifying and transcending it in important ways. Parenthood is labor, inasmuch as it requires the exertion of effort for the sake of a larger goal: the well-being and development of a child. But, unlike other forms of care work, which likewise aim at the well-being of another, parenthood is specified by the asymmetrical but reciprocal relationship between caregiver and child that is contextualized within a kin relationship. This relationship is unrepeatable because it aims at the good of a particular child. Sandra Sullivan-Dunbar observes that caregiving often expresses Christian love in a particular and exclusive way within specific interpersonal relationships and can therefore appear to be in tension with the Christian commitment to agape as an ideal of universal love. However, such a contrast owes more to failures of moral imagination influenced by accepted dichotomies and moral boundaries than to the demands of Christian love.[4] Christian love is not an ephemeral universal ideal but instead is always particularized in specific relationships. As Richard Gaillardetz writes,

> Perhaps the most important point to make about the call to love is that love is, from a Christian point of view, less an attitude than an actual relationship. Love in this most basic sense is a call to be with and for another or others in concrete and determinate ways. It means constituting one's life practices within determinate networks of love relationships. As a concrete relationship, love will be accompanied by attitude and affect, but it is the relationship itself that is primary.[5]

Interpersonal relationships should not foreclose further forms of communion or expressions of solidarity but may instead form people through experiences of self-giving love to encounter others with greater awareness and self-possession.[6] In its ideal, Christian parenthood is characterized by a depth of love that expresses itself in both specific relational commitments and a willingness to extend the bonds of love to meet the needs of others.

Although parental relationships are always unique and specific, they are not always predictable. Like the neighbor in the parable of the Good Samaritan, the specific identity of a parent is discovered in and through commitment and actual acts of caregiving.[7] The Christian baptismal identity is expressed in willingness to extend love on account of the needs of others and therefore creates possibilities for unplanned or unexpected realizations of parenthood. Parenthood as a moral reality has less to do with specific legal or biological commitments and more to do with relational openness and a willingness to shape one's life in relation to the needs of another. Through this joining of lives, a parental vocation is begun, in which loving commitment to another, and the relational reciprocity this initiates, create the context for growth and self-discovery as a person and parent. Consequently, regardless of parenting style or family structure, the relational intimacy of parenthood that is created through investing one's life and interest in the good of another creates the context for growth. As Darlene Fozard Weaver writes, "The actions by which we deepen or evade intimacy are precisely those by which we share or withhold ourselves and welcome or refuse the other. This means that our actions contribute to the gain or loss of the other, that we experience that gain or loss not as an extrinsic verdict on our actions but as their inner reality."[8]

Moreover, the vocational reality of parenthood is expressed not only through an intimate communion of life but also in the binding of the good of both parent and child to an outward orientation that recognizes and responds to the needs of others.[9] That is, parenthood is intimate but not private, and it remains rooted in the baptismal call to communion and solidarity that extends beyond the parent–child relationship.[10] Such commitments may be expressed through charitable acts and social advocacy, or may also be realized in expressions of solidarity and extensions of kinship, even to the point of creating new parental identities through response to a child's need. Hence, in the relational dimension of parenthood, baptismal identity is primary because it creates the vocational context for self-giving love and solidarity with others that may come to be actualized and recognized within a specific parental relationship. For this same reason, parenthood always occurs within or gives rise to a family as a community of love.

As a form of work, however, parenthood is associated with certain tasks and is divisible, such that multiple unique parental relationships with a particular child can coexist simultaneously. Three important aspects of parenthood's divisibility are worth special consideration. First, parenthood is not a zero-sum game. In a two-parent household, both parents may be equally and fully parents to a child, even as in a single-parent household only one adult might fulfill this role. Parenthood may also be divided more broadly, as can happen in stepfamilies or among adoptive or foster parents where multiple individuals might participate in parenting either simultaneously or across time. As such, the identification of any single individual as a parent does not inherently limit the same or similar identification of others.

Second, parenthood is unequally divisible. That is, individuals may participate in acts of parenthood to greater or lesser extents. Often, extended family members such as grandparents fulfill significant parental roles even while biological or adoptive parents remain primary parents. For example, formal education is a commonly subdivided parental role. Catholic teaching and Western societies broadly agree that legal parents are responsible for children's education, but legal parents rarely fulfill this role directly within educational structures.[11] As this demonstrates, parental responsibilities are frequently "outsourced" at the specific level, such as teaching mathematics or learning to play the violin. Because such education is a responsibility of parenthood, it is in essence a parental act, but the relational connection may still differentiate it from an act of parenthood. In other words, teachers participate in the duties of parenthood but do not necessarily parent their pupils, although they may. Between formal institutions of outsourced parental responsibilities and the inclusion of significantly involved co-parents lies a large gradation of interpersonal relationships. Given these fuzzy boundaries, in ambiguous circumstances the determination of parenthood—in its moral, interpersonal sense—relies largely on the judgment of the individuals involved who are best suited to assess their relationships.

Third and finally, parenthood originates in time. That is, someone may become a parent to a child by fulfilling the duties of parenthood and by establishing a specific kin relationship. In other words, parents are not created ex nihilo at a child's birth. Parenthood may begin before or after the birth of a particular child, according to the establishment of relationships and corresponding actions. Moreover, the emergence of a fully parental relationship can be relatively quick or happen gradually over time. The latter arises within foster care or other caregiving arrangements where individuals fulfill the duties of caregiving and move in greater or lesser degrees to the fuller relational realities of parenthood.

Although persons become parents within time, it is less clear if and to what extent a fully parental relationship might end. Someone once regarded as a parent by a particular individual may no longer be considered a parent to that same individual at a later point. Nonetheless, if someone was a parent in the full moral and interpersonal sense of the word, his or her influence necessarily constitutes an aspect of the parented individual's identity thereafter. As such, the common term "estranged parent" best captures the reality of a parent who was but is no longer regarded as a parent. That is, the recognized kinship dimension of parenthood may end such that interpersonal obligations cease, but the relational reality of parenthood in time cannot simply be erased because it constitutes a developmental reality of the parented individual. The reciprocal nature of the relational labor of parenthood further implies that the inerasable nature of a true parental relationship applies to both parent and child.

This potential difference between parental identity and present regard as a parent admits to greater ambiguity with negative parental experiences that may be colored by abuse, trauma, or neglect. Although parenting shapes those who are parented, this is never unconditionally positive and in some circumstances is largely or overwhelmingly negative. At some point, damaging interpersonal relationships are no longer parenthood, morally considered and regardless of legal standing, because the relational and labor dimensions would be misdirected or go unfulfilled. That is, beyond the extent of influence on shaping another's life, the quality of this influence must be considered a dimension of parenthood morally considered. This suggests that parenthood has a teleological character of its own and remains open to normative assessments of human goods beyond subjective experience. In healthy and fulfilling parental relationships, the divisions between subjective and normative should generally align; but under unhealthy and harmful circumstances, the tensions become more pronounced. As such, parenting can to a greater or lesser extent fulfill its purposes across a wide range of differentiated experiences and moral complexity. Moreover, this complexity enters the sphere of the morally tragic in circumstances when parents are to various extents committed to the well-being of their child while simultaneously being sources of active harm. Once again in the moral domain, as in its experiential reality, parenthood admits to fuzzy boundaries and occasionally conflictual realities.

Returning again to its relational dimension, parenthood is differentiated from other forms of relationship by the particular kin identity that binds parents and children. This defines parenthood as an ongoing relationship based in mutual obligations, even as the forms of parental labor shift substantially over time. An older parent offering advice to an adult child remains concerned for his or her child's well-being even while their efforts are directed in radically different ways from those of someone parenting an infant. Nonetheless, parenting remains parenting across time through the ongoing relational connection of parent to child, even as the specific acts of parenting change dramatically. Although the kin obligations that support parenthood are mutual between parent and child, they are not reciprocally equivalent. Yet, once again, this imbalanced quality likewise varies across time.

Care for young children is based on a mutual understanding of relational obligations but is profoundly unequal in the labor exerted. In contrast, care for an elderly or ill parent can reverse the exertion of labor within the parent–child relationship. Nonetheless, a child may become a caregiver to a parent without abrogating the parent–child relationship. Although a child may well fulfill a parenting role, framing parenthood as only a matter of dependence on a caregiver too narrowly construes parenthood and underappreciates the radically interdependent nature of human life. As Sandra Sullivan-Dunbar observes, despite a pervasive ideological willingness to believe in our own unencumbered independence, dependency is more basic to human experience than autonomy. Moreover, Christian theological commitments equalize our common human dependence on the Creator, while care is a pervasive and constitutional reality of interpersonal and social experience.[12] As such, associating parenting with the act of caregiving alone does not adequately attend to the common reality of dependence.[13] Although some level of autonomy and responsibility over another is associated with the parental role, parenthood is not singly defined by this particular imbalance between parties. Instead, such differentiated obligations remain contextualized within kin commitments and the larger social realities of dependence such that a reversal of this role does not fully constitute a reversal of parental identity.

Given our present position in history, the majority of parental relationships today are spent in relations with adult children that create the conditions for greater reciprocal mutuality in relationships and labor. Parenting infants and young children is an intense and ever-changing commitment of both physical and emotional effort, but it is ultimately fleeting in relation to the decades now commonly spent sustaining adult parent–child relationships. Despite transitions in care and responsibility throughout the life course and their relative distributions in time, kinship continues to bind the parent–child relationship. The fact that it is not always easy for older adults to relinquish their autonomy and caretaking responsibilities to their children, even when necessity dictates that such roles must reverse, speaks to the profound impact of parenthood in shaping individuals as persons, but need not suggest it is bound only to these aspects of care.

Both parenthood and caregiving are rooted in a general human capacity to extend concern to another and intentionally respond to another's needs for the sake of their well-being. However, not all caregiving constitutes parenthood because not all caregiving is framed by a particular parent–child kin relationship. Admittedly, distinctions can be imprecise, given that kinship is a *recognized set of obligations* based on an *interpretation* of underlying states of being. As such, parental obligations admit to diverse interpretations across various social circumstances, but they share common ground in the uniquely unequal and other-directed relationship of parenthood.

Kinship, like parenthood, may also emerge over time in response to relationships fostered between persons. The unique kin obligations specific to parenthood are commonly based in interpretations of kin obligations stemming from the realities of biological motherhood and fatherhood. Nonetheless, not all biological parents are parents in the full moral sense of the term, even while other forms of relatedness can and do give rise to parenthood in this sense. The creation of a parental kin relationship may come about decisively in acts such as adoption, in which a legal reality parallels a commitment to parent a child, but can also arise gradually or be understood in retrospect as the extent of a relational commitment and its impact are recognized.

Consequently, parenthood is in one sense chosen and in another sense is given, while the balance can vary across experiences. As Sullivan-Dunbar observes, "We determine with whom we interact, to a large degree, by where we live, what we choose as a vocation, and what pressing human need in some other part of the world we choose to aid (or not). Our encounters are not so random as to neutralize the many individual and social decisions that place us in proximity to particular needy neighbors (or comfortably distant from needy persons who live in poorer countries or worse neighborhoods)."[14]

Consequently, both direct decisions and realities that are beyond our control as well as the consequences and interactions of a wide range of our choices set possibilities for different relational experiences. As such, family formation and the experience of parenthood often grow largely out of moral decisions about what proximity to new possibilities for relationship potential parents are willing to occupy. Commitment to Christian love as an expression of our baptismal identity calls for openness to other's needs across the life course, not merely in reproductive choices, such that all Christians are called to the possibility of caregiving relative to the needs of others they encounter and their own individual capacities. For some, this common call to love and service of neighbor is realized in the specific vocation of parenthood that is enacted within or gives rise to a family.

FURTHER THEOLOGICAL SUPPORTS

The Catholic tradition consistently upholds education and evangelization as tasks essential to the labor dimension of parenthood. Within this slim list, the first is also among the corporal acts of mercy and the second is an obligation of all Christians in relation to their baptismal identity. Consequently, the specific moral reality of parenthood specifies these obligations within the life of the family but can easily be obscured when family structure is prioritized over function. Setting aside the bias toward gender norms and sexual ethical issues in the prevailing framework that leads to an emphasis on family structure, where Christian ideas of parenthood differ most markedly from broader cultural practices is in the identification and extension of parenthood's relational dimension. As documented in the previous chapter, Christians historically have extended kin obligations based on the slimmest of underlying connections, down to simply the fact of another's need itself. The common creation of all persons in God and the common identity given to Christians in baptism have served as powerful fundamental realities upon which Christian kin obligations are interpreted. The parable of the Good Samaritan's creation of neighbor-love is perhaps the best-known story of such meagerly manufactured kin obligations. Remarkably, this story has been re-created throughout history as Christians have voluntarily cared for children both with and without the ties of biological relatedness.

The personalist tradition underlies the progression in contemporary Catholic teaching on the family that moves from a theological account of human persons, including the desire and need for relationships, to a normative vision of the family with its attendant ethical norms. Along the way, reflections on the family include questions about the nature of gender, sexuality, and marriage before arriving at parenthood. Although this progression is defensible, it has led to relative inattention to the anthropological realities of parenthood as the prioritized matters of gender and sexual ethics have consumed theological attention. Even when Catholic teaching specifically addresses parenthood, it often has a "natalist" bent driven in no small part by concern about moral sexual activity and means of procreation. The educational task of parenthood has been consistently upheld, yet the theological foundations for this duty—including its theological anthropological roots, its relation to parenthood as a vocation, and the personal qualities and capabilities required to educate effectively—have received relatively limited attention.

The enthusiasm with which matters related to sexuality, gender, and marriage are debated is often defended as reflecting the fundamental importance of these issues for the family, even as the debates themselves have actively detracted attention from the actual workings of families and practices of parenthood. Regardless of the defensibility of contemporary magisterial teaching related to sexuality and gender, the likelihood of the polarization on these issues decreasing in the near future, and thereby opening the way for greater attention to parenthood, is vanishingly small. Yet parenthood remains a formative experience for countless Catholics that shapes their self-understanding and growth as persons.

The present climate obscures the reception of theological accounts of parenthood that extend much beyond conception and birth or are actively inclusive of diverse family forms, and it is unlikely to change. Therefore, at a practical level, alternative avenues for reflecting on the theological realities of parenthood are called for as a means of communicating the faith to families while significant and deeply held disagreements remain. Diverging from the model of gender to marriage to sex to procreation that guides the prevailing framework, a path oriented around the labor and relational dimensions of parenthood can proceed from a basic appreciation of human dignity and interconnectedness to the value of work as beneficial for persons and increasing solidarity to the unique capabilities and commitments needed for the specific vocation of parenting. This framework maintains the same personalist trajectory while significantly shifting the terms of its progression.

The central question for this possible alternative is whether reflection on parenthood *must start specifically with sexual anthropology*. If this is not the case, then broader anthropological foundations might well be expected to lead to meaningful reflection on the theological reality of parenthood as disclosed within the Catholic tradition. Interestingly, John Paul II suggests the latter possibility in his presentation of work as the foundation of family; inasmuch as it is the source of the material necessities of family life as well as a shaping force in the process of education. This assertion is obviously not intended to undermine his own concern for interpersonal sexual complementarity as a foundation for the family, but nonetheless points to possible additional anthropological paths for considering theological aspects of the family.[15]

Mapping such a pathway will certainly shed new light on the subject and provide reasons to reconsider aspects of the prevailing framework in light of the broader points of reflection being introduced. Nonetheless, as long as these both constitute reasonable frameworks for conceptualizing parenthood, mapped along the personalistic commitment to the good of the human person and in dialogue with the tradition, such points of critical tension ought to be regarded as opportunities for faithful discernment. In order to begin this new path, we now turn to anthropological insights expressed in Catholic Social Teaching that have not typically been included by the prevailing paradigm but are suited for the framework being proposed.

THE ANTHROPOLOGY OF *LABOREM EXERCENS*

As is characteristic of John Paul II's personalist approach, *Laborem exercens* explores the reality of human labor by offering a reflection on humanity through the context of work.[16] His vision is based in a relational anthropology, in which the gift of self leads to both self-knowledge and solidarity with others. Accordingly, he describes labor's ultimate purpose as elevating "unceasingly the cultural and moral level of the society."[17] Humans are called to work, while work itself has an essential human dimension.

Laborem exercens offers a unique resource for reflection on parenthood because it clearly views parenting as a form of labor while substantially bypassing the gender and sexual issues that are characteristic of the prevailing framework. The encyclical's vision of work, which proceeds in a personalist fashion from the person to the act, is essentially gender-neutral in its concern for the reality of work in the context of persons generally considered. Nonetheless, gendered presuppositions clearly inform its presentation of particular forms of labor.[18]

This mismatch between an inclusive scope and gendered presuppositions limits the document's intent to affirm the dignity and value of domestic work.

The problem is exacerbated by John Paul II's propensity for dividing public and private life along with masculine and feminine gender identities while linking the latter firmly with domestic life. Christine Firer Hinze counts the limited integration of parenting in the encyclical's larger vision of labor as a significant weakness as it restricts engagement with the gendered suppositions within its view of domestic labor.[19]

Laborem exercens does make strides in its use of gender-inclusive terms when considering employment such as "adult who is responsible for a family" and "spouse."[20] This inclusivity departs markedly from the earlier pattern of Catholic Social Teaching that associated men alone with wage labor and appears influenced by John Paul II's concern to engage the actual realities of female employment and reassert women's legitimate role in public life.[21] However, just a few lines after this gender-inclusive approach is exemplified, *Laborem exercens* singly associates motherhood with domestic labor. Hinze argues the document "cuts in several directions" as different facets of its agenda "work at cross purposes, preventing Catholic Social Teaching from mounting an effective social-ethical agenda for supporting the work of the home."[22] This point is demonstrated clearly within the encyclical as it notes the Bible's "praise for the work of women" with a reference to Proverbs 31.[23] However, the "wife of noble character" described in scripture manages both domestic and economic duties while little emphasis is placed on her motherhood. She does feed and dress children, but she also feeds the slaves and dresses her husband. Moreover, the biblical wife labors, invests, and creates, while her arms are strong from her physical efforts.[24]

Although the encyclical envisions women participating alongside men in the labor force, men are not reciprocally envisioned as active partners in domestic life. Even the task of education, which has historically landed within the ideological purview of fatherhood, is here associated with mothers alone.[25] And though "mother" and "father" both occur five times within the document, every occurrence of "mother" comes within paragraph nineteen's concerns about domestic life, whereas every occurrence of "father" refers to God. Such unevenness permits the encyclical's concern about the realities of employment to be undermined by its own inability to apply the same standards to the family's domestic life.[26]

This halting attempt at gender inclusivity may also owe to Catholic Social Teaching's earlier assumption of vocations as singular realities. In foundational early documents, Leo XIII and Pius XI both confidently assumed men's vocation to be a singular career, with women's being the work of the home. This simplistic vision served gendered expectations but neither adequately reflected the diversities of family life and labor back then nor does it prove very helpful in the complex realities of the present. Like many parents before them, parents today are tasked with negotiating their vocational identities in relation to uncertain horizons that contain myriad possibilities for potential familial and occupational roles.

Laborem exercens reflects the crossroads to which John Paul II has come at his point in history. On one hand, it seeks to engage the realities of contemporary experience; on the other hand, it seeks to develop the inherited tradition of social thought. Its own perspective also remains conditioned by gendered presuppositions that complicate engagement with experiential realities. As a result, women are left split between two worlds of labor within a document that still tends to conceive of vocations as singular, while men continue to occupy a singular and stable role as wage earners despite changing social realities. This unevenness is amplified by the document's distinction of "human work" from "the work of women," which it repeats twice while enumerating forms of work recognized in scripture.[27]

Even so, the document provides resources for responding to the tensions brought on by its own assumptions. Following John Paul II's concern for the subjective realities of work, the introduction of multiplicity and flexibility in individual vocations appears to only heighten possibilities for self-discovery and growth in humanity. John Paul II seems to envision a single profession as a potential source of growth and transformation (e.g., an electrician growing in excellence as an electrician). However, there is little evident reason why this could not be extended across multiple domains, even as it requires a focus on more basic skills and capacities (e.g., an electrician turned computer tech turned salesman growing in excellence as an adaptable and diligent professional). Household and parental responsibilities could well be added to the multitude of vocational trajectories in which persons grow in their skills and self-understanding. *Laborem exercens* provides a limited internal rationale for why male and female vocations must be patterned in the way it presents them but instead offers rich, but unfortunately underutilized, foundations for considering the broad capacities for individuals to develop as persons through vocations that span diverse public and private roles.

These gendered tensions replicate the priorities for the prevailing conception of parenthood that have been outlined in previous chapters. On one hand, the experience of parenthood seems to relate to basic human capacities and realities; on the other hand, specific gendered norms inform how parenthood is conceived. Between the common human capabilities required for the tasks of parenting and the gendered expectations of how individuals are to fulfill these tasks lies an unexplained conceptual gap that is supported through appeals to socially conservative gender norms. Such conceptual gaps are likewise evident in *Laborem exercens*'s treatment of labor because it too is informed by a conceptual division of male and female work despite its vision of work being ostensibly inclusive. John Paul II recognized that the reality of labor in many people's lives means that women are often employed in physically challenging wage labor, yet this regard stands at odds with his ideal of femininity marked by passivity and domestic maternal care.

Concerns to preserve socially conservative gender norms without apparent theological warrants seem to muddle the clarity of magisterial arguments across a range of issues and directly affect teaching on both labor and parenthood. These disjunctions between gender norms and more inclusive visions of labor and parenthood are a cause for special attention because they point to competing conceptual pathways that the documents themselves rarely make explicit. Setting the interests in gender norms aside in order to focus on the functional aspects of these realities allows for a clearer view of the common anthropological realities being described. By doing this, the vision of labor within *Laborem exercens* can be placed alongside a desire to conceptualize parenthood and more fully understand its dimension as labor.

The first challenge in utilizing *Laborem exercens* in this way is the document's own imprecision on what exactly it includes in its understanding of work. On one hand, the document appeals to a sweeping vision of work that includes virtually all manual or intellectual activities having to do with the sustenance or betterment of individuals and society—or, more accurately, individuals within society. On the other hand, John Paul II's paradigm for labor is clearly informed by industry, trades, and craftsmanship. These specific forms of labor are prototypical for the encyclical's guiding description of labor as acts wherein a subject, who is a worker, applies effort to transform an object of the material world in order to produce something.[28] This vision of labor continues the themes of earlier documents of Catholic Social Teaching, centered as they were on the rights of workers after the Industrial Revolution, but relies on an absolute subject/object divide that is not inclusive of all human work.

Utilizing Genesis, the idea of dominion frames John Paul II's conception of work, while the phrase "subdue the earth" is repeated throughout the text. This view is also clearly rooted in *Gaudium et spes,* which posits dominion over creation as humanity's calling.[29] Consequently, a hierarchy of human subject over nonhuman object permeates John Paul II's account of work. However, the work of parenthood, and also many other forms of labor, is not done within such a subject–object relationship. Parenting is not directed at a material object but at another person and their well-being such that the subject–object relationship is replaced with an interpersonal relationship.

Because the conceptual paradigm for labor in *Laborem exercens* centers on a subject–object relation, it is unclear how labor within interpersonal relationships can be included within its paradigm. The encyclical does consider intersubjective relations between employer and employee that condition mutual respect,[30] but its conception of work itself prioritizes the subjective worker over the object of the work.[31] Such a prioritization is not possible when another person is taken to be the object of labor because it would violate John Paul II's personalist moral commitments.

John Paul's personalism extended Immanuel Kant's (1724–1804) assertion that persons ought never be treated only as means by rejecting any treatment of persons "as a mere means."[32] In *Love and Responsibility,* the future John Paul II articulates his premise that the "personalist norm, in its negative aspect, states that the person is the kind of good which does not admit of use and cannot be treated as an object of use and as the means to an end."[33] Reiterating a similar point later in *Crossing the Threshold of Hope,* John Paul II states that "love for a person excludes the possibility of treating him as an object of pleasure."[34] Consequently, John Paul II differs from Kant in shifting away from condemning the reduction of a person to a means to more fully condemning the treatment of a person as a means in any sense. Yet his occasional use of qualifying language suggests that John Paul II's prohibition on use is not as all-encompassing as these statements imply but is based upon a more fundamental understanding of persons and their nature.[35] In contrast, he is very comfortable with the exertion of human control over raw materials, animals, and other nonhuman creation as all are mere objects and can be treated as such.[36]

Positively stated, John Paul II insists that persons must always be engaged through love in their full personhood, which does not admit to objectification understood as abuse or misuse with regard to human nature, whereas Kant had simply insisted that a person always be treated as more than an object. This higher standard has particular relevance for *Laborem exercens*'s unequal engagement with forms of labor, in which the object of the labor seems to be a human person (e.g., ministry, education, and parenting). Such forms of work are included in the encyclical's broad intentions but are a conspicuously ill fit for the paradigm of labor employed throughout. Nonetheless, the encyclical gives no indication that intersubjective work, such as parenthood, is not work in its proper sense. In fact, it insists the opposite.

It could be argued that this tension is only apparent and can be resolved by clarifying the object of the labor within interpersonal forms of labor. For example, with respect to education, one might argue that the object of labor is the acquisition of knowledge itself.[37] The problem with such an approach is that it drives a wedge precisely through the human relationship of teacher and taught. In order to save a definition, it undermines personalism's concern for the subjective and intersubjective dimensions of personhood.[38] Considered in its subjective reality, the tasks of teaching are directed at the shaping of persons, such that the object of any particular act of teaching is properly the person being taught. Shifting the object to knowledge itself undermines an essential dimension of teaching as an interpersonal reality. At the same time, the reality that teaching is in fact a form of labor is also undeniable. Even more evidently, the tasks of parenting are directed at the health, well-being, and development of persons such that the object of parental labor must be the child himself or herself.

The tension between the encyclical's subject–object paradigm and interpersonal forms of labor emerges throughout its engagement with domestic labor. For example, *Laborem exercens* identifies labor as human participation "in the activity of God himself, his creator."[39] In so doing, it connects labor to the same vision of participation that has been associated with both procreation and the education of children throughout modern magisterial teaching. This bolsters the encyclical's position that parenting is a form of labor.

The same paragraph includes a reflection on Christ as a "man of work." However, rather than focusing on the laborious dimensions of Jesus's ministry, which are illustrated in multiple ways throughout the Gospels,[40] John Paul II focuses on his background as a craftsman.[41] This links divine concern to human work, but strikingly fails to acknowledge the interpersonal work that characterized Jesus's public and interpersonal ministry. Likewise, *Laborem exercens* clearly affirms parenthood as labor in its reflection on the relationship of work and family. According to the encyclical, work begins with a subjective dimension, then passes through the family to the greater good of society.[42] Throughout, the document clearly includes interpersonal labor as labor in its full theological sense and yet remains ambiguous as to how such work ought to be reconciled with the paradigm being employed.

To shore up this reliance on subject/object dichotomies, Ruth Yoemon has introduced the concept "worthy objects." Such objects—be they persons, institutions, animals, and the like—contain their own value and therefore have a role in dictating how they are to be treated by the subject. She writes that "being attentive to worthy objects requires an emotional engagement which is both satisfying to us because we are able to experience the objective features of meaningful work, and represents an appropriate response to the nature of the object."[43] Such a view seems to better encompass experiences of interpersonal labor in which interdependence and solidarity are experienced not indirectly through the mediation of the product of labor but directly through an interpersonal relationship that nonetheless contains a labor dimension. Although such a bridge seems essential for connecting John Paul II's thought on labor to the actual labor of parenthood, as well as for shoring up internal inconsistencies within *Laborem exercens*, John Paul II himself seems to provide little guidance on how such a move could avoid conflicting with his articulation of the personalistic norm.

Nonetheless, Yeoman's proposal may have purchase because it creates space for a morally realist account of subject-worthy object interactions that would seem to protect John Paul II's underlying commitments. Yeoman recognizes that not only must the subject be responsive to a worthy object, but the treatment of a worthy object by a subject is always interpreted.[44] On the face of it, providing space for interpretation accounts for historical variability in childrearing practices despite consistence in the object (i.e., the child). However, from a Catholic moral perspective, this also allows for the insertion of realist claims based in normative interpretations of human nature. Hence, a person as an object of labor could be considered a type of worthy object that by his or her very nature does not admit to abuse or misuse, which, as Kevin Rickert has argued, is simply a Thomistic expression of John Paul II's personalistic norm.[45]

The disjunctions created by parenthood's apparent inclusion and exclusion as a form of labor does not plague reflections on the intransitive dimension of labor presented in *Laborem exercens* nearly as much as those of the transitive dimension. Because the intransitive dimension of labor is a primary point of emphasis that shapes the encyclical's anthropological reflections, there remains much to be gained for an account of parenthood regarding its personal and vocational aspects.[46] Following John Paul II's argument, parenting, like all forms of work, has the subjective effect of shaping persons. As stated above, this reality of parenthood seems to disallow a complete discontinuation of parenthood, even when the relational aspect has deteriorated. That is, the relational work of parenting shapes the parent such that its reality in time cannot be disavowed, even as the continuation of an interpersonal relationship may be. John Paul II's recognition of the transformative subjective reality of labor also helps to clarify how parents become parents in time. That is, the relational labor of parenting itself reveals a person's subjective recognition of their identity as a parent. Parenthood is discovered subjectively both through the relationship it fosters and through the intransitive effects of parental labor whereby individuals realize capacities and aspects of the self that had not previously been realized in the same way. Clarifying this intransitive dimension of work, John Paul II writes: "As a person, man is therefore the subject of work. As a person he works, he performs various actions belonging to the work process; independently of their objective content, these actions must all serve to realize his humanity, to fulfill the calling to be a person that is his by reason of his very humanity."[47]

Such a view also permits a greater understanding of parenthood as a vocation. That is, like other forms of labor, parenthood can be a path toward fuller realization of the self through service to others. Capturing perhaps one of the greatest truths of parenthood, John Paul II recognizes that the goodness of labor lies in part in the difficulties it entails.[48] Fulfilling work implies challenges that take concerted effort to overcome. Such challenges also create the possibility for individual growth and personal transformation.[49]

Moreover, *Laborem exercens* argues that a moral evaluation of work requires consideration of its humanizing impact on the workers themselves.[50] As John Paul II writes, "there is no doubt that human work has an ethical value of its own, which clearly and directly remain[s] linked to the fact that the one who carries it out is a person, a conscious and free subject, that is to say a subject that decides about himself."[51] The human person is the central purpose of work, no matter what specific form that labor takes. By focusing on the intransitive effect of labor on the subject, and setting aside the complications of inserting another subject into a paradigm framed by the hierarchy of subject over object noted above, this affirmation, applied to parenthood, suggests that parenting is not ordered only toward the well-being and development of children but also pertains to the development of parents as persons. Moreover, this is not merely an indirect consequence of the work of parenting but is instead an essential feature of its reality.[52] Parenting, it seems, ought to be good for people in all its dimensions.

Taking this aspect of parenting seriously aids in rethinking how tightly parenting is defined within a recent tradition that has operated primarily out of a private, biological nuclear vision of the family. Family systems are complex, and children may have multiple adults who they count as parents during their development or at different points in their lives. Commitment to a child's well-being and the transformative effects of the laborious efforts dedicated to serving this good define the reality of parenthood. The realization of such a personal transformation through the experiences of parenting neither depends on the existence of a biological relationship nor on the number of co-parents who are likewise concerned for the child.

Furthermore, *Laborem exercens* helps root the capacity to parent in common human capabilities. There is a clear parallel in the purpose of work and the purpose of the family, in that both are aimed at solidarity across generations and across society. As John Paul II writes, "the essence and role of the family are in the final analysis specified by love. Hence the family has the mission to guard, reveal and communicate love, and this is a living reflection of and a real sharing in God's love for humanity and the love of Christ the Lord for the Church His bride."[53] Solidarity is a basic ethical expression of love as the fundamental value of the family. In this view, the language of self-gift that is so central to John Paul II's anthropology might be considered an intimate form of solidarity. Moreover, John Paul II presents work as an essential anthropological reality that communicates God's design for humanity and defines the human person. This suggests that we should not be surprised to find that the capabilities to perform specific forms of labor are rooted deeply within humanity. Parenting, it seems, calls forth and actualizes innate capacities for commitment to another person's well-being and, in this way, can realize and develop capacities for solidarity through its acts.[54] In these parental acts, concern extends beyond the self to the child, and in this extension, individuals are formed as parents. As a vocation, this growth in self-identity and ability also constitutes growth in relation to the divine, inasmuch as the child is another in whom one encounters Christ.[55]

Parenthood entails myriad social pressures that can fuel alienation from the self, many of which stem from a perceived need to meet expectations of devoted motherhood and fatherhood in ways that do not match personal capacities or familial contexts. This alienation depersonalizes the relational work of parenthood and separates individuals from more fulfilling realizations of the grace of their parental vocation. Viewing parenthood from the perspective of labor rather than gender may create greater space for the subjective well-being and development of parents as persons, inasmuch as it distances parenthood from highly influential gendered expectations. Although contemporary Catholic teaching has frequently warned against viewing children as objects, it has not meaningfully recognized how often parenthood is characterized by objectification because parents are themselves treated as means to an end by their children and by the social and religious forces that shape expectations without concern for personal context or capabilities. Consequently, a key dimension of the subjective reality of parenting is the task of resisting objectification, so far as conditions permit. To do so, theological perspectives on parenthood must come to recognize the necessity of conflict within parent–child relations that is so often covered over by saccharine idealizations of harmonious family life.

Resistance on the part of parents to the objectifying demands of children trains children to regard others as persons who cannot be treated as objects of their own gratification. For decades, feminist scholars have noted the lack of reflection on love of self within the Catholic tradition's tendency to promote self-sacrifice. In *Centessimus annus*, John Paul II warns of alienation and writes of the danger of refusing to live out of "self-giving and the formation of authentic human community."[56] This view of self-giving must be balanced with an appropriate affirmation of dignity and self-love. Parents should not be pressured to forfeit their subjective dignity and well-being for the sake of their children. As a vocation of solidarity, mutual respect as well as self-giving are required from both parents and children, even as children must learn to grow into this mutuality over time in developmentally appropriate ways. This affirmation of self-love and resistance to objectification is a challenging task of parenthood, not a natural given within ideally structured families.

Parenthood, then, is a deep form of solidarity based in a free and loving gift of self that aims at the well-being of another and transforms both the parent and parented. Parenting also reaches beyond this interpersonal encounter to the greater social and historical inheritance of humanity as participation in parenting joins parents in solidarity both among their peers and across generations. John Paul II's description of how work can draw the worker into relationships of solidarity serves as a fitting metaphor:

> A man can easily see that *through his work he enters into two inheritances*: the inheritance of what is given to the whole of humanity in the resources of nature, and the inheritance of what others have already developed on the basis of those resources. . . . In working, man also "enters into the labour of others." Guided both by our intelligence and by the faith that draws light from the word of God, we have no difficulty in accepting this image of the sphere and process of man's labour. It is *a consistent image, one that is humanistic as well as theological*. . . . If some dependence is discovered in the work process, it is dependence on the Giver of all the resources of creation, and also on other human beings, those to whose work and initiative we owe the perfected and increased possibilities of our own work [emphasis in the original].[57]

Parenting participates explicitly in the ongoing inheritance of humanity through both the reception of life and the concerted effort to guide the child's well-being with the resources that our place in history and relations to others make available. In parenting, individuals participate in relationships of solidarity with the children who are the objects of their care, with other parents, with caregivers, and with other involved individuals—and with the greater social, ecclesial, and historic communities in which they are situated.

In these many ways, the anthropological reflections on the realities of human work offered within *Laborem exercens* help to expand and clarify the human realities of parenthood. Although these are merely reflections offered toward a most robust theological anthropology, they are substantive enough to suggest that the central theological realities of parenthood can be articulated from a different standpoint than the prevailing framework of parenthood typically acknowledges. Without prioritizing sexual ethical or gender norms, anthropological reflections on the reality of parenthood as a form or labor can meaningfully engage parental experiences within a theological frame.

THE ANTHROPOLOGY OF *LAUDATO SI'*

An important question left unanswered in this engagement with *Laborem exercens* is how such a view of parenthood as labor can be fully rooted within the encyclical's theological vision, given that its own paradigm for labor relies on a subject–object relation that does not fit the actual experiences of parenthood. Although the potential avenue of introducing the concept of "worthy object" was suggested, the basic challenge itself rests in John Paul II's propensity for dualistic categories, which he tends to present as contrasting and absolute. This tendency makes it difficult to see how a subject could ever be counted as an object of labor, while the document itself does not seem aware of the tension or the exclusion of particular forms of interpersonal labor it creates. As considered in chapter 3, Pope Francis has largely continued in the same trajectory of John Paul II's thought about the topics of gender and sexuality. However, in other areas his thought demonstrates a greater willingness to explore anthropological realities that are defined by their interrelatedness rather than distinctions.

Although John Paul II draws a strong distinction between the human person and all nonhuman creation, as did *Gaudium et spes*, Francis's *Laudato si'* challenges assumptions of human uniqueness, dominance, and control over nonhuman creation.[58] The encyclical's revision of dichotomous relationships is guided by its commitment to the Catholic sacramental imagination. Instead of strict lines of division, the encyclical emphasizes the interconnectedness of beings as a consequence of existence within a universe that images the Triune God.[59] God dwells in intimate relation to this interrelated creation, which, permeated by divine grace, contains an essential, Eucharistic dimension.[60]

Moreover, as Celia Dean-Drummond argues, Francis "sees interconnection as important to a theological approach to the world that is concerned with right relationships in justice and that combines care for the natural world with care for oneself and care for right relationships within the human community."[61] In referring anthropology to the Trinity, Francis shows that dignity and relationality are not opposed. This allows a shift not only away from an isolated focus on individuals but on humanity as well and still arrives at an affirmation of dignity through a different anthropological key that is more cognizant of the deep relational character of human existence.

The relational anthropology of *Laudato si'* centers on its observation that humanity was not created in isolation but was born from within a larger web of reality to which persons relate with a specific identity and tasks.[62] In this view, the "dominion" proper to the human race is not centered on a subject/object dichotomy or control and submission but instead on the particular relations and responsibilities that humans have within and for wider creation. As such, the communal structure of existence calls individuals out of themselves and into relationship.[63] In doing so, the anthropological centrality of self-gift is preserved, as is the conviction that in this outward relational movement toward the other, persons come to know and understand themselves. As *Laudato si'* explains, "The human person grows more, matures more and is sanctified more to the extent that he or she enters into relationships, going out from themselves to live in communion with God, with others and with all creatures."[64]

As such, the interconnected nature of our existence supports the notion of self-gift so central to John Paul II's personalist moral vision. However, for him, the language of self-gift centers on interpersonal relationships, while the subject–object relation that defines his reflection on labor exhibits self-gift in a more indirect way as the material products of labor can carry this to other persons. In contrast, *Laudato si'* allows these relationships to extend beyond humans through its emphasis on God's loving presence mediated through all created beings, which thereby take on a certain subjective dimension as conduits of grace. Nonhuman creation is "open to God's transcendence,"[65] such that the spirit of life in-dwells "every living creature and calls us to enter into relationship with [God]."[66] Quoting Patriarch Bartholomew, the encyclical states, "It is our humble conviction that the divine and the human meet in the slightest detail in the seamless garment of God's creation, in the last speck of dust of our planet."[67] *Laudato si'* places human existence within a world that cannot constrain itself from proclaiming God's glory and is consequently a world that is abundantly open to relationships.

Bringing such a theological vision into dialogue with *Laborem exercens* allows for a softening of the subject/object divide, because it rejects the association of any created thing as a "mere object." Because all things are rooted in the Creator, all things bear the marks of their creation and may mediate divine love. In such a sacramental theological vision, to treat any being as *merely* an object neglects its openness to transcendent reality. This does not entirely bridge the human/subject, nonhuman/object divide, but it forestalls dualistic differentiation between human and nonhuman because even nonhuman creation can reveal its creator and therefore speak in a deeply personal way to the sacramentality of creation. This vision reaffirms the understanding of work as always relational work in both its transitive and intransitive dimensions, not only in an extended indirect way but also because there is an "other" behind every object of work, be it a material object or a human person. All things stand in relation to God and as such offer the possibility of sacramental encounter when recognized in their full realities.

Although John Paul II also held a sacramental understanding of creation, his views tended toward differentiations, while the anthropological vision introduced in *Laudato si'* tends toward connections. To some extent, Francis simply allows these differing anthropological realities to stand in tension, such that the encyclical does not present an entirely unified perspective.[68] Nonetheless, the sacramental-relational emphasis of *Laudato si'* read into *Laborem exercens* frees the latter from the possibility of isolating labor from actual relationships, regardless of the particular object. It is possible to read *Laborem exercens* as describing an almost entirely isolated subjective experience of labor, in which an individual exerts effort on a mere lump of matter while the subjective transformation of the worker comes through the consequences of his or her own exertion reflected back upon himself or herself. The anthropological perspective introduced in *Laudato si'* disallows this possibility by making relational encounter fundamental to human existence, not just interpersonally as John Paul II emphasized, but as constituent of encounters with any part of God's creation.

Labor in its full human reality cannot be isolating, even when done in the absence of another human person. Instead, the external exertion of one's creativity and efforts in the world always implies the possibility of encounter with an irreducible other. As such, the challenge is not personalism's concern for reducing persons to mere objects so much as the theological possibility of belief in mere objects within God's sacramental creation. Estrangement, isolation, greed, and delusions of grandeur define sin in the personalist context of both popes. But whereas John Paul II presented sin as the failure to recognize the other as a irreducible subject in his or her own right, Francis presents sin as a failure to recognize the sacramental nature of our existence and the relationships in which we are bound.[69] Humans are relational creatures, called to discover and become ourselves within and through these relationships.

The relational anthropology of *Laudato si'* insists on the interconnectedness of all things, and on the human person's constitutive need for relationships. Human persons are only known, and only know ourselves, through our foundational relationships with God, other humans, and nonhuman creation. Rightly understanding ourselves within God's creation involves seeing our dependence on and moral obligations toward nonhuman creation as we cannot come to know ourselves in isolation.[70] The true price of a rigid dichotomy between the person and the rest of the material world is that it makes the human person foreign to a universe that God has proclaimed good. In asserting that God, humanity, and nonhuman creation form an integrated communion, each unknowable without the others, the relational anthropology of *Laudato si'* reveals that the full dimensions of our anthropological reality cannot be abstracted from the conditions of existence within the sacramental web of creation.

Reintegrating these anthropological observations into a theological view of parenthood, we can see that parenthood is a relational form of labor not least because all forms of labor are relational. As such, the problem is not so much that interpersonal labor does not fit the paradigm of *Laborem exercens* but that the paradigm of *Laborem exercens* fails to take the sacramental commitments of the Catholic tradition to their full theological implications. Although it is clear that labor directed at nonhuman material objects is meaningfully different from labor directed at other persons, these do not stand in a strictly dichotomous relationship. And though the "worthy object" remains a helpful category for objects that offer norms for use, this becomes a matter of degree because nothing is entirely without its own internal meaning or significance. As such, children may be understood as both properly the objects of acts of parenthood and also fully persons in themselves. Moreover, as the object of concerned parental labor, children may come to be recognized explicitly as sacramental to their parents. This sacramental encounter is in part conditioned on the concerted effort that parents exert through their acts of parenting, in which they come to discover the richness of the personhood of their object of care, including his or her reality as a gift from God who incarnates God's loving presence within the world.

This sacramental-relational vision of parenthood, which *Laudato si'* helps to clarify, is only intended as an indication toward a theological pathway to understanding parenthood in richer anthropological dimensions. Likewise, this vision of the sacramental nature of parenthood is not contingent on a prior reflection on sexual ethics or gender norms; instead, it begins with the interpersonal reality of parenthood as a form of labor within the context of a sacramental worldview.

CONCLUSION

Although this alternative framework for parenthood based in relational labor has been sketched above in very broad and incomplete terms, its implications and ability to fit within a contemporary Catholic moral theological framework are evident. Because parenthood does not involve only sexual activity or the realization of innate gendered propensities, shifting to consider parenthood as relational labor allows a pathway to understanding contours of parenthood as an anthropological reality that the prevailing framework has left unattended. Importantly, it is the anthropological insights of recent popes that prove informative for beginning to articulate this pathway toward a broader engagement with parenthood as rooted in common human capabilities. In this, we find the important dimensions of parenthood as a relational act that seeks the good of both parents and parented within the context of the larger human society and sacramental creation.

NOTES

1. "Child" within this context refers simply to the person who is parented, not strictly young persons. Such a relationship generally begins in childhood but continues beyond. The position of child implies a trajectory toward maturity, along which parental labor directs the child's development and growth.
2. John Paul II, *Redemptoris custos*, secs. 7, 21.
3. John Paul II, sec. 8.
4. Sullivan-Dunbar, *Human Dependency*, 142–43.
5. Gaillardetz, "School," 130.
6. Such a view is supported by research suggesting that "interdependence" and "independence" are not mutually exclusive categories. Instead, high levels of interdependence can and do coexist with high levels of independence. See Lee, "Persons," 321–27.
7. Sullivan-Dunbar, *Human Dependency*, 38.
8. Weaver, *Acting Person*, 89.
9. See Rubio, *Family Ethics*.
10. Millare, "Towards a Common Communion," 610.
11. Homeschooling diverges from this pattern, but even here education is commonly shared among multiple adults within and beyond a school system. It might also be noted that this was written during the 2020 COVID-19 pandemic, a point at which parents in the United States were broadly fulfilling this role of direct formal education to the best of our abilities.
12. Sullivan-Dunbar, *Human Dependency*, 225.
13. The perspective being developed shares clear points of connection with the ethics of care and may help to advance the dialogue between Catholic theological commitments and this relatively recent but much needed rebuttal to traditional modes of Western ethical discourse. Unfortunately, an adequate engagement with such possibilities is not possible here because it lies beyond the scope of this book.

14. Sullivan-Dunbar, *Human Dependency*, 120.
15. Baum, "*Laborem exercens*," 530.
16. John Paul II, *Laborem exercens*, sec. 1.
17. John Paul II, *Laborem exercens*, "Introductory Blessing."
18. Dorr, *Option*, 321.
19. Hinze, "Women."
20. John Paul II, *Laborem exercens*, sec. 19.
21. Vatican II, *Gaudium et spes*, sec. 29.
22. Hinze, "Women," 63.
23. John Paul II, *Laborem exercens*, sec. 26.
24. Prov. 31:15–17.
25. John Paul II, *Laborem exercens*, sec. 19.
26. A chapter written by female students of Ursuline High School in *Visions and Vocations*, a recent publication of the Catholic Women Speak Network, stresses the multiple vocations they seek to fulfill within their lifetimes as well as the desire that their male counterparts be held to the same standards of commitment to a vocation within family life. See Students of the Ursuline High School, Wimbledon, "Letter."
27. John Paul II, *Laborem exercens*, sec. 26.
28. Baum, "*Laborem exercens*," 531. Commentators disagree on the relationship between the Polish movement, Solidarity, and the arguments of the encyclical. Certainly, the pope's concern for the events in Poland colored his perspective and may have helped focus his thought on the industrial working class. Lamoureux, "Commentary," 391.
29. Vatican II, *Gaudium et spes*, sec. 34.
30. Finn, "Human Work," 882.
31. Tablan, "Catholic Social Teachings," 295.
32. John Paul II, *Veritatis splendor*, sec. 48.
33. Wojtyla, *Love*, 41.
34. John Paul II, *Crossing the Threshold*, 201.
35. Rickert, "Wojtyla's Personalistic Norm," 677.
36. John Paul II, *Laborem exercens*, sec. 5.
37. Gregory Baum briefly considers Hannah Arendt's distinction between work and action which may be relevant to this discussion. For Arendt, "The objects of work . . . are the things people produce. . . . By contrast, the object of action is the reordering of human relations. Work has to do with making, action with doing." This might help to explain the subject/object divide because only "work" in this analysis would imply a nonhuman object. But *Laborem exercens* itself suggests no such distinction. Moreover, Arendt's view still appears to raise the question of whether education, ministry, and parenthood, which take persons and relationships as their objects, are work or action. Baum, "*Laborem exercens*," 534.
38. John Paul II also recognizes the interpersonal significance of parenting, teaching, and pastoral care in his earlier encyclical on mercy, *Dives in misericordia*. See John Paul II, *Dives in misericordia*, sec. 14.
39. John Paul II, *Laborem exercens*, sec. 26.
40. Cf. Luke 9:58, Matt. 8:20, and John 4:31–35.
41. John Paul II, *Laborem exercens*, sec. 26.
42. John Paul II, sec. 10.
43. Yeoman, "Conceptualizing Meaningful Work," 245.
44. Yeoman.

45. Rickert, "Wojtyla's Personalistic Norm," 677.
46. See Brady, *Essential Catholic Social Thought*.
47. John Paul II, *Laborem exercens*, sec. 6.
48. John Paul II, sec. 9.
49. John Paul II.
50. Baum, "*Laborem exercens*," 529.
51. John Paul II, *Laborem exercens*, sec. 6.
52. John Paul II, sec. 6.
53. John Paul II, *Familiaris consortio*, sec. 17.
54. Naughton and Lacniak, "Theological Context," 992.
55. Weaver, *Acting Person*, 74.
56. John Paul II, *Centessimus annus*, sec. 41.
57. John Paul II, *Laborem exercens*, sec. 13.
58. See Kohlhaas and McLaughlin, "Loving."
59. Francis, *Laudato si'*, sec. 239.
60. Francis, sec. 236.
61. Deane-Drummond, "New Anthropology?" 191.
62. Christiansen, "Cosmic Family."
63. McDonald, "*Laudato Si'*."
64. Francis, *Laudato si'*, sec. 240.
65. Francis, sec. 79.
66. Francis, sec. 88.
67. Francis, sec. 9.
68. Deane-Drummond, "New Anthropology?" 191.
69. Francis, *Laudato si'*, sec. 50.
70. Millare, "Towards a Common Communion," 610.

Conclusion

This book has explored the emergence and consequences of a broadly influential contemporary framework for Catholic thought on the family and parenthood. This framework emerged after the Industrialization Revolution, in parallel with the development of modern Catholic Social Teaching, and it carries certain presumptions about marriage, the family, gender, and parenting that stem from the cultural forces that shaped the modern West. Notably, Catholic teaching on the family incorporated a conceptual divide between the male-public sphere of social leadership and wage earning and the female-private sphere of domestic concerns and childrearing. In about the mid–twentieth century, this framework was transformed as the reforms of Vatican II recognized marriage as a partnership between equals and affirmed women's right to participate in public life. At the same time, however, Catholic teaching remained wary of the sexual revolution and the displacement of traditional gender norms. Consequently, the publication of *Humanae vitae* marks a key moment of development in this history, for Paul VI reaffirmed Catholic opposition to contraception, including the newly available birth control pill, while linking "responsible parenthood" to sexual behavior. In the ensuing intra-Catholic disagreements that revolved around *Humanae vitae*'s judgment but ultimately included a much larger web of intersecting concerns, conceptions of parenthood centered more narrowly on sexual-reproductive issues.

In this context, John Paul II presented a unified theological vision informed by the personalist turn in moral theology, while firmly upholding traditional sexual ethical norms. Moreover, he praised women and supported women's rights to participate in the public sphere while remaining stalwart on the significance of gender difference and women's central place within the family. His concern for the family also led to significant contributions across moral and social teaching that highlighted the social dimensions of family life while tending to idealize the biological, nuclear family. In doing so, the diversities of family experiences and the theological values traditionally associated with adoptive parenthood received relatively little attention. At the same time, increasing social acceptance of homosexuality and developments in reproductive technology elicited increasingly forceful magisterial appeals to the meaning and value of sexual differences and biological procreation. The effect was to solidify the contemporary framework for parenthood around the private, biological nuclear family, rooted in the gendered realities of bodily existence and traditional Catholic sexual ethical norms. Despite some loosening of particular pastoral applications and a clear desire to mercifully meet families in their actual circumstances, Pope Francis has largely affirmed and continued the prevalence of this framework, while his adamant rejection of "gender theory" has further positioned magisterial teaching in opposition to contemporary academic discourse.

For their part, many academic theologians have critiqued aspects of contemporary magisterial teaching, notably including its opposition to contraception, gender essentialism, and developments in moral teaching related to homosexuality and same-sex partnerships. Yet given these particular points of tension, academic criticisms have also tended to replicate the concerns of the prevailing framework for parenthood with limited divergence from its basic assumptions.

Like any conceptual frame, the prevailing Catholic framework for parenthood has informed engagement while also concealing issues that lie beyond the boundaries it establishes. Retracing its emergence in modern history reveals its influence over time but cannot itself assess the framework's moral value. In this normative step, I have suggested that the contemporary framework for parenthood is, in fact, detrimental to considerations of parenthood in its full theological-anthropological realities as it restricts conceptual possibilities by focusing attention on the particular issues of sexual ethics and gender while obstructing from view both the common anthropological roots of parental capabilities and Christian parenthood's foundation in baptismal identity.

In an attempt to overcome the tunnel vision that keeps Catholic thought on parenthood fixated on these issues, the second part of this book has explored various resources for reconsidering the terms of the prevailing framework. To this end, the second part has presented interpretive options within the tradition, introduced themes from the social sciences regarding child well-being and compared these with those of contemporary Catholic teaching, engaged historical diversity in Christian expressions of kinship, and considered a model of parenthood as relational labor in conversation with John Paul II's anthropology of work. These explorations have sketched a different path for conceptualizing parenthood that may overcome particular limitations of the presently dominant framework. The contribution to theological discourse made in these pages is offered as a well-grounded yet provisional starting point that might open new possibilities for thinking about parenthood within the Catholic tradition.[1]

IMPLICATIONS

Supposing that the ideas offered in this book do, in fact, constitute a meaningful contribution to a Catholic theological anthropology of parenthood, they cannot help but have consequences at the level of moral judgment and pastoral application. Personalist moral methodology typically maps a trajectory from theological anthropology to moral theology such that the vision of the human person informs moral obligations. With respect to the moral issues related to parenthood, recent years have seen widespread uncertainty and disagreement on the implications of Catholic moral teaching as various Catholic institutions have addressed such issues differently.

As social acceptance of diverse family forms has increased, contemporary magisterial teaching has continued to firmly insist that the foundation of the family lies within the relationship formed by a man and woman in marriage. Meanwhile, applications of magisterial teaching to specific situations have often proven complex, inconsistent, unpopular, and at times quite damaging to the public perception of Catholic institutions.[2] Throughout the last two decades, high-profile cases have included Catholic denials of public services; terminations of parish, hospital, and school staff members; and refusals to baptize or fully welcome children of same-sex parents into Catholic parishes and schools. In response to each of these actions, Catholics have remained firmly and sometimes viscerally divided.

This book opened with a review of one such episode in Illinois, wherein Catholic adoption agencies lost access to government contracts as a result of conflicts between antidiscrimination legislation and the agencies' religious commitments. This case was presented to draw attention to the continued development of Catholic teaching in recent years along with the misalignment between this teaching and direct concern for actual parental abilities. In Illinois, Catholic agencies argued that their religious convictions absolutely prohibited placing children with same-sex couples, even as they did not articulate what parental capabilities such couples necessarily lacked. Moreover, their argument for religious freedom hinged on a recent clarification from the Congregation for the Doctrine of the Faith that was signed by a prefect who himself had employed a less restrictive interpretation of this teaching as an archbishop only a few years earlier. Within their theological context, such arguments simultaneously acknowledge the ongoing development of Catholic thought and suppose immediate reception by which magisterial clarifications can be equated with deeply held religious convictions. This immediate, authoritarian view of religious convictions betrays a naive understanding of the Catholic tradition that undermines the importance of reception by the faithful, the role of the conscience, and other processes in moral theological discernment fit for a community that values both its tradition and meaningful experiential engagement.

Present uncertainty about the practical application of Catholic moral norms related to families stems from the obvious reality that there is ongoing uncertainty about the potential developments of Catholic belief on these matters. Although some will gladly argue that the Magisterium ought to remove all such uncertainty through the force of authority, this betrays a religious mind-set and ecclesial understanding that are not shared by all Catholics. Moreover, a simple review of recent history confirms that authoritative teaching is ineffective in removing ambiguity in the actual life of the Church when the experiences of the faithful present contrary evidence. This being the case, Catholic institutions must deliberately and carefully discern how moral standards ought to apply in diverse situations. In considering the specific case of adoption by same-sex couples, the arguments advanced within this book suggest that the concerns for gender complementarity and sexual ethical norms are exaggerated within present magisterial judgments and require balance within a broader framework for parenthood. With such an approach, the Catholic public's responses to the phenomenon of same-sex parenting could speak directly to this reality on its merits *as parenting* rather than the current framing as disordered sexual relationships that claim more social rights than they justly deserve. Not only would this approach speak more directly to the issue as it is publicly understood; it also avoids weakening the central interests in children's well-being that are often communicated through a primary concern for sexual relationships.

The framework developed in the preceding pages suggests that contemporary magisterial teaching is justified in its insistence that no one can claim a right to a child. Children are first and foremost persons, and they ought to be treated accordingly—meaning that they cannot be an object of possession. Nonetheless, society at large, and those charged with the care of children in particular, are morally obligated to respond to the needs of children and secure their well-being as far as conditions allow. The standards of "best care" and "best interest of the child" that are commonly applied in legal decisions of guardianship well reflect these moral priorities.

Presumed sexual activity among adults is not a suitable categorical standard in such assessments. First, this is because there is little evidence that this influences a child's well-being on the same level as the instability of foster or institutional care, with the lack of long-term parental relationships that such situations often entail. And second, it is because the standard is inconsistently applied across adoptive couples and is therefore unfair. Although homo-genital sex acts are absolutely proscribed by Catholic moral teaching, so too are contraception, masturbation, and the viewing of pornography. These objective evils cannot be assessed by the gender of partners alone, and yet they are pervasive throughout the sexual lives of married Catholics. Conversely, the existence of any sexual relationship, as realized through specific genital acts, is not a given within all marriages or intimate partnerships. As such, the gendered identity of partners is not a sufficient standard for assessing the moral standing of their sexual lives.

Moreover, this line of argument suggests a flawed conception of the complexity of human relationships. Although immoral sexual practices may be significant enough to outweigh the moral goods of a particular relationship, recognizing this reality does not imply a general principle that the objective existence of sexual immorality absolutely corrupts all relationships.[3] Not only is this standard once again being unevenly applied; it also fails to recognize that relationships are greater than acts. This priority follows from the Catholic understanding of sexuality as a key factor in the human drive toward relationships themselves.[4] Because sexuality serves relationships, sexual immorality alone cannot determine a relationship's entire moral content, although it may outweigh its moral value. It is a regrettable but evident reality that individuals are capable of behaving immorally in certain areas of their lives while managing others more appropriately. As such, the existence of sexual immorality must be set within the context of the relationship itself, holistically considered.

Gender complementarity has provided support for a second key line of the argument against adoption by same-sex couples. Here, Catholic teaching is justified in its assertion that children's full development is aided by the influence of adults who differently model mature, gendered personhood both independently and in relationships of mutuality. However, restricting the requirement for gender complementarity to married spouses alone relies on a paltry view of the family and parenthood. Open and inclusive families, the sort praised by some documents of magisterial teaching, also mean more expansive opportunities for various adult influences. Once again, though parental gender complementarity is presented as absolute for same-sex couples, the same standard is not applied consistently because single parents are excused from such an absolute requirement. Instead, in these situations, Catholic teaching acknowledges the importance and influence of caring adults beyond primary parents. Moreover, because single parenthood, adoptive parenthood, and care for children by vowed religious have all been accepted without protest on the grounds of parental capabilities, within the tradition the capacity for direct caregiving does not appear to be essentially related to gender complementarity among caregivers. Consequently, parental capabilities appear to be widespread among adults, such that the gender or number of parents does not, in fact, decisively determine what counts as at least a minimally acceptable parental relationship with regard to children's needs.

The implication of examining these lines of argument is that same-sex adoptive parenthood should not be absolutely proscribed on the basis of either sexual acts or gender complementarity as these are presently defended. Although many of the questions raised in Catholic teaching remain important and informative, they do not rise to such a high standard as absolute prohibition. Accepting parenthood's foundation in basic human capacities and the Christian tradition's commitment to responding to the needs of children, same-sex couples who seek to offer homes to children should be regarded more generously. Moreover, present realities witness to many same-sex couples that do, in fact, desire to raise their children within the Catholic Church, which has caused many current uncertainties at the pastoral level.

When parenthood is conceived as relational labor based on common human capacities, the moral evaluation of fitness for parenthood likewise shifts to concern for abilities to form and sustain relationships and to effectively perform the specific labor that parenthood demands. A relational anthropology, as well as the actual history of Christian caregiving practices, suggests that most otherwise capable adults can demonstrate and develop these capabilities. Likewise, taking seriously the idea that labor is good for persons introduces issues for the human development of parents or potential parents themselves. Although no one can claim a right to initiate parenting, parenting itself remains a human good and a potential vocation that can lead to growth in humanity. For this reason, any power to discriminate among who may become a parent must be wielded with due recognition for the loss of a potential good denying this opportunity entails. Certainly, adults who are able to maintain healthy, stable, and committed marriages are also likely to have the relevant capacities for parenthood, but this does not mean that these capacities are strictly limited to such persons. Standards for adoptive parents should be based on realistic expectations of serving children's best interests, not idealizations.

Having applied this expanded framework for parenthood to this book's original test case, it appears that an absolute prohibition of adoption for same-sex couples is both overly assertive and inadequately informed. This conclusion does not imply that all adoptions to same-sex couples are thereby justified, but simply that they should not be categorically excluded. Instead, a more nuanced approach is required to evaluate specific cases, both in terms of parental fitness and in light of social and contextual factors. The prioritization of child well-being requires that the inability to reasonably improve a child's prospects is prohibitive for initiating a new parental relationship, regardless of the capabilities of potential parents. Considering such situations, it is important to note that the anthropological perspective developed here does not imply an identification of parenthood in its moral theological sense with legal guardianship. Many children throughout history have found parents beyond their legal guardians, while the Christian tradition on kinship implies openness to serving the needs of others as its most essential aspect. Authentic expressions of parenthood can and do occur in diverse circumstances.

FURTHER TRAJECTORIES

Throughout the modern era, gender and sexual ethics have played increasingly important roles in Catholic conceptions of parenthood. This distinctive trend is marked more by tendencies rather than explicit rejections of broader views, as aspects of wider traditions have been retained and reasserted throughout this period. Examples include the convictions that adoptive parenthood is a paradigmatic expression of the nature of Christian parenthood, that the most important function of the Christian parent is the spiritual education of children, that families are versatile and open social units that function over time, and that nurturing and caregiving capacities are common human attributes. Although biological kinship, the marriage-based family structure, and moral means of procreation are important dimensions of parenthood, their recent dominance has overshadowed other significant ideals.

An account of Christian parenthood centered on parenthood as relational labor attends to child well-being through its concern for adult capabilities. This conception implies care for the physical, emotional, and educational needs of children when it is guided by the moral pursuit of authentic human flourishing and understands children fundamentally as gifts from God.[5] Christian parents, through their committed interpersonal relationship and concerted acts of parental care, manifest their vocation for parenthood and in so doing assist their children in seeking their ultimate good in friendship with God.[6] Christian parenthood is a form of evangelization not because it is unique but because it is a vocation rooted in the Christian baptismal identity, which calls for solidarity with others in service to their well-being holistically considered.

The nature of solidarity as it applies to the family and among families is one specific trajectory that requires greater reflection in this anthropological development. The participation of nonparents in parenting and parenting by non–legally recognized parents are particular manifestations of solidarity that require greater attention. Not all caregivers are parents; but all those who care for children participate to some extent in the reality of parenthood. Such an exploration would help differentiate the specific dimensions of the Christian vocation of parenthood from the more fundamental implications of the common Christian obligation to care for others that is given in baptism.

The limitations of parenthood also require attention. Following Kant's dictum, "ought implies can," a person should not be expected to morally assent to an obligation that they cannot reasonably fulfill. Parenthood has been presented as an emergent reality that becomes evident through the commitments and acts of parenting itself. Consequently, a current lack of development of parental capacities does not necessarily imply a future absence of parental capacities—in fact, such capacities are typically realized over time. Nonetheless, there are circumstances in which the initiation or continuation of a parental relationship may cease to serve a child's well-being or be harmful to the development of the parents themselves. Although an established parental relationship implies a prima facie duty to continue parenting, based on the relational dimension of parenthood, serious reasons could require that this be set aside. Circumstances can change significantly over the course of a child's development, and therefore an assessment of parental capability must attend to reasonably foreseeable developments and adaptations in parental abilities.[7] Parents who surrender their parental duties out of concern for a child's best interest represent an important consideration along this trajectory, because such acts may both fulfill parental obligations while discontinuing an interpersonal parental relationship.[8] Thus, a fuller account of Christian parenthood may provide insight on family dissolution as well as family formation.

Furthermore, the balance of the specific differentiations of fatherhood and motherhood requires attention. Within contemporary Catholic teaching, there is very little suggestion that men can nurture children directly, despite the existence of primary caregiver fathers as a small but significant reality.[9] Magisterial thought directs paternal involvement through the motherhood of a man's spouse and counts an assisting, indirect role as sufficient for male nurture.[10] This view cuts both ways because it links women to essential parental tasks while limiting the view of male abilities. As men increasingly partake in more egalitarian parental experiences, such gendered characterizations unfortunately dismiss both their human adaptability and the developmental nature of parenthood itself. John Paul II argued that motherly nurture grows out of women's *experience* of bearing children, and he thereby suggests that parental traits are to some extent learned. This reaffirms the labor dimension of parenthood while hinting that even gendered parental expectations may arise from typically gendered experiences rather than innately differentiated capacities. Greater attention to human adaptability in fulfilling parental roles could facilitate more nuanced responses to cultural developments that are relevant to the family and gender norms.

Moreover, this book has suggested that common human capacities ground the necessary conditions for parenthood. Both the view that parental capabilities and specific duties of parenthood are essentially governed by gender, and the view that parental capabilities and proclivity for parental behaviors are unshaped by gender shortchange the complexities of actual embodied human experience. An adequate approach must attend to the fact that human gender does shape dispositions and propensities through both physiological and social processes while also recognizing the significance of common human capabilities and adaptability. Certain capabilities are simply too important to the human person to be the sole domain of a single gender. Failure to recognize this constitutes a failure to recognize the essential unity of human experience.[11] Therefore, when a capability appears to constitute an essential aspect of personhood, theological conversation must shift to how gender shapes its expression, not its existence.

Framing parenthood within commitments to the unity of human experience and the human potential for development does not settle the problematic of gender but does mark out important parameters. If parental functioning relies on both common human capabilities and the development of these through experience, it is difficult to imagine motherhood and fatherhood as essentially dichotomous realities without excluding nonbiological mothers from authentic motherhood. But parenthood is also an embodied activity, and therefore gender differentiation cannot be entirely ignored. For these reasons, contemporary discussions of parenthood rest on an anthropological tension between the observable realities of human embodiedness and the possibilities of human potential.

Finally, children and the nature of childhood require greater attention. The relative lack of theological and moral attention to children as legitimate subjects of concern in their own right is evident. Examples of this lacuna range from theological writings based on male experience that largely ignore the topics of children and childcare to feminist theological writings that presume children to be entirely included within the interests of women. In magisterial writings, similar biases have influenced three distinct trends in addressing children. The first, as in much modern theology, simply places the topic of children under the concerns of the family. Care for the child is often divided among gendered lines, with nurture coming from the mother and provision and education coming from the father. The second trend is evident in the "natalist" bent of modern teaching through the dominance of moral questions about procreation, reproductive technologies, and protection of the unborn. The final trend is a tendency to translate concern for children's well-being quickly into rights claims. There are significant reasons to question the application of rights language to children inasmuch as rational free adults are the original subjects of this perspective. Additionally, rights language has been widely criticized as a rather sparse tool for asserting ethical claims that respect the full dignity and complexity of human persons. Without sustained theological attention to children and childhood, rights claims remain some of the few available tools for expressing legitimate concern for children, even though they do so imperfectly.

CONCLUSION

Throughout recent decades, American Catholics have faced numerous questions about the nature of marriage, the family, and, ultimately, parenthood that have led to acrimonious disagreements. Differing responses have often hinged largely on social and political commitments and self-identities as well as religious convictions (the distinctions are often blurry). Same-sex relationships seem to occupy a unique focal point for wide-ranging disagreements—so much so that a person's stance on the subject serves as effective shorthand for indicating to which camp one belongs. A majority of US Catholics are comfortable with same-sex marriage, a statistic that grows stronger among young Catholics. However, roughly one-third are opposed, and this group also tends to be the most religiously active.[12] Recently, growing social awareness of transgender experiences has led to similar divisiveness and partisanship among US Catholics. Although the human drive to politically and religiously regulate human sexual behavior is well known, it is not so clear that Catholic theology must continually attempt to pass through this contemporary quagmire of culture war contentiousness centered on gender and sexuality in order to say something meaningful about parenthood. This book constitutes one attempt to argue for a new path forward.

Even as US Catholics are unlikely to come to a widespread agreement any time soon on issues of gender and sexual behavior, Catholic parents still share a great deal in common through their experiences of caring for their children. Although readers may disagree with some of the conclusions I have drawn, I hope the research and arguments offered here have provided an opportunity to reflect on the common experiences that unite Catholics called to the vocation of parenthood through work, love, and the sacramental realities of our daily lives.

NOTES

1. Traina, *Feminist Ethics,* 320.
2. Although Catholics are not in consistent agreement on how specific situations ought to be handled, there is concern across Catholic views about the inconsistency evident in these applications. E.g., Patrick Reilly, the founder of the Newman Society, praises the Congregation for Catholic Education's recent document "Male and Female He Created Them" for its clear guidance on gender norms but identifies the document's shortcomings in its lack of clarity on its specific implications for Catholic institutions. See Reilly, "Educators.'"
3. This recognition is implicit in *Persona humana*'s objection to same-sex relationships but has rarely been acknowledged since. See Congregation for the Doctrine of the Faith, *Persona humana,* sec. 8.
4. Ferder and Heagle, "Tender Fires," 20.
5. The understanding of the moral life as a pursuit of human flourishing is central to the Catholic moral tradition, whereas the conception of children as gifts dates to early Christianity and has appeared repeatedly in magisterial writing on the family since *Casti connubii.* See Pius XI, *Casti connubii,* secs. 15, 53.
6. Paul VI, *Evangelii nuntiandi,* sec. 71.
7. The fact that human needs, desires, and abilities change over time is central to Nussbaum's approach to Capabilities Theory. See Nussbaum, *Creating Capabilities,* 25.
8. Post, "Adoption," 160–61. Cultural pressures that label birth mothers who choose to relinquish parental claims as failed mothers, and de facto failed woman, are the cause of great harm to both women and children.
9. A conception of direct male nurture cannot be entirely ruled out because it could be implied in the relatively brief considerations of single parenthood and is present in statements by the US Catholic bishops.
10. John Paul II, "Letter to Families," sec. 16.
11. This is based on the Patristic dictum, "what has not been assumed has not been saved." Feminist theologians have rightly raised concern about explanations of gender that appear to affect basic personhood. See Reuther, *Sexism,* 93–138.
12. Lipka, "Young US Catholics."

BIBLIOGRAPHY

Aasgaard, Reider. "Paul as a Child: Children and Childhood in the Letters of the Apostle." *Journal of Biblical Literature* 126, no. 1 (2007): 129–59.

African Pastors. *Christ's New Homeland: Africa—Contribution to the Synod on the Family by African Pastors.* San Francisco: Ignatius, 2015.

"Agathonicê." In *Women in Early Christianity: Translations from Greek Texts,* edited by Patricia Cox Miller, 45. Washington, DC: Catholic University of America Press, 2005.

Alison, James. *On Being Liked.* New York: Crossroad, 2004.

Allen, Ann Taylor. *Feminism and Motherhood in Western Europe, 1890–1970.* New York: Palgrave Macmillan, 2005.

American Psychological Association. *Lesbian and Gay Parenting.* Washington, DC: American Psychological Association, 2005.

Anderson, Herbert. "Between Rhetoric and Reality: Women and Men as Equal Partners." In *Mutuality Matters: Family, Faith, and Just Love,* edited by Herbert Anderson, Edward Foley, Bonnie Miller-McLemore, and Robert Schreiter, 67–82. New York: Rowman & Littlefield, 2004.

Anonymous. "Sins of Admission; Why *Wouldn't* Gay Parents Pick a Catholic School?" *Commonweal,* April 23, 2010. https://www.commonwealmagazine.org/sins-admission.

Aquinas, Thomas. *Summa contra Gentiles.* Trans. Vernon J. Bourke. Garden City, NY: Hanover House, 1956.

———. *Summa theologica.* Trans. Fathers of the English Dominican Province. New York: Benziger Brothers, 1911–25.

Ariès, Philipe. *Centuries of Childhood: A Social History of Family Life.* Trans. Robert Baldick. New York: Random House, 1962.

Assistant Secretary for Planning and Evaluation. "Children Adopted from Foster Care: Child and Family Characteristics, Adoption Motivation and Well-Being." US Department of Health and Human Services, May 2011. http://aspe.hhs.gov/hsp/09/NSAP/Brief1/rb.pdf.

Associated Press. "Priest Tells Court 'Fornication'—Not Pregnancy—Reason Unwed Teacher Fired." *Crux,* September 12, 2019. https://cruxnow.com/ap/2019/09/12/priest-tells-court-fornication-not-pregnancy-reason-unwed-teacher-fired/.

Atkinson, Clarissa W. "'Wonderful Affection': Seventeenth-Century Missionaries to New France on Children and Childhood." In *The Child in Christian Thought,* edited by Marcia J. Bunge, 227–46. Grand Rapids: William B. Eerdmans, 2001.

Augustine. *On the Morals of the Manicheans. New Advent.* https://www.newadvent.org/fathers/1402.htm.

Aulette, Judy Root. *Changing American Families.* Boston: Pearson, 2007.

Bader, Jennifer. "Engaging the Struggle." In *Human Sexuality in the Catholic Tradition,* edited by Kieran Scott and Harold Daly Horrel, 91–110. New York: Rowman & Littlefield, 2007.

Bartel, Sarah, and John S. Grabowski, eds. *A Catechism for Family Life: Insights from Catholic Teaching on Love, Marriage, Sex, and Parenting.* Washington, DC: Catholic University of America Press, 2018.

Bartholet, Elizabeth. *Family Bonds: Adoption and the Politics of Parenting.* Boston: Houghton Mifflin, 1993.

Baum, Gregory. "*Laborem exercens.*" In *The New Dictionary of Catholic Social Thought,* edited by Judith A. Dwyer and Elizabeth Montgomery, 527–35. Collegeville, MN: Liturgical Press, 1994.

Bendroth, Margaret. "Horace Bushnell's *Christian Nurture.*" In *The Child in Christian Thought,* edited by Marcia J. Bunge, 350–64. Grand Rapids: William B. Eerdmans, 2001.

———. "Mainline Protestants and Children." In *Children and Childhood in American Religions,* edited by Don S. Browning and Bonnie J. Miller-McLemore, 25–41. New Brunswick, NJ: Rutgers University Press, 2009.

Benedict XVI. *Caritas in veritate.* Encyclical letter. Vatican website. June 29, 2009. www.vatican.va/content/benedict-xvi/en/encyclicals/documents/hf_ben-xvi_enc_20090629_caritas-in-veritate.html.

———. *Deus caritas est.* Encyclical letter. Vatican website. December 25, 2005. www.vatican.va/holy_father/benedict_xvi/encyclicals/documents/hf_ben-xvi_enc_20051225_deus-caritas-est_en.html.

———. "The Human Person, The Heart of Peace." Message on World Day of Peace. Vatican website. January 1, 2007. www.vatican.va/holy_father/benedict_xvi/messages/peace/documents/hf_ben-xvi_mes_20061208_xl-world-day-peace_en.html.

———. *Spe salvi.* Encyclical letter. Vatican website. November 30, 2007. http://w2.vatican.va/content/benedict-xvi/en/encyclicals/documents/hf_ben-xvi_enc_20071130_spe-salvi.html.

Bishops' Committee for Pastoral Research and Practices. *Parenthood.* Washington, DC: Office for Publishing and Promotion Services, US Catholic Conference, 1990.

Borestein, Michelle. "DC Archdiocese: Denying Communion to Lesbian at Funeral Was Against 'Policy.'" *Washington Post,* February 29, 2009. www.washingtonpost.com/local/dc-archdiocese-denying-communion-to-lesbian-at-funeral-was-against-policy/2012/02/28/gIQAlIxVgR_story.html.

Boswell, John Eastburn. "*Exposito* and *Oblatio*: The Abandonment of Children and the Ancient and Medieval Family." *American Historical Review* 89, no. 1 (February 1984): 10–33.

Bourg, Florence Caffery. *Where Two or Three Are Gathered: Christian Families as Domestic Church.* Notre Dame, IN: University of Notre Dame Press, 2004.

Brady, Bernard. *Essential Catholic Social Thought,* 2nd ed. Maryknoll, NY: Orbis, 2017.

Bramlett, Matthew D. "The National Survey of Adoptive Parents: Benchmark Estimates for School Performance and Family Relationship Quality for Adopted Children." US Department of Health and Human Services, June 2011. http://aspe.hhs.gov/hsp/09/NSAP/Brief1/rb.pdf.

Brazal, Agnes M. "Maternal Migration and Paternal Responsibility in the Philippines." In *Catholic Women Speak: Bringing Our Gifts to the Table,* edited by Catholic Women Speak Network, 150–54. New York: Paulist Press, 2015.

Brekus, Catherine A. "Children of Wrath, Children of Grace: Jonathan Edwards and the Puritan Culture of Child Rearing." In *The Child in Christian Thought,* edited by Marcia J. Bunge, 300–328. Grand Rapids: William B. Eerdmans, 2001.

Brodzinski, David M., and Evan B. Donaldson Adoption Institute. "Expanding Resources for Children III: Research-Based Best Practices in Adoption by Gays and Lesbians." October 2011. http://adoptioninstitute.org/publications/expanding-resources-for-children-iii-research-based-best-practices-in-adoption-by-gays-and-lesbians/.

Brown, Peter. *The Body and Society: Men, Women and Sexual Renunciation in Early Christianity.* New York: Columbia University Press, 1988.

Browning, Don S. *Christian Ethics and the Moral Psychologies.* Grand Rapids: William B. Eerdmans, 2006.

Browning, Don S., and John Witte Jr. "Christianity's Mixed Contributions to Children's Rights." *Zygon* 46, no. 3 (September 2011): 713–32.

Buchanan, Wyatt. "Catholic Charity Might Stop Adoptions / Vatican Prohibits Placement with Same-Sex Couples." *SFGate,* March 11, 2006. www.sfgate.com/bayarea/article/SAN-FRANCISCO-Catholic-charity-might-stop-2539650.php.

Bunge, Marcia J. "Introduction." In *The Child in Christian Thought,* edited by Marcia J. Bunge, 1–28. Grand Rapids: William B. Eerdmans, 2001.

Cahill, Lisa Sowle. "Catholic Families: Theology, Reality, and the Gospel." In *Catholic Women Speak: Bringing Our Gifts to the Table,* edited by Catholic Women Speak Network, 57–61. New York: Paulist Press, 2015.

———. *Family: A Christian Social Perspective.* Minneapolis: Augsburg Fortress, 2000.

———. "Same-Sex Marriage and Catholicism." In *More Than a Monologue: Sexual Diversity in the Roman Catholic Church—Volume 2: Inquiry, Thought, and Expression.* New York: Fordham University Press, 2014.

———. *Sex, Gender & Christian Ethics.* Cambridge: Cambridge University Press, 1996.

———. *Theological Bio-Ethics: Participation, Justice, Change.* Washington, DC: Georgetown University Press, 2005.

Callahan, Daniel. *The Catholic Case for Contraception.* New York: Macmillan, 1969.

Carmona, Victor. "Mixed-Status Families and Brokenness: Will Our Fractured Relationships Heal?" In *Human Families, Identities, Relationships, and Responsibilities,* edited by Jacob M. Kohlhaas and Mary Roche Doyle. New York: Orbis, 2021.

———. "Mixed Status Families, Solidarity, and *Lo Cotidiano.*" In *Sex, Love & Families: Catholic Perspectives,* edited by Jason King and Julie Hanlon Rubio, 199–210. Minneapolis: Liturgical Press, 2020.

Carp, E. Wayne, ed. *Adoption in America.* Ann Arbor: University of Michigan Press, 2002.

Catechism of the Catholic Church, 2nd ed. Vatican City: Vatican Press, 1997.

"Catholic Charities in San Francisco Severs Links to Homosexual Adoptions." Catholic News Agency, October 5, 2008. www.catholicnewsagency.com/news/catholic_charities_in_san_francisco_severs_links_to_homosexual_adoptions/.

Catholic News Service. "Father George Clements, Pioneering Chicago Priest, Dies." *America,* December 1, 2019. www.americamagazine.org/faith/2019/12/01/father-george-clements-pioneering-chicago-priest-dies.

Cecero, John J. "Toward Christian Sexual Maturity." In *Human Sexuality in the Catholic Tradition,* edited by Kieren Scott and Michael Warren, 33–46. New York: Rowman & Littlefield Publishers, 2007.

Center for Marriage and Families. "Family Structure and Children's Educational Outcomes." Institute for American Values, November 2005. www.americanvalues.org/pdfs/researchbrief1.pdf.

———. "Research Brief 1: Family Structure and Children's Educational Outcomes." Institute for American Values, November 2005. www.americanvalues.org/catalog/pdfs/researchbrief1.pdf.

Choi, Hoon. "Beyond 'Helping Out': Fathers as Caregivers." In *Sex, Love & Families: Catholic Perspectives*, edited by Jason King and Julie Hanlon Rubio, 69–78. Collegeville, MN: Liturgical Press, 2020.

Cholij, Roman. "Priestly Celibacy in Patristics and in the History of the Church." Vatican website, January 1, 1993. www.vatican.va/roman_curia/congregations/cclergy/documents/rc_con_cclergy_doc_01011993_chisto_en.html.

Christensen-Nuges, Charlotte. "Parental Authority and Freedom of Choice: The Debate on Clandestinity and Parental Consent at the Council of Trent (1545–63)." *Sixteenth Century Journal* 45, no. 1 (Spring 2014): 51–72.

Christiansen, Drew. "A Cosmic Family." *America*, July 20–27, 2015.

Chrysostom, John. "An Address on Vainglory and the Right Way for Parents to Bring Up Their Children." In *Christianity and Pagan Culture in the Later Roman Empire*, trans. Max L. W. Laistner. Ithaca, NY: Cornell University Press, 1951.

Clarke-Stewart, Alison, and Cornelia Brentano. *Divorce: Causes and Consequences*. New Haven, CT: Yale University Press, 2006.

Cloutier, David. "*Humanae vitae* and *Amoris laetitia*: Seeking the Catholic Both/And." Presentation at Catholic Theological Society of America Annual Convention, Indianapolis, June 8, 2018.

———. "Wanting 'the Best' for 'Our Kids': Parenting and Privilege." In *Sex, Love & Families: Catholic Perspectives*, edited by Jason King and Julie Hanlon Rubio, 259–70. Minneapolis: Liturgical Press, 2020.

Code of Canon Law: In English Translation. London: Collins, 1983.

Cole, Basil. "An Introduction to the Concept 'Basic Goods' in the Writings of Germain Grisez." *Angelicum* 70, no. 1 (1993): 35–65.

Collier, Elizabeth W., and Charles R. Strain, with Catholic Relief Services. *Global Migration: What's Happening, Why, and a Just Response*. Winona, MN: Anselm Academic, 2017.

Collins, Patricia Hill. *Black Feminist Thought: Knowledge, Consciousness, and the Politics of Empowerment*, 2nd ed. New York: Routledge, 2000.

"Conclusions of the Congress on 'Paternity of God and Paternity in the Family.'" In *Enchiridion on the Family: A Compendium of the Church Teaching on Family and Life Issues from Vatican II to the Present*, 1st ed., edited by Pontifical Council for the Family, section 5.14. Boston: Pauline Books and Media, 2004.

Congregation for Catholic Education. "'Male and Female He Created Them': Towards a Path of Dialogue on the Question of Gender Theory in Education." Vatican website. February 2, 2019. www.educatio.va/content/dam/cec/Documenti/19_0997_INGLESE.pdf.

Congregation for the Doctrine of the Faith. "Considerations Regarding Proposals to Give Legal Recognition to Unions between Homosexual Persons." Vatican website, July 31, 2003. www.vatican.va/roman_curia/congregations/cfaith/documents/rc_con_cfaith_doc_20030731_homosexual-unions_en.html.

———. *Donum vitae*. Vatican Website. February 22, 1987. www.vatican.va/roman_curia/congregations/cfaith/documents/rc_con_cfaith_doc_19870222_respect-for-human-life_en.html.

———. *Letter to the Bishops of the Catholic Church on the Pastoral Care of Homosexual Persons*. Washington, DC: US Catholic Conference, 1986.

———. *Persona humana*. Vatican website, December 29, 1975. www.vatican.va/roman_curia/congregations/cfaith/documents/rc_con_cfaith_doc_19751229_persona-humana_en.html.

———. "Some Considerations Concerning the Response to Legislative Proposals on the Non-Discrimination of Homosexual Persons." Vatican website, July 22, 1992. www.vatican.va/roman_curia/congregations/cfaith/documents/rc_con_cfaith_doc_19920724_homosexual-persons_en.html.

Coontz, Stephanie. *Marriage, a History: How Love Conquered Marriage*. New York: Penguin, 2006.

———. *The Way We Never Were: American Families and the Nostalgia Trap*, revised and updated edition. New York: Basic Books, 2016.

Cooper, Tanya Asim. "Racial Bias in American Foster Care: The National Debate." *Marquette Law Review* 97, no. 2 (Winter 2013): 215–77.

Coran, Christina. "Teacher Marries Her Girlfriend, and Then Catholic School Fires Her." *New York Times*, February 17, 2018. www.nytimes.com/2018/02/17/us/gay-teacher-fired.html.

Crane, Russel D., and Tim B. Heaton, eds. *Handbook of Families and Poverty*. Los Angeles: Sage, 2008.

Creagh, Dianne. "The Baby Trains: Catholic Foster Care and Western Migration, 1873–1929." *Journal of Social History* 46, no. 1 (2012): 197–218.

Cruz, Gemma Tulud. "It Takes a Global Village: Families in the Age of Migration." In *Sex, Love & Families: Catholic Perspectives*, edited by Jason King and Julie Hanlon Rubio, 211–22. Minneapolis: Liturgical Press, 2020.

Cunningham, Hugh. *Children and Childhood in Western Society Since 1500*, 2nd ed. New York: Routledge, 2005.

Curran, Charles E. *The Development of Moral Theology: Five Strands*. Washington, DC: Georgetown University Press, 2013.

———. "*Evangelium vitae* and Its Broader Context." In *John Paul II and Moral Theology*, edited by Charles E. Curran and Richard A. McCormick, 239–51. Mahwah, NJ: Paulist Press, 1998.

———. "Masturbation and Objectively Grave Matter: An Exploratory Discussion." *Catholic Theological Society of America Proceedings* 21 (1966): 95–109.

———. *The Moral Theology of Pope John Paul II*. Washington, DC: Georgetown University Press, 2005.

Curran, Charles E., and Richard A. McCormick, eds. *Dialogue about Catholic Sexual Teaching*. New York: Paulist Press, 1993.

Curran, Charles E., and Julie Hanlon Rubio, eds. *Marriage*. Mahwah, NJ: Paulist Press, 2009.

D'Angelo, Mary R. "Ευσεβεια: Roman Imperial Family Values and Sexual Politics of 4 Maccabees and the Pastorals." *Biblical Interpretation* 11, no. 3 (2003): 139–65.

de Haro, Raymond Garcia. *Marriage and the Family in the Documents of the Magisterium: A Course in the Theology of Marriage*. Trans. William E. May. San Francisco: Ignatius Press, 1993.

Deane-Drummond, Celia. "A New Anthropology? *Laudato Si'* and the Question of Interconnectedness." In *Laudato Si' and the Environment: Pope Francis' Green Encyclical*, edited by Robert McKim, 189–201. New York: Routledge, 2019.

Dearman, J. Andrew. "The Family in the Old Testament." *Interpretation* 52, no. 2 (April 1998): 117–29.

Destro, Adriana, and Mauro Pesce. "Fathers and Householders in the Jesus Movement: The Perspective of the Gospel of Luke." *Biblical Interpretation* 11, no. 3 (2003): 211–38.

Digmann, Anthony J. *Sign of Contradiction: Contraception, Family Planning & Catholicism.* Dayton, OH: One More Soul, 2015.

Dixon, Suzanne. *The Roman Mother.* London: Croom Helm, 1988.

Donahue, Charles, Jr. "The Canon Law on the Formation of Marriage and Social Practice in the Later Middle Ages." *Journal of Family History* 8 (1983): 144–58.

Dorr, Donal. *Option for the Poor and for the Earth: Catholic Social Teaching.* Maryknoll, NY: Orbis, 2012.

Doucet, Andrea. "'It's Just Not Good for a Man to Be Interested in Other People's Children': Fathers, Public Displays of Care, and 'Relevant Others.'" In *Displaying Families: A New Concept for the Sociology of Family Life,* edited by Esther Dermott and Julie Seymour, 81–101. New York: Palgrave Macmillan, 2012.

Elliott, John H. "The Jesus Movement Was Not Egalitarian but Family-Oriented." *Biblical Interpretation* 11, no. 3 (2003): 173–210.

Ellison, Marvin M. *Making Love Just: Sexual Ethics for Perplexing Times.* Minneapolis: Fortress Press, 2012.

England, Paula, and Kathryn Edin, eds. *Unmarried Couples with Children.* New York: Russell Sage Foundation, 2007.

"Every Child Has a Right to a Mother and a Father." *For Your Marriage,* April 23, 2014. www.foryourmarriage.org/every-child-has-a-right-to-a-mother-and-a-father/.

Fahey, Michael. "Christian Family as Domestic Church at Vatican II." In *The Family,* edited by Lisa S. Cahill and Dietmar Mieth, *Concillium* 4 (1995): 85–92.

Failinger, Marie A. "Co-Creating Adoption Law: A Lutheran Perspective." *Dialog: A Journal of Theology* 51, no. 4 (Winter 2012): 266–75.

Fairtlough, Anna. "Growing Up with a Lesbian or Gay Parent: Young People's Perspectives." *Health and Social Care in the Community* 16, no. 5 (2008): 521–28.

Fanucci, Laura Kelly. *Everyday Sacrament: The Messy Grace of Parenting.* Collegeville, MN: Liturgical Press, 2014.

Farley, Margaret A. *Just Love: A Framework for Christian Sexual Ethics.* New York: Continuum, 2010.

Feldman, Ruth, and Marian J Bakermans-Kranenburg. "Oxytocin: A Parenting Hormone." *Current Opinion in Psychology* (June 15, 2017): 13–18.

Ferder, Fran, and John Heagle. "Tender Fires: The Spiritual Promise of Sexuality." In *Human Sexuality in the Catholic Tradition,* edited by Kieran Scott and Harold Daly Horell, 15–27. New York: Rowman & Littlefield, 2007.

Filteau, Jerry. "Catholic Charities in Boston Archdiocese to End Adoption Services." Catholic News Service, March 13, 2006. www.catholicnews.com/data/stories/cns/0601456.htm.

Finch, Andrew J. "Parental Authority and the Problem of Clandestine Marriage in the Later Middle Ages." *Law and History Review* 8, no. 2 (Autumn 1990): 189–204.

Finn, Daniel. "Human Work in Catholic Social Thought." *American Journal of Economics and Sociology* 71, no. 4 (October 2012): 874–85.

Flores, Nichole M. "Latina/o Families: Solidarity and the Common Good." *Journal of the Society of Christian Ethics* 33, no. 2 (Fall–Winter 2013): 57–72.

Francis. *Amoris laetitia.* Apostolic exhortation. Vatican website. March 19, 2016. https://w2.vatican.va/content/dam/francesco/pdf/apost_exhortations/documents/papa-francesco_esortazione-ap_20160319_amoris-laetitia_en.pdf, sec. 251.

———. *Evangelii gaudium*. Apostolic exhortation. Vatican website. November 24, 2013. www.vatican.va/content/francesco/en/apost_exhortations/documents/papa-francesco_esortazione-ap_20131124_evangelii-gaudium.html.

———. *Laudato si'*. Encyclical letter. Vatican website. May 24, 2015. www.vatican.va/content/francesco/en/encyclicals/documents/papa-francesco_20150524_enciclica-laudato-si.html.

Fry, Timothy, ed. *The Rule of St. Benedict*. Collegeville, MN: Liturgical Press, 1982.

Gaillardetz, Richard R. *A Daring Promise: A Spirituality of Christian Marriage*. New York: Crossroad, 2002.

———. "A School for Love: Marriage as Christian Friendship." In *Sex, Love & Families: Catholic Perspectives*. Minneapolis: Liturgical Press, 2020.

Gajiwala, Astrid Lobo. "Challenging Families: Indian Women Speak from the Margins." In *Catholic Women Speak: Bringing Our Gifts to the Table*, edited by Catholic Women Speak Network, 141–45. New York: Paulist Press, 2015.

Gallagher, John. "Magisterial Teaching from 1918 to the Present." In *Change in Official Catholic Moral Teachings*, edited by Charles E. Curran, 227–47. Mahwah, NJ: Paulist Press, 2003.

Gates, Gary J. "Family Focus on . . . LGBT Families." *National Council on Family Relations* FF51 (Winter 2011): F1–F4.

———. "LGBT Parenting in the United States." Williams Institute, February 2013. www.law.ucla.edu/williamsinstitute.

———. "Same-Sex and Different-Sex Couples in the American Community Survey: 2005–2011." Williams Institute, March 2013. www.law.ucla.edu/williamsinstitute.

Gerstel, Naomi. "Rethinking Families and Community: The Color, Class, and Centrality of Extended Kin Ties." *Sociological Forum* 26, no. 1 (March 2011): 1–20.

Gettler, Lee T., Thomas W. McDade, Alan B. Feranil, and Christopher W. Kuzawa. "Longitudinal Evidence that Fatherhood Decreases Testosterone in Human Males." *Proceedings of the National Academy of the Sciences of the United States of America* 108, no. 39 (2011): 16194–99.

Giris, Sherif, Robert P. George, and Ryan T. Anderson. "What Is Marriage?" *Harvard Journal of Law and Public Policy* 34, no. 1 (Winter 2010): 245–87.

Gittins, Anthony J. "In Search of Goodenough Families: Cultural and Religious Perspectives." In *Mutuality Matters; Family, Faith, and Just Love*, edited by Herbert Anderson, Edward Foley, Bonnie Miller-McLemore, and Robert Schreiter, 167–82. New York: Rowman & Littlefield, 2004.

Glauber, Rebecca. "Race and Gender in Families and at Work: The Fatherhood Wage Premium." *Gender and Society* 22, no. 1 (February 2008): 8–30.

Gordon, Linda. *The Great Arizona Orphan Abduction*. Cambridge, MA: Harvard University Press, 2001.

Gudorf, Christine E. *Body, Sex, and Pleasure: Reconstructing Christian Sexual Ethics*. Cleveland: Pilgrim Press, 1994.

———. "A New Moral Discourse on Sexuality." In *Human Sexuality in the Catholic Tradition*, edited by Kieran Scott and Harold Daly Horell, 51–70. New York: Rowman & Littlefield, 2007.

———. "Western Religion and the Patriarchal Family." In *Perspectives on Marriage: A Reader*, edited by Kieren Scott and Michael Warren, 285–304. New York: Oxford University Press, 2000.

Gundry-Volf, Judith M. "The Least and the Greatest: Children in the New Testament." In *The Child in Christian Thought*, edited by Marcia J. Bunge, 29–60. Grand Rapids: William B. Eerdmans, 2001.

Guroian, Vigen. "The Ecclesial Family; John Chrysostom on Parenthood and Children." In *The Child in Christian Thought*, edited by Marcia J. Bunge, 61–77. Grand Rapids: William B. Eerdmans, 2001.

Guzman, Lina, Suzanne Ryan, and Zakia Redd. "Research Brief: What Is 'Healthy Marriage'? Defining the Concept." *Child Trends*, September, 2004. http://acf.gov/healthymarriage/pdf/Child_Trends-2004.pdf.

Hacsi, Timothy A. *Second Home: Orphan Asylums and Poor Families in America*. Cambridge, MA: Harvard University Press, 1997.

Hadebe, Nontando. "Reading the Signs of the Times: Maternal Mortality and Reproductive Rights." In *Catholic Women Speak: Bringing Our Gifts to the Table*, edited by Catholic Women Speak Network, 146–50. New York: Paulist Press, 2015.

Harris, Emma Jane. "Conscience and Contraception: Telling Our Stories." In *Catholic Women Speak: Bringing Our Gifts to the Table*, edited by Catholic Women Speak Network, 103–5. New York: Paulist Press, 2015.

Harvard Men's Health Watch. "Marriage and Men's Health." Harvard Health Publishing, June 5, 2019. www.health.harvard.edu/mens-health/marriage-and-mens-health.

Harvey, A. E. *A Companion to the New Testament*, 2nd ed. Cambridge: Cambridge University Press, 2004.

Hauser, Daniel. *Marriage and Christian Life: A Theology of Christian Marriage*. Lanham, MD: University Press of America, 2005.

Hebblethwaite, Peter. *Paul VI: The First Modern Pope*. New York: Paulist Press, 1993.

Heijst, Annelies van. *Models of Charitable Care: Catholic Nuns and Children in Their Care in Amsterdam, 1852–2002*. Leiden: Brill, 2008.

Herlihy, David. *Medieval Households*. Cambridge, MA: Harvard University Press, 1985.

Hillman, Eugene. *Polygamy Reconsidered: African Plural Marriages and the Christian Churches*. New York: Orbis, 1975.

Hinze, Bradford. *Practices of Dialogue in the Roman Catholic Church: Aims and Obstacles, Lessons and Laments*. New York: Continuum, 2006.

Hinze, Christine Firer. "Catholics and Feminists on Work, Family, and Flourishing." In *Sex, Marriage & Family: Catholic Perspectives*, edited by Jason King and Julie Hanlon Rubio, 247–58. Minneapolis: Liturgical Press, 2020.

———. "Women, Families, and the Legacy of *Laborem exercens*: An Unfinished Agenda." *Journal of Catholic Social Thought* 6, no. 1 (2009): 63–92.

Hogan, Richard M., and John M. LeVoir. *Covenant of Love: Pope John Paul II on Sexuality, Marriage, and Family in the Modern World*. Garden City, NY: Doubleday, 1985.

Holt, Marilyn Irvin. *The Orphan Trains: Placing Out in America*. Lincoln: University of Nebraska Press, 1992.

Holy Roman Rota. "The Order of the Purposes of Matrimony." In *Matrimony*, 541–58. Trans. Michael J. Byrnes. Boston: Saint Paul Editions, 1963.

Holy See Press Office. *Synodus Episcoporum Bulletin*. Vatican website. October 17–21, 2012. www.vatican.va/news_services/press/sinodo/documents/bollettino_25_xiii-ordinaria-2012/02_inglese/b21_02.html.

hooks, bell. "Revolutionary Parenting." In *Feminist Theory: From Margin to Center*. Boston: South End Press, 1984.

Huston, Aletha C., Kaeley C. Bobbitt, and Alison Bently. "Time Spent in Child Care: How and Why Does It Affect Social Development." *Developmental Psychology* 51, no. 5 (2015): 621–34.

"Illinois Religious Freedom Protection and Civil Unions Act." Illinois General Assembly, June 1, 2011. www.ilga.gov/legislation/ilcs/ilcs3.asp?ActID=3294&ChapterID=59.

James, David. "The Integration of Masculine Spirituality." In *Perspectives on Marriage: A Reader*, edited by Kieran Scott and Michael Warren, 313–30. New York: Oxford University Press, 2001.

Janssens, Louis. "Particular Goods and Personalist Morals." *Ethical Perspectives* 6 (1999): 55–59.

Jenkins, Philip. *The Lost History of Christianity: The Thousand-Year Golden Age of the Church in the Middle East, Africa, and Asia—and How It Died.* New York: Harper One, 2009.

John Jay College of Criminal Justice. *The Nature and Scope of Sexual Abuse of Minors by Catholic Priests and Deacons in the United States 1950–2002.* Washington, DC: US Conference of Catholic Bishops, 2004.

———. *2006 Supplementary Report: The Nature and Scope of Sexual Abuse of Minors by Catholic Priests and Deacons in the United States 1950–2002.* Washington, DC: US Conference of Catholic Bishops, 2006.

John Jay College Research Team. *The Causes and Context of Sexual Abuse of Minors by Catholic Priests in the United States, 1950–2010.* Washington, DC: US Conference of Catholic Bishops, May 2011.

John Paul II. "Address of the Holy Father John Paul II to the Meeting of the Adoptive Families Organized by the Missionaries of Charity." Vatican website, September 5, 2000. www.vatican.va/content/john-paul-ii/en/speeches/2000/jul-sep/documents/hf_jp-ii_spe_20000905_adozioni.html.

———. "Address of John Paul II to the Members of the Pontifical Council on the Family." Vatican website, June 4, 1999. http://w2.vatican.va/content/john-paul-ii/en/speeches/1999/june/documents/hf_jp-ii_spe_04061999_family.html.

———. *Blessed Are the Pure of Heart.* Boston: Pauline Books & Media, 1988.

———. *Catechesis tradendae.* Apostolic exhortation. Vatican website, October 16, 1979. www.vatican.va/content/john-paul-ii/en/apost_exhortations/documents/hf_jp-ii_exh_16101979_catechesi-tradendae.html.

———. *Centessimus annus.* Encyclical letter. Vatican website, May 1, 1991. www.vatican.va/content/john-paul-ii/en/encyclicals/documents/hf_jp-ii_enc_01051991_centesimus-annus.html.

———. *Crossing the Threshold of Hope.* New York: Alfred A. Knopf, 1994.

———. *Dives in misericordia.* Encyclical letter. Vatican website, November 30, 1980. www.vatican.va/content/john-paul-ii/en/encyclicals/documents/hf_jp-ii_enc_30111980_dives-in-misericordia.html.

———. *Evangelium vitae.* Encyclical letter. Vatican website, March 25, 1995. www.vatican.va/holy_father/john_paul_ii/encyclicals/documents/hf_jp-ii_enc_25031995_evangelium-vitae_en.html.

———. *Familiaris consortio.* Apostolic exhortation. Vatican website, November 22, 1981. www.vatican.va/content/john-paul-ii/en/apost_exhortations/documents/hf_jp-ii_exh_19811122_familiaris-consortio.html.

———. "General Audience." Vatican website, August 27, 1980. http://vatican.va/content/john-paul-ii/it/audiences/1980/documents/hf_jp-ii_aud_19800827.html.

———. "General Audience." Vatican website, January 12, 1983. www.vatican.va/content/john-paul-ii/it/audiences/1983/documents/hf_jp-ii_aud_19830112.html.

———. *Gratissimam sane*. Encyclical letter. Vatican website, February 2, 1994. www.vatican.va/holy_father/john_paul_ii/letters/documents/hf_jp-ii_let_02021994_families_en.html.

———. "Interpreting the Concept of Concupiscence." Vatican website, October 8, 1980. www.vatican.va/content/john-paul-ii/it/audiences/1980/documents/hf_jp-ii_aud_19801008.html.

———. *Laborem exercens*. Encyclical letter. Vatican website, September 14, 1981. www.vatican.va/content/john-paul-ii/en/encyclicals/documents/hf_jp-ii_enc_14091981_laborem-exercens.html.

———. "Letter to Families." Vatican website, February 2, 1994. www.google.com/search?q=john+paul+ii+letter+to+families&rlz=1C1GTPM_enUS798US798&oq=john+paul+II+letter+to+fami&aqs=chrome.0.0j46j69i57j0l3.4805j0j4&sourceid=chrome&ie=UTF-8.

———. *Man and Woman He Created Them: A Theology of the Body*. Trans. Michael Waldstein. Boston: Pauline Books and Media, 2006.

———. *Memory and Identity: Conversations at the Dawn of a Millennium*. New York: Rizzoli, 2005.

———. *Mulieris dignitatem*. Apostolic letter. Vatican website, August 15, 1988. www.vatican.va/content/john-paul-ii/en/apost_letters/1988/documents/hf_jp-ii_apl_19880815_mulieris-dignitatem.html.

———. "The Mystery of Woman Is Revealed in Motherhood." General audience. Vatican website, March 12, 1980. www.vatican.va/content/john-paul-ii/en/audiences/1980/documents/hf_jp-ii_aud_19800312.html.

———. "The Nuptial Meaning of the Body." General audience. Vatican website, January 9, 1980. http://w2.vatican.va/content/john-paul-ii/en/audiences/1980/documents/hf_jp-ii_aud_19800109.html.

———. "The Paternity of God and Paternity in the Family." In *Enchiridion on the Family: A Compendium of the Church Teaching on Family and Life Issues from Vatican II to the Present*, 1st ed., edited by Pontifical Council for the Family, section 7.11. Boston: Pauline Books and Media, 2004.

———. *Redemptor hominis*. Encyclical letter. Vatican website, March 4, 1979. www.vatican.va/content/john-paul-ii/en/encyclicals/documents/hf_jp-ii_enc_04031979_redemptor-hominis.html.

———. *Redemptoris custos*. Apostolic exhortation. Vatican website, August 15, 1989. www.vatican.va/content/john-paul-ii/en/apost_exhortations/documents/hf_jp-ii_exh_15081989_redemptoris-custos.html.

———. "The Rights of the Elderly and the Family." In *Enchiridion on the Family: A Compendium of the Church Teaching on Family and Life Issues from Vatican II to the Present*, 1st ed., edited by Pontifical Council for the Family, section 6.13. Boston: Pauline Books and Media, 2004.

———. *Veritatis splendor*. Encyclical letter. Vatican website, August 6, 1993. www.vatican.va/content/john-paul-ii/en/encyclicals/documents/hf_jp-ii_enc_06081993_veritatis-splendor.html.

———. "Woman, Spouse and Mother, in the Family and in Society." In *Enchiridion on the Family: A Compendium of the Church Teaching on Family and Life Issues from Vatican II to the Present*, 1st ed., edited by Pontifical Council for the Family, section 5.11. Boston: Pauline Books and Media, 2004.

John XXIII. *Mater et magistra*. Encyclical letter. Vatican website, May 15, 1961. www.vatican.va/holy_father/john_xxiii/encyclicals/documents/hf_j-xxiii_enc_15051961_mater_en.html.

———. *Pacem in terris*. Encyclical letter. Vatican website, April 11, 1963. www.vatican.va/holy_father/john_xxiii/encyclicals/documents/hf_j-xxiii_enc_11041963_pacem_en.html.

Joyce, Mary Rosera. *The Meaning of Contraception*. Staten Island: Alba House, 1970. Reprinted as "The Meaning of Contraception," in *Why* Humanae Vitae *Was Right: A Reader*, edited by Janet E. Smith. San Francisco: Ignatius Press, 1993.

Jung, Patricia Beattie. "God Sets the Lonely in Families." In *More Than a Monologue: Sexual Diversity in the Roman Catholic Church—Volume 2: Inquiry, Thought, and Expression*, edited by Christine Firer Hinze and J. Patrick Hornbeck II, 115–33. New York: Fordham University Press, 2014.

Jussen, Bernhard. *Spiritual Kinship as Social Practice: Godparenthood and Adoption in the Early Middle Ages*. Trans. Pamela Selwyn. Newark: University of Delaware Press, 2000.

Keenan, James F. *Catholic Theological Ethics Past, Present, and Future: The Trento Conference*. New York: Orbis, 2011.

———. *Catholic Theological Ethics in the World Church*. London: Continuum, 2007.

———. *History of Catholic Moral Theology in the Twentieth Century: From Confessing Sins to Liberating Consciences*. New York: Continuum, 2010.

Keenan, Marie. *Child Sexual Abuse & the Catholic Church: Gender, Power, and Organizational Culture*. New York: Oxford University Press, 2012.

Kelly, David F. *Contemporary Catholic Health Care Ethics*. Washington, DC: Georgetown University Press, 2004.

Kidder, Clark. "West by Orphan Train." *Wisconsin Magazine of History* 87, no. 2 (Winter 2003–4): 30–39.

Kohlhaas, Jacob M., and Ryan Patrick McLaughlin. "Loving the World We Are: Anthropology and Relationality in *Laudato si'*." *Journal of Religious Ethics* 47, no. 3 (September 2019): 501–24.

Kotsko, Adam. *Neoliberalism's Demons: On the Political Theology of Late Capital*. Stanford, CA: Stanford University Press, 2018.

Krueger, Patrick M., Douglas P. Jutte, Luisa Franzini, Irma Elo, and Mark D. Hayward. "Family Structure and Multiple Domains of Child Well-Being in the United States: A Cross-Sectional Study." *Population Health Metrics* 13, no. 6 (2015): 1–11.

Lamoureux, Patricia A. "Commentary on *Laborem exercens (On Human Work)*." In *Modern Catholic Social Teaching: Commentaries and Interpretations*, edited by Kenneth R. Himes, 389–414. Washington, DC: Georgetown University Press, 2005.

Lawler, Michael G. *Marriage and the Catholic Church; Disputed Questions*. Wilmington, DE: Michael Glazier Books, 2002.

———. *What Is and What Ought to Be*. New York: Continuum, 2005.

Lawler, Michael G., and William P. Roberts, eds. *Christian Marriage and Family: Contemporary Theological and Pastoral Perspectives*. Collegeville, MN: Liturgical Press, 1996.

Lee, Su Li. "Persons as Gifts: Understanding Interdependence through Pope John Paul II's Anthropology." *Catholic Social Science Review* 14 (2009): 321–27.

Leo XIII. *Arcanum divinae sapientiae.* Encyclical letter. Vatican website, February 10, 1880. www.vatican.va/holy_father/leo_xiii/encyclicals/documents/hf_l-xiii_enc_10021880_arcanum_en.html.

Leven, Yigel. "Jesus 'Son of God' and 'Son of David': The 'Adoption' of Jesus into the Davidic Line." *Journal for the Study of the New Testament* 28, no. 4 (2006): 415–42.

Lipka, Michael. "Young US Catholics Overwhelmingly Accepting of Homosexuality." Pew Research, October 16, 2014. www.pewresearch.org/fact-tank/2014/10/16/young-u-s-catholics-overwhelmingly-accepting-of-homosexuality/.

Llewellyn, Dawn, and Paul Middleton. "Motherhood, Martyrdom, and the Threat to Christian Identity: Voicing a Modern and Ancient Taboo." Presentation at meeting of American Academy of Religions, Baltimore, 2013.

Lofquist, Daphne. "Same-Sex Couple Households." US Census Bureau, American Communities Survey Brief 10-3, September 2011. www2.census.gov/library/publications/2011/acs/acsbr10-03.pdf.

Mackin, Theodore. "The Primitive Christian Understanding of Marriage." In *Perspectives on Marriage; A Reader*, edited by Kieran Scott and Michael Warren, 22–28. New York: Oxford University Press, 2001.

Martins, John W. "A Scriptural Look at Jesus' Teachings on Marriage and Divorce." *America Magazine*, November 6, 2015. www.americamagazine.org/faith/2015/11/06/scriptural-look-jesus-teachings-marriage-and-divorce.

May, William E. "Moral Theologians and 'Veritatis Splendor.'" *Homiletic and Pastoral Review*, December 1994. Reproduced online by EWTN. www.ewtn.com/library/THEOLOGY/MORALVS.HTM.

May, William E., Ronald Lawler, and Joseph Boyle Jr. *Catholic Sexual Ethics: A Summary, Explanation, & Defense*, 3rd ed. Huntington, IN: Our Sunday Visitor, 2011.

McCarthy, Davod Matzko. *Sex & Love in the Home: A Theology of the Household*, 2nd ed. Eugene, OR: Wipf & Stock, 2010.

McCormick, Richard. "Ambiguity in Moral Choice." In *Doing Evil to Achieve Good: Moral Choice in Conflict Situations*, edited by Richard McCormick and Paul Ramsey, 7–53. Chicago: Loyola University Press, 1978.

McDonald, Kevin. "*Laudato si'*: An Ecclesiological Perspective." Paper presented at Exploring *Laudato si'*, Saint Mary's University, Twickenham, November 17, 2015. www.stmarys.ac.uk/news/wp-content/uploads/2015/09/Archbish-McDonald-speech.pdf.

McEwen, Erwin. "FY12 Foster Care and Adoption Contracts." Scribd.com, July 8, 2011. www.scribd.com/doc/59782549/Catholic-Charities-Foster-Care-and-Adoption-Contracts-Illinois-Department-of-Children-Family-Services-Letter.

McNabb, Vicent. *On Christian Marriage.* New York: Sheed & Ward, 1933.

McNeil, John J. *The Church and the Homosexual*, 4th ed. Boston: Beacon Press, 1993.

Medlin, Maryann. "Illinois Bishops Announce Shutdown of Adoption Services." Catholic News Agency, November 15, 2011. www.catholicnewsagency.com/news/illinois-bishops-announce-shutdown-of-adoption-services.

Meilaender, Gilbert C. *Not by Nature but by Grace: Forming Families through Adoption.* Notre Dame, IN: University of Notre Dame Press, 2016.

Millare, Roland. "Towards a Common Communion: The Relational Anthropologies of John Zizioulas and Karol Wojtyla." *New Blackfriars* 98, no. 1077 (September 2017): 599–614.

Miller, Timothy S. *The Orphans of Byzantium: Child Welfare in the Christian Empire.* Washington, DC: Catholic University of America Press, 2003.

Moffett, Samuel Hugh. *A History of Christianity in Asia: Beginnings to 1500.* Maryknoll, NY: Orbis, 1992.

Momigliano, Anna. "Why Some Catholics Defend the Kidnapping of a Jewish Boy: It's Not About the Church's Relationship with Jews; It's About the Culture War Inside the Church." *Atlantic*, January 24, 2018. www.theatlantic.com/international/archive/2018/01/some-catholics-are-defending-the-kidnapping-of-a-jewish-boy/551240/.

Monroe, Kristen Renwick. "Explanations from Evolutionary Biology." In *The Heart of Altruism; Perceptions of a Common Humanity.* Princeton, NJ: Princeton University Press, 1996.

Moore, Kristin Anderson, Susan M. Jekielek, Jacinta Bronte-Tinkew, and Emmanuel Mounier. *Personalism.* Notre Dame, IN: University of Notre Dame Press, 1952.

Moore, Kristin Anderson, Susan M. Jekielek, and Carol Emig, MPP. "Marriage from a Child's Perspective: How Does Family Structure Affect Children, and What Can We Do About It?" *Child Trends*, June 2002. www.childtrends.org/?publications=marriage-from-a-childs-perspective-how-does-family-structure-affect-children-and-what-can-we-do-about-it.

Murphy, David, Tawana Bandy, Hannah Schmitz, and Kristin Anderson Moore. "Caring Adults: Important for Positive Child Well-Being." *Child Trends*, December 2013. www.childtrends.org/?publications=caring-adults-important-for-positive-child-well-being.

National Conference of Catholic Bishops. "Economic Justice for All: Pastoral Letter on Catholic Social Teaching and the US Economy." November 1986. www.usccb.org/upload/economic_justice_for_all.pdf.

Naughton, Michael, and Gene R. Lacniak. "A Theological Context of Work from the Catholic Social Encyclical Tradition." *Journal of Business Ethics* 12, no. 12 (December 1993): 981–94.

Neuger, Christie. "Gender Narratives and the Epidemic of Violence in Contemporary Families." In *Mutuality Matters; Family, Faith, and Just Love*, edited by Herbert Anderson, Edward Foley, Bonnie Miller-McLemore, and Robert Schreiter, 83–92. New York: Rowman & Littlefield, 2004.

New Oxford Notes. "The Future of Marriage in America." *New Oxford Review* 54, no. 3 (April 2012): 12–14.

Nussbaum, Martha C. *Creating Capabilities: The Human Development Approach.* Cambridge, MA: Harvard University Press, 2011.

Obach, Robert. *The Catholic Church on Marital Intercourse.* Lanham, MD: Rowman & Littlefield, 2009.

Office of the Attorney General, Commonwealth of Pennsylvania. "Report I of the 40th Statewide Investigative Grand Jury: Redacted." Pennsylvania Attorney General, July 27, 2018. www.attorneygeneral.gov/report/.

Oord, Thomas Jay. "Morals, Love, and Relations in Evolutionary Theory." In *Evolution and Ethics; Human Morality in Biological & Religious Perspective*, edited by Philip Clayton and Jeffery Schloss, 287–301. Grand Rapids: William B. Eerdmans, 2004.

Osborne, Catherine R. "Migrant Domestic Careworkers: Between the Public and the Private in Catholic Social Teaching." *Journal of Religious Ethics* 40, no. 1 (March 2012): 1–25.

Osiek, Carolyn. "Pietas In and Out of the Frying Pan." *Biblical Interpretation* 11, no. 3 (2003): 166–72.

Ostdiek, Gilbert. "More Than a Family Affair: Reflections on Baptizing Children and Mutuality." In *Mutuality Matters: Family, Faith, and Just Love*, edited by Herbert Anderson, Edward Foley, Bonnie Miller-McLemore, and Robert Schreiter, 57–66. New York: Rowman & Littlefield, 2004.

Ozment, Steven. *When Fathers Ruled: Family Life in Reformation Europe*. Cambridge, MA: Harvard University Press, 1983.

Parent, Justin, Deborah J. Jones, Rex Forehand, Jessica Cuellar, and Erin K. Shoulberg. "The Role of Coparents in African American Single-Mother Families: The Indirect Effect of Coparent Identity on Youth Psychosocial Adjustment." *Journal of Family Psychology* 27, no. 2 (2013): 252–62.

Parsons, Susan Frank. *The Ethics of Gender*. Malden, MA: Blackwell, 2002.

Paul VI. *Evangelii nuntiandi*. Apostolic exhortation. Vatican website, December 8, 1975. www.vatican.va/content/paul-vi/en/apost_exhortations/documents/hf_p-vi_exh_19751208_evangelii-nuntiandi.html.

———. *Humanae vitae*. Encyclical letter. Vatican website. July 25, 1968. www.vatican.va/content/paul-vi/en/encyclicals/documents/hf_p-vi_enc_25071968_humanae-vitae.html.

———. "Pope Paul VI to the Teams of Our Lady." In *Why* Humanae vitae *Was Right*. San Francisco: Ignatius Press, 1993.

———. *Populorum progressio*. Encyclical letter. Vatican website. March 26, 1967. www.vatican.va/content/paul-vi/en/encyclicals/documents/hf_p-vi_enc_26031967_populorum.html.

Paulson, Michael. "Gay Marriages Confront Catholic School Rules." *New York Times*, January 22, 2014. www.nytimes.com/2014/01/23/us/gay-marriages-confront-catholic-school-rules.html?_r=0.

Perpetua, "The Martyrdom of Perpetua." In *In Her Words: Women's Writing in the History of Christian Thought*, edited by Amy Oden, 26–37. Nashville: Abingdon Press, 1994.

Pitkin, Barbara. "'The Heritage of the Lord': Children in the Theology of John Calvin." In *The Child in Christian Thought*, edited by Marcia J. Bunge, 160–93. Grand Rapids: William B. Eerdmans, 2001.

Pius IX. *Quanta cura*. Encyclical letter. Vatican website, December 8, 1864. www.vatican.va/content/pius-ix/la/documents/encyclica-quanta-cura-8-decembris-1864.html.

Pius XI. *Casti connubii*. Encyclical letter. Vatican website, December 31, 1930. www.vatican.va/holy_father/pius_xi/encyclicals/documents/hf_p-xi_enc_31121930_casti-connubii_en.html.

———. *Divini illius magistri*. Encyclical letter. Vatican website, December 31, 1929. www.vatican.va/holy_father/pius_xi/encyclicals/documents/hf_p-xi_enc_31121929_divini-illius-magistri_en.html.

Pius XII. "Allocution to Associations of the Large Families." In *Matrimony*, 434–43. Trans. Michael J. Byrnes. Boston: Saint Paul Editions, 1963.

———. "Allocution to Fathers of Families." In *Matrimony*, 397–404. Trans. Michael J. Byrnes. Boston: Saint Paul Editions, 1963.

———. "Allocution to the International Congress of Catholic Doctors." In *Matrimony*, 383–85. Trans. Michael J. Byrnes. Boston: Saint Paul Editions, 1963.

———. "Allocution to the Members of the II World Congress of Fertility and Sterility." In *Matrimony*, 482–92. Trans. Michael J. Byrnes. Boston: Saint Paul Editions, 1963.

———. "Allocution to the Members of the Seventh Congress on Hematology." In *Matrimony*, 513–25. Trans. Michael J. Byrnes. Boston: Saint Paul Editions, 1963.

———. "Allocution to Midwives." In *Matrimony*, 405–34. Trans. Michael J. Byrnes. Boston: Saint Paul Editions, 1963.

———. "Allocution to Newlyweds (1941)." In *Matrimony*, 325–28. Trans. Michael J. Byrnes. Boston: Saint Paul Editions, 1963.

———. "Allocution to Newlyweds (1942): Indissolubility Is Demanded by Nature." In *Matrimony*, 346–52. Trans. Michael J. Byrnes. Boston: Saint Paul Editions, 1963.

———. "Allocution to Newlyweds (1942): The Nuptial Bond." In *Matrimony*, 340–46. Trans. Michael J. Byrnes. Boston: Saint Paul Editions, 1963.

———. "Allocution to Parish Priests and Lenten Preachers of Rome." In *Matrimony*, 359–60. Trans. Michael J. Byrnes. Boston: Saint Paul Editions, 1963.

———. "Letter *Testes obsequie*." In *Matrimony*, 385–86. Trans. Michael J. Byrnes. Boston: Saint Paul Editions, 1963.

———. "Radio Message to French Families." In *Matrimony*, 360–63. Trans. Michael J. Byrnes. Boston: Saint Paul Editions, 1963.

———. "Radio Message to the World." In *Matrimony*, 352–53. Trans. Michael J. Byrnes. Boston: Saint Paul Editions, 1963.

———. *Summi pontificatus*. Encyclical letter. Vatican website, October 20, 1939. www.vatican.va/content/pius-xii/en/encyclicals/documents/hf_p-xii_enc_20101939_summi-pontificatus.html.

Pleck, Joseph H., and Jeffery L. Stueve. "A Narrative Approach to Paternal Identity: The Importance of Parental Identity 'Conjointness.'" In *Conceptualizing and Measuring Father Involvement*, edited by Randal D. Day and Michael E. Lamb, 83–108. Mahwah, NJ: Lawrence Erlbaum, 2004.

Pontifical Council for the Family. "Charter of the Rights of the Family." Vatican website, October 22, 1983. www.vatican.va/roman_curia/pontifical_councils/family/documents/rc_pc_family_doc_19831022_family-rights_en.html.

———. "Family, Marriage and 'De Facto' Unions." Vatican website, November 9, 2000. www.vatican.va/roman_curia/pontifical_councils/family/documents/rc_pc_family_doc_20001109_de-facto-unions_en.html.

Pontifical Council for Legislative Texts. "On the Admissibility to the Sacred Communion of the Divorced People Who Have Returned to Marry." Vatican website, June 24, 2000. www.vatican.va/roman_curia/pontifical_councils/intrptxt/documents/rc_pc_intrptxt_doc_20000706_declaration_sp.html.

Pope, Stephen. "Scientific and Natural Law Analysis of Homosexuality: A Methodological Study." *Journal of Religious Ethics* 25, no. 1 (Spring 1997): 89–126.

Popenoe, David. "The American Family 1988–2028: Looking Back and Looking Forward." Center for Marriage and Families, Research Brief 13, August 2008. http://americanvalues.org/catalog/pdfs/researchbrief13.pdf.

Post, Stephen G. "Adoption Theologically Considered." *Journal of Religious Ethics* 25, no. 1 (1997): 1–5.

Pui-lan, Kwok. *Introducing Asian Feminist Theology*. Sheffield, UK: Sheffield Academic Press, 2000.

Rawson, Beryl. "The Roman Family in Recent Research: State of the Question." *Biblical Interpretation* 11, no. 3 (2003): 119–38.

Reese, Thomas J. "Looking Back at the 1980 Synod on the Family." *National Catholic Reporter*, September 12, 2014. www.ncronline.org/blogs/faith-and-justice/looking-back-1980-synod-family.

———. "Report from the Synod." *America*, October 11, 1980. www.scribd.com/document/239453850/A-Report-From-the-Synod.

Reilly, Patrick. "Educators Need More Than 'Male and Female He Created Them.'" Cardinal Newman Society, July 18, 2019. https://newmansociety.org/educators-need-more-than-male-and-female-he-created-them/.

Reimer-Barry, Emily. "How to Be Fired from Your Job at a Catholic Institution: It's Easier Than You Think!" *Catholic Moral Theology*, June 18, 2013. https://catholicmoraltheology.com/how-to-be-fired-from-your-job-at-a-catholic-institution-it-is-easier-than-you-think/.

Resnick, Irven M. "Marriage in Medieval Culture: Consent Theory and the Case of Joseph and Mary." *Church History* 69, no. 2 (June 2000): 350–71.

Rickert, Kevin. "Wojtyla's Personalistic Norm: A Thomistic Analysis." *Nova et Vetera* 7, no. 3 (2009): 653–78.

Rivaux, Stephanie L., Joyce James, Kim Wittenstrom, and Donald Baumann. "The Intersection of Race, Poverty, and Risk: Understanding the Decision to Provide Services to Clients and to Remove Children." *Child Welfare* 87, no. 2 (2008): 151–68.

Roberts, Dorothy E. "Prison, Foster Care, and the Systemic Punishment of Black Mothers." *UCLA Law Review* 59 (2012): 1475–1500.

Roche, Mary M. Doyle. *Schools of Solidarity: Families and Catholic Social Teaching.* Collegeville, MN: Liturgical Press, 2015.

Rubin, David M., Amanda L. R. O'Reilly, Xianqun Luan, and A. Russell Localio. "The Impact of Placement Stability on Behavioral Well-Being for Children in Foster Care." *Pediatrics* 119, no. 2 (2007): 336–44.

Rubio, Julie Hanlon. *A Christian Theology of Marriage and Family.* New York: Paulist Press, 2003.

———. *Family Ethics: Practices for Christians.* Washington, DC: Georgetown University Press, 2010.

Ruddick, Sara. "On 'Maternal Thinking.'" *Women's Studies Quarterly* 37, nos. 3–4 (Fall–Winter 2009): 305–8.

Ruether, Rosemary Radford. "Christianity and the Family: Ancient Challenge, Modern Crisis." *Conrad Grebel Review* 19, no. 2 (Spring 2001): 83–95.

———. *Christianity and the Making of the Modern Family.* Boston: Beacon Press, 2000.

———. *Sexism and God-Talk: Toward a Feminist Theology.* Boston: Beacon Press, 1993.

Rutherford, Adam. *A Brief History of Everyone Who Ever Lived: The Human Story Retold Through Our Genes.* New York: The Experiment, 2017.

Sahlins, Marshall. *What Kinship Is and Is Not.* Chicago: University of Chicago Press, 2013.

Salzman, Todd A. *What Are They Saying about Catholic Ethical Method?* New York: Paulist Press, 2003.

Salzman, Todd A., ed. *Method and Catholic Moral Theology: The Ongoing Reconstruction.* Omaha: Creighton University Press, 1999.

Salzman, Todd A., Thomas M. Kelly, and John J. O'Keefe. *Marriage in the Catholic Tradition.* New York: Crossroad, 2004.

Salzman, Todd A., and Michael G. Lawler. *Sexual Ethics: A Theological Introduction.* Washington, DC: Georgetown University Press, 2012.

———. *The Sexual Person: Towards a Renewed Catholic Anthropology.* Washington, DC: Georgetown University Press, 2008.

Sarkisian, Natalia, Mariana Gerena, and Naomi Gerstel. "Extended Family Integration among Mexican and Euro Americans: Ethnicity, Gender, and Class." *Journal of Marriage and Family* 69, no. 1 (February 2007): 40–54.

Schmalz, Valerie. "SF Catholic Charities Cuts Ties to Homosexual Adoptions." *Our Sunday Visitor*, October 12, 2008. www.osv.com/tabid/7621/itemid/4093/Catholic-Charities-cuts-homosexual-adoption-ties.aspx; www.catholicnewsagency.com/news/catholic_charities_in_san_francisco_severs_links_to_homosexual_adoptions/.

Schmidt, John. "Summary Court Order." Scribd.com, August 18, 2011. www.scribd.com/doc/62597962/Illinois-Circuit-Court-Summary-Judgment-Order-in-Catholic-Charities-Foster-Care-Adoption-Services-Case.

Schwartz, Ann. "Connective Complexity: African American Adolescents and the Relational Context of Kinship Foster Care." *Child Welfare* 87, no. 2 (2008): 77–97.

Scott, Kieran, and Michael Warren. *Perspectives on Marriage: A Reader.* New York: Oxford University Press, 2001.

Selling, Joseph. "Regulating Fertility and Clarifying Moral Language." *Heythrop Journal* 55, no. 6 (2014): 1033–43.

Shivanandan, Mary. "Conjugal Spirituality and the Gift of Reference." *Nova et Vetera*, English Edition 10, no. 2 (2012): 485–506.

Silverman, Hollie, and Carma Hassan. "A Teacher Fired from a Catholic School for Being Gay Has Reached a Settlement." CNN, July 9, 2019. www.cnn.com/2019/07/09/us/catholic-school-fires-teacher-settlement/index.html.

Smith, Janet E. "Natural Law and Personalism in *Veritatis splendor.*" In *John Paul II and Moral Theology*, edited by Charles E. Curran and Richard A. McCormick, 67–84. Mahwah, NJ: Paulist Press, 1998.

Smith, Janet E., ed. *Why* Humanae vitae *Was Right: A Reader.* San Francisco: Ignatius Press, 1993.

Smith, Lesley. "Who Is My Mother? Honouring Parents in Medieval Exegesis of the Ten Commandments." In *Motherhood, Religion, and Society in Medieval Europe, 400–1400*, edited by Conrad Leyser and Lesley Smith, 155–72. Burlington, VT: Ashgate, 2011.

Smithers, Gregory D. "American Abolitionism and Slave-Breeding Discourse: A Re-evaluation." *Slavery & Abolition* 33, no. 4 (December 2012): 551–70.

Soltis, Kathryn Getek. "Family Relationships and Incarceration." In *Sex, Love & Families: Catholic Perspectives*, edited by Jason King and Julie Hanlon Rubio, 163–74. Minneapolis: Liturgical Press, 2020.

Southon, Emma. "Family Planning." In *Marriage, Sex and Death: The Family and the Fall of the Roman West.* Amsterdam: Amsterdam University Press, 2017.

"The State of our Unions: Marriage in America 2011." University of Virginia National Marriage Project and Institute for American Values, 2011. http://stateofourunions.org/2011/SOOU2011.pdf.

Strohl, Jane E. "The Child in Luther's Theology: 'For What Purpose Do We Older Folks Exist, Other Than to Care for . . . the Young?'" In *The Child in Christian Thought*, edited by Marcia J. Bunge, 134–59. Grand Rapids: William B. Eerdmans, 2001.

Students of the Ursuline High School, Wimbledon. "A Letter to Pope Francis—from Ten Young Catholic Women, Ages 14 to 17." In *Visions and Vocations*, edited by Tina Beattie and Diana Culbertson, 63–73. Mahwah, NJ: Catholic Women Speak Network, 2018.

Sullivan-Dunbar, Sandra. *Human Dependency and Christian Ethics.* Cambridge, UK: Cambridge University Press, 2017.

———. "Valuing Family Care." In *Sex, Love & Families: Catholic Perspectives*, edited by Jason King and Julie Hanlon Rubio, 151–62. Minneapolis: Liturgical Press, 2020.

Synod of Bishops. "*Relatio post disceptationem.*" *National Catholic Reporter*, October 15, 2014. www.ncronline.org/news/vatican/relatio-post-disceptationem-2014-synod-bishops-family.

———. *Relatio synodi.* Vatican website, October 18, 2014. www.vatican.va/news_services/press/sinodo/documents/bollettino_25_xiii-ordinaria-2012/02_inglese/b21_02.html.

Tablan, Ferdinand. "Catholic Social Teachings: Toward a Meaningful Work." *Journal of Business Ethics* 128, no. 2 (May 2015): 291–303.

Taylor, Charles. *A Secular Age*. Cambridge, MA: Belknap Press of Harvard University Press, 2007.

Tentier, Leslie Woodcock. *Catholics and Contraception: An American History*. Ithaca, NY: Cornell University Press, 2004.

Thecla. "The Acts of Paul and Thecla." In *In Her Words: Women's Writing in the History of Christian Thought*, edited by Amy Oden, 21–25. Nashville: Abingdon Press, 1994.

Traina, Christina L. H. *Feminist Ethics and Natural Law: The End of Anathemas*. Washington, DC: Georgetown University Press, 1999.

———. "How Gendered in Marriage?" In *Sex Love & Families: Catholic Perspectives*, edited by Jason King and Julie Hanlon Rubio, 79–90. Collegeville, MN: Liturgical Press, 2020.

———. "A Person in the Making; Thomas Aquinas on Children and Childhood." In *The Child in Christian Thought*, edited by Marcia J. Bunge, 103–33. Grand Rapids: William B. Eerdmans, 2001.

US Conference of Catholic Bishops. "Between Man and Woman: Questions and Answers about Marriage and Same-Sex Unions." November 2003. www.usccb.org/issues-and-action/marriage-and-family/marriage/promotion-and-defense-of-marriage/questions-and-answers-about-marriage-and-same-sex-unions.cfm.

———. "Discrimination against Catholic Adoption Services." 2012. www.usccb.org/issues-and-action/religious-liberty/fortnight-for-freedom/upload/Catholic-Adoption-Services.pdf.

———. "Economic Justice for All: Pastoral Letter on Catholic Social Teaching and the US Economy." November 1986. www.usccb.org/upload/ economic_justice_for_all.pdf.

———. *Follow the Way of Love*. Washington, DC: US Conference of Catholic Bishops, 1994.

———. "Frequently Asked Questions about the Defense of Marriage." www.usccb.org/issues-and-action/marriage-and-family/marriage/promotion-and-defense-of-marriage/frequently-asked-questions-on-defense-of-marriage.cfm.

———. "Marriage, Love, and Life in the Divine Plan." November 2009. www.usccb.org/issues-and-action/marriage-and-family/marriage/love-and-life.

———. "Putting Children and Families First: A Challenge for Our Church, Nation and World." Priests for Life, November 1986. www.priestsforlife.org/magisterium/bishops/91-11puttingchildrenandfamiliesfirstuscc.htm, sec. VI.B.4.

US Conference of Catholic Bishops, Ad Hoc Committee for Religious Liberty. "Our First, Most Cherished Liberty: A Statement on Religious Liberty." March 2012, www.usccb.org/issues-and-action/religious-liberty/upload/Our-First-Most-Cherished-Liberty-Apr12-6-12-12.pdf.

US Conference of Catholic Bishops, Committee on Doctrine. "Inadequacies in the Theological Methodology and Conclusions of *The Sexual Person: Toward a Renewed Catholic Anthropology* by Todd A. Salzman and Michael G. Lawler." September 15, 2010. www.usccb.org/doctrine/Sexual_Person_2010-09-15.pdf.

US Department of Health and Human Services. "Marriage and Cohabitation in the United States: A Statistical Portrait Based on Cycle 6 (2002) of the National Survey of Family Growth." *Vital and Health Statistics* 23, no. 28 (February 2010): 1–12.

Vandivere, Sharon, and Karen Malm. *Adoption USA: A Chartbook Based on the 2007 National Survey of Adoptive Parents*. Washington, DC: U.S. Department of Health and Human Services, Office of the Assistant Secretary for Planning and Evaluation, 2009.

Vatican II. *Apostolicam actuositatem*. Vatican website, November 18, 1965. www.vatican.va/archive/hist_councils/ii_vatican_council/documents/vat-ii_decree_19651118_apostolicam-actuositatem_en.html.

———. *Gaudium et spes*. Counciliar constitution. Vatican website, December 7, 1965. www.vatican.va/archive/hist_councils/ii_vatican_council/documents/vat-ii_const_19651207_gaudium-et-spes_en.html.

———. *Gravissimum educationis*. Vatican website, October 28, 1965. www.vatican.va/archive/hist_councils/ii_vatican_council/documents/vat-ii_decl_19651028_gravissimum-educationis_en.html.

———. *Lumen gentium*. Vatican website, November 21, 1964. www.vatican.va/archive/hist_councils/ii_vatican_council/documents/vat-ii_const_19641121_lumen-gentium_en.html.

———. *Optatem totius*. Vatican website, October 28, 1965. www.vatican.va/archive/hist_councils/ii_vatican_council/documents/vat-ii_decree_19651028_optatam-totius_en.html.

Von Hildebrand, Dietrich. *The Encyclical* Humane vitae, *A Sign of Contradiction: An Essay on Birth Control and Catholic Conscience*. Chicago: Franciscan Herald Press, 1969.

Wall, Glenda, and Stephanie Arnold. "How Involved Is Involved Fathering? An Exploration of the Contemporary Culture of Fatherhood." *Gender and Society* 21, no. 4 (August 2007): 508–27.

Ware, Ann Patrick. "The Vatican Letter: Presuppositions and Objections." In *The Vatican and Homosexuality; Reactions to the "Letter to the Bishops of the Catholic Church on the Pastoral Care of Homosexual Persons,"* edited by Jeannine Gramick and Pat Fury, 28–32. New York: Crossroad, 1988.

Weaver, Darlene Fozard. *The Acting Person and the Christian Moral Life*. Washington, DC: Georgetown University Press, 2011.

———. "Adoption, Social Justice, and Catholic Tradition." *Journal of Catholic Social Thought* 13, no. 2 (Summer 2016): 197–213.

———. "Water Is Thicker Than Blood: Adoptive Families and Catholic Tradition." *Concilium*, no. 2 (2016): 98–110.

Weaver, Natalie Kertes. *Marriage and Family: A Christian Theological Foundation*. Winona, MN: Anselm Academic, 2009.

West, Christopher. *Good News about Sex & Marriage: Answers to Your Honest Questions about Catholic Teaching*. Rev. ed. Cincinnati: Servant Books, 2004.

Wilcox, W. Bradford, ed. "The State of Our Unions; Marriage in America 2011." University of Virginia National Marriage Project and Institute for American Values. December 2011. http://stateofourunions.org/2011/SOOU2011.pdf.

Wilcox, W. Bradford, Linda Waite, and Alex Roberts. "Marriage and Mental Health in Adults and Children." Center for Marriage and Families, Research Brief 4, February 2007. http://americanvalues.org/catalog/pdfs/researchbrief4.pdf.

Williams, Susan L., and Wayne L. Villemez. "Seekers and Finders: Male Entry and Exit in Female-Dominated Jobs." In *Doing Women's Work: Men in Non-traditional Occupations*, edited by Christine L. Williams, 64–90. Newbury Park, CA: Sage, 1993.

Winfield, Nicole. "Memoir of Jewish Boy Taken from Home by Pius IX; Altered in Translation." *Crux*, April 20, 2018. https://cruxnow.com/vatican/2018/04/memoir-of-jewish-boy-taken-from-home-by-pius-ix-altered-in-translation/.

Wojtyla, Karol. *The Acting Person*. Boston: D. Reidel, 1979.

———. "The Anthropological Vision of *Humanae vitae.*" Trans. William E. May. *Nova et Vetera,* English Edition 7, no. 3 (2009): 731–50.

———. *Love and Responsibility.* San Francisco: Ignatius Press, 1993.

Wooden, Cindy. "Birth of an Encyclical: Priest Documents Preparation of *Humanae vitae.*" *National Catholic Reporter,* July 23, 2018. www.ncronline.org/news/vatican/birth-encyclical-priest-documents-preparation-humanae-vitae.

Yeoman, Ruth. "Conceptualizing Meaningful Work as a Fundamental Human Need." *Journal of Business Ethics* 125, no. 2 (December 2014): 235–51.

INDEX

ABOUT THE AUTHOR

Jacob M. Kohlhaas, who received his PhD from Duquesne University in 2015, is an associate professor of moral theology at Loras College in Dubuque, Iowa. He teaches a range of courses in theology, ethics, and general education, and he serves as director of the college's Honors Program. His work has been published in *Theological Studies, Journal of Religious Ethics, Journal of Moral Theology,* and *Religious Studies Review,* as well as *America* and *US Catholic* magazines.

CPSIA information can be obtained
at www.ICGtesting.com
Printed in the USA
BVHW030724070422
633636BV00001B/4

9 781647 121129